The Encyclopedia of Nails

Hairdressing and Beauty Industry Authority Series – related titles

Beauty Therapy

Beauty Therapy – The Foundations: The Official Guide to Level 2
Lorraine Nordmann

Professional Beauty Therapy: The Official Guide to Level 3
Lorraine Nordmann, Lorraine Appleyard and Pamela Linforth

Aromatherapy for the Beauty Therapist Valerie Ann Worwood

Indian Head Massage Muriel Burnham-Airey and Adele O'Keefe

An Holistic Guide to Anatomy and Physiology Tina Parsons

The Complete Nail Technician Marian Newman

The Encyclopedia of Nails Jacqui Jefford and Anne Swain

The World of Skin Care: A Scientific Companion Dr John Gray

Safety in the Salon Elaine Almond

Hairdressing

Start Hairdressing: The Official Guide to Level 1 Martin Green and Leo Palladino

Hairdressing – The Foundations: The Official Guide to Level 2 Leo Palladino

Professional Hairdressing: The Official Guide to Level 3
Martin Green, Lesley Kimber and Leo Palladino

Men's Hairdressing: Traditional and Modern Barbering Maurice Lister

African-Caribbean Hairdressing Sandra Gittens

The World of Hair: A Scientific Companion Dr John Gray

Salon Management Martin Green

Essensuals, Next Generation Toni & Guy: Step by Step

Mahogany Hairdressing: Steps to Cutting, Colouring and Finishing Hair
Martin Gannon and Richard Thompson

Mahogany Hairdressing: Advanced Looks Martin Gannon and Richard Thompson

Patrick Cameron: Dressing Long Hair Patrick Cameron and Jacki Wadeson

Patrick Cameron: Dressing Long Hair Book 2 Patrick Cameron

Bridal Hair Pat Dixon and Jacki Wadeson

Trevor Sorbie: Visions in Hair Kris Sorbie and Jacki Wadeson

The Total Look: The Style Guide for Hair and Make-up Professionals Ian Mistlin

Art of Hair Colouring David Adams and Jacki Wadeson

The Encyclopedia
of Nails

Jacqui Jefford and Anne Swain

HABIA
Hairdressing And Beauty Industry Authority

THOMSON
™

Australia • Canada • Mexico • Singapore • Spain • United Kingdom • United States

THOMSON

The Encyclopedia of Nails

Copyright © Jacqui Jefford and Anne Swain 2002

The Thomson logo is a registered trademark used herein under licence.

For more information, contact
Thomson, High Holborn House, 50–51 Bedford Row, London, WC1R 4LR
or visit us on the World Wide Web at: http://www.thomsonlearning.co.uk

British Library Cataloguing-in-Publication Data
A catalogue record for this book is available from the British Library

Reprinted 2002, 2003 and 2005

ISBN-13: 978-1-86152-836-1
ISBN-10: 1-86152-836-1

Typeset by Meridian Colour Repro Ltd, Pangbourne-on-Thames, Berkshire

Printed in Italy by G. Canale & C.

Contents

Foreword

One of the exciting parts of my job is reviewing new books and writing the foreword. You see, I get this wonderful opportunity to look at each book some months before it hits the bookshelves. I'm constantly impressed by the abilities and the range of talented people working in the nail industry and Jacqui Jefford and Anne Swain are no exception.

This excellent book takes you in clear concise steps from starting your career, learning about nails, right through to managing your salon. Not only is it logically written but I personally found it a fascinating read.

If you're starting your career as a nail technician, this book will be your constant companion. Jacqui Jefford and Anne Swain show just how rewarding a career in nails can be. Follow their advice and be the best in your field. Your clients will thank you.

Alan Goldsbro
Chief Executive Officer
Hairdressing and Beauty Industry Authority

Acknowledgements

We would like to dedicate this book to Gigi Rouse, our friend and mentor, without whose love, support and time we would not be where we are today, thank you.

We would like to express our thanks to:

- our husbands Ian and Bob for their patience and computer skills without which this book would not have been possible
- Sue Marsh for taking nail skills beyond anyone's imagination
- Doug Schoon for constantly inspiring us
- Creative Nail Design for all they have taught us
- Designer Nails for photos and products
- Rachel Myatt at K-Sa-Ra for Nail Art Products
- Tracy Maddox and Liesl Silcock for their beautiful nail art
- Diane Plummer and Katherine Rae for their inspirational airbrush skills
- Gigi Rouse for all the photographs of the step-by-steps
- Bob Jefford Associates.
- Jane Cook for the Grim Reaper
- Richard and James for photography
- John Grace at Essential Nails
- Richard Batten Edwards
- Models: Blue, Chrissy, Gillian, Kelly, Kim, Michelle, Sam, Tracy
- Alex Fox

About this book

The nail industry has become one of the biggest growth industries in the UK today. Nail technicians are now becoming recognised as professionals in their own right and have a selection of work areas never dreamed of in the past. This book is for a novice just entering the nail world, but it will also help those technicians already qualified and wanting to look at other career options within the industry today. All of the information in this Encyclopedia will guide you through any nail qualification you need to achieve to gain recognition with insurance companies, trade associations, employers and local authorities for licences. You will find here all the information you need to match the National Occupational Standards laid down by the Hairdressing and Beauty Industry Authority (HABIA) and a lot more. There are those within the industry who would wish to see a 'nail only' qualification and, hopefully, in the near future this will be achieved. The extra chapters that we have included may become part of a new qualification in the future but, if not, they certainly offer career options for a nail technician wishing to progress on to other areas of work within the nail industry.

This book concentrates exclusively on the nail technician and the information they need to perform their job effectively within the rules and regulations laid down by Health and Safety legislation and by the industry's National Training Organisation, HABIA. The information included in this Encyclopedia is generic and refers to no specific product, product company or set procedure. Everyone reading this will understand that our product companies are very important and the information they provide to help us on our journey through the nail industry is essential. They supply valuable information on chemicals, products and their usage and this book makes no attempt to replace that. Product manufacturers and companies can offer valuable input to your training and it's worth remembering to make good use of this resource.

We hope that you find the book informative, helpful and – most important – enjoyable. Good luck to all of you on your journey through this wonderful industry.

The salon and working environment

The professional nail industry is one of the fastest growing industries in the UK today. Nail treatments have, until recently, taken second place to hair and beauty, with technicians renting desks within hair and beauty salons. However, this situation has now changed and there are many successful nail salons and even chains of nail salons developing across the UK. This chapter takes you through the various career opportunities available once you have completed your basic training. You may decide to follow more than one career route at the same time depending on what suits your lifestyle and background. We will try to guide you through the points you need to consider when deciding where you want to be: the right environment, whether you want to be mobile or static, the salon as a whole including its layout and decor, and security aspects both for yourself and for your equipment and stock. This chapter also touches on the other professionals you will need to consult at the outset to help you establish a business plan and to set up your working space.

In this chapter we will consider the following aspects:

- **starting out**
- **salon layout and environment**
- **salon security and staff safety**
- **reception**
- **effective stock control**

Starting out

Learning objectives

In this section you will learn about:

- **areas of work, whether as a home-based technician, a mobile technician or as a technician based in a salon, in the media or fashion world**

- **training, skills and qualifications**

- **getting a job**

- **professional associations**

- **setting up your own business, employing people, drawing on advice from professional advisers, insurance, advertising, and ways of financing your business**

The professional nail industry is one of the fastest growing and most exciting. Men and women have been extending and decorating their nails and fingers for centuries so nail technology is nothing new. The Ancient Egyptians were great nail artists and not only decorated their nails but extended them with papyrus and gold ornaments. At the present time, nail technology is improving continuously and every week there are new products coming on to the market and new techniques being made available. Every technician should make it their goal to keep up to date with trends in fashion and technology by attending workshops and by reading trade magazines.

The nail industry is all about people. A successful nail technician will have good people skills as well as good technical skills and before embarking on any training this requirement should be borne in mind. You will be with your clients for more hours a week than with your family and you need to be adaptable, good natured, personable and able to communicate with people from all walks of life. There are many areas to consider when starting out in the nail industry and we will look at how to start up and where to go for training, what products to use and which area you wish to work in. Remember to plan the start of your career carefully as you will find that the sky is the limit – anything is achievable as long as you remain focused on your goals.

Areas of work

Until a few years ago the range areas where a nail technician could work were quite limited. However, the industry today has more career routes than ever and with good quality training, experience and the enthusiasm to succeed, you may choose any of the following career paths:

- home-based technician
- mobile technician
- technician based in a salon, whether employed or self-employed, working at a desk in a hairdressing salon, a sports centre, beauty salon, boutique, dedicated nail salon, or even on a cruise liner or at an airport
- in media or fashion as a photographic nail artist or at catwalk shows
- setting up or owning your own salon
- teaching at an FE college, private training centre or acting as an educator/trainer for a product company
- in sales, either as a sales demonstrator for a product company at trade shows, or a sales representative out on the road

You will eventually have a choice of all of the above paths, but you need to make a start as some of the areas will require more experience than others. It is impossible to train for a period of a few days and then perform nail treatments to a high skill level and salon standard. You will need to spend a certain amount of time doing an apprenticeship under the wing of a mentor, tutor or employer.

Home-based technician

There are many excellent, high profile technicians working in today's industry who started out at home, built a successful clientele and then went on to achieve great success in education or media work. It is hard to build a clientele when you are first starting out, but with determination and motivation this can be achieved.

Once you have completed your training, look at how practical it will be to work at home. Consider the following points before committing yourself to working at home.

- Are young children likely to be there during working hours?
- Have you a dedicated room for your nail desk?
- Do your family mind the intrusion of your clients?

- Will your mortgage lender allow you to run a business from home?
- Can you get permission from your local Borough Council?
- What parking facilities are available in your area?
- Would your neighbours mind? You do need to ask their opinion.

If your home is where you want to work, then go through the above checklist and make sure you have the consent and permissions that you need. There is nothing worse than building a healthy business only to have a neighbour make a complaint to the local council about your clients parking in their spaces. You need to look at where you will be working and make sure that it is comfortable for your clients. Think, also, about somewhere for your clients to wait. It is also important to consider where and how you will store your products, especially if you have young children at home. Use a desk or cupboard that has lockable drawers or doors.

Working from home can be extremely cost effective as the overheads are very low, there is little or no travelling, and hours can be arranged to suit you and your family. You do, however, need to be careful when allowing strangers into your home: be aware that new clients are strangers and you know nothing about them. This is why a designated area of the house, preferably with its own entrance, is better than inviting them into a living area where they can see your possessions. This also creates a more professional impression.

Safety Tip

Make sure you observe all the safety rules for storage, ventilation and hygiene, as you do not want your family to have to live with the odours from your products.

Mobile technician

Becoming a mobile technician can be very satisfying and financially rewarding.

There are a few main points to take into consideration before choosing this career path:

- reliable transport
- business insurance for your vehicle and products in transit
- the possibility of unsociable hours of work
- the radius of the area that you will travel
- your treatment prices should take into account petrol costs and travelling time
- be aware of the areas you will be travelling to, the availability of safe parking and whether you will have far to walk

- have a well stocked kit as it is frustrating to run out of products or forget an item when you have travelled to a client
- carry a small amount of retail items with you
- have a mobile phone that has good network coverage
- be prepared for your clients not to have a suitable surface for you to work on
- bear in mind that your clients may have children or pets; ensure you can work safely in such situations
- take your rubbish away with you and dispose of it yourself
- make sure that a family member or friend knows your movements for the day/night
- always contact your client the day before to check they still want their appointment rather than making a wasted journey

Mobile work can be stressful and exhausting, especially if working within an inner city where traffic is heavy. Also, especially in winter, you need to be aware of weather conditions and that you may get wet and cold. On the other hand, it can be very rewarding to have your own business and to be in command of the hours that you work. Make sure that you cover all the areas such as insurance, health and safety and finance arrangements that you would normally do for any business. Remember that your clients may think that as a mobile technician your charges will be lower than those in a salon but, in fact, the opposite is true. Consider all of your running costs and the time involved and charge accordingly. If you are good at what you do, clients will pay for your services.

In a salon

A desk in a hairdressing salon, sports centre, beauty salon or boutique

When setting up a desk in any form of established premises, you will have access to an instant clientele. Whilst clients are having their hair done, they will be watching you working at your desk and curious about what you are doing. Use this to your advantage. The points to take into consideration when setting up a desk in another environment are:

- The cost – will you pay a weekly rent or a percentage of your takings?
- Who will be responsible for supplying furniture and products?

- Will the salon advertise for you or will you operate a separate price list?
- Will their receptionist book appointments for you?
- Will you have to contribute towards printing, telephone, other staff?
- Will you need to have your own insurance?
- Can you be a keyholder, allowing you to work outside their opening hours?
- Will other facilities such as washroom, staffroom and parking be available to you and your clients?
- Will there be space available for your retail stock and who will handle any money?
- Will you be responsible for taking your own payments?

When considering working or renting a desk in someone else's premises one of the first things you must do is draw up a written agreement defining the rules and regulations of the agreement between you and them. If you do not do this then you may find you have built up a healthy business only to be disappointed when the owners of the premises want to change the rules, forcing you to leave or, worse still, asking you to leave and employing someone else in your place.

There are many positive aspects to working in a salon where you are the only technician. It is less lonely than working at home or as a mobile technician as you will always have others to chat to which can be particularly helpful when you have an awkward client. As well as being seen working, you can ask the other staff members to wear your nails and nail art as this will be a constant source of advertising. You could give staff a discount or swap treatments with them. It is cheaper to share newspaper advertising and take part in any promotional days. Always negotiate a trial period before committing yourself to a long rent – you will need to know whether or not you can fit in with the environment and the other staff.

Being employed within a nail salon

Good nail technicians are hard for salon owners to find, as most successful technicians usually establish businesses of their own and do not want to work for other people.

Working as an employed technician, however, can be very rewarding and there are a number of advantages to consider:

- working to set hours each day
- having a regular income each week
- being mentored by a employer or other colleagues

- being part of a team of professionals
- having constant access to updated products and training
- not having to worry about ordering and paying for stock
- reducing demands from clients to work unsocial hours

A salon owner will usually want to interview you before taking you on and they will probably want to see evidence of your nail skills and any other areas of expertise that you have. It is worthwhile making sure that you are up-to-date on all issues within the nail industry before attending an interview, as this will show that you take your profession seriously. You may find that a salon owner will ask you to use a different system or product from the one you are currently using or have been trained with. Don't be afraid to say if this is the case and ask if they are willing to do some training with you rather than throwing you in at the deep end with new clients.

Always make sure before taking the job that you agree on salary, hours of work, etc. with your potential employer and that you receive a written contract within twelve weeks of starting.

On a cruise liner

If you would like to travel the world whilst working, then cruising may be the choice for you. No one will pretend that it is not hard work, but the rewards can be immense. You will need to have an independent personality and be keen and free to travel the world. Good social skills are imperative to this type of work.

Here are a few points to take into consideration when applying for work on cruise liners:

- living with another person you may never have met before in a small cramped cabin for six months or more
- working very long hours – sometimes 12 hours a day, 6 days a week, with little time off
- the pay is not too good, but the tips can be
- experience is essential as you will have a strict interview
- you may have to spend 2–6 weeks in a training school before setting off on a ship
- you will be away for at least 6–8 months at a time
- you will be living, working and socialising with the same people for 6–8 months

- when in port you will have the opportunity to see areas of the world you would not necessarily visit
- you can make friendships that will last a lifetime
- you should be able to save money – living expenses are low and there is nowhere to spend your money
- there is usually a good social life on board ship

If you choose this career path you must remember that once you have joined the cruise ship you cannot come home until your contract has finished. If you find you are homesick, do not like the job or that you clash with other staff, you would have to pay to come home, and this may not be financially possible. Consider carefully whether you are likely to be suited to this lifestyle before committing yourself.

At an airport

When working in an airport you will usually be based in the departure lounge, although some long haul carriers are starting to offer in-flight beauty treatments. You will usually need to have good quick nail skills and will almost always be working under pressure as clients have to catch their planes. Security is a priority in all airports and you will have to undergo a security check before you are taken on. You will then be given a security pass with your photograph and this must be worn at all times – leave it at home and you may not be able to get into work. The services offered by the salon will determine the skills you will need. Try to find this information out before attending an interview and so avoid wasting your time.

Within the media and fashion spheres

In the media as a photographic nail artist

This career route is really only for the experienced technician who has already served an apprenticeship in the areas they intend to offer to photographers, editors, designers and stylists. It is hard work but can be very rewarding and lucrative. This is a relatively new area of work in our industry and, as such, we feel it is important enough to give it a section on its own. You will find further information in Chapter 8.

Working in the fashion industry at catwalk shows

Once again, this is an area for an experienced technician who is multi-skilled and is not for those who are learning their craft. As with photographic work it is a relatively new avenue for nail technicians. The work is very low paid – if there is any pay at all – can be extremely demanding and stressful, and is therefore not for the faint-hearted. Fashion work is highly skilled and is also covered in more detail in Chapter 8.

Owning your own salon

It is a wise technician who gains some experience before embarking on running and owning a salon. There are many points to consider before going down this path. No amount of training can replace experience gained from time spent working on members of the public. When thinking of opening your own salon you will need to involve other professionals and invest large sums of money. The process requires total commitment and can be both time consuming and stressful. Think carefully about the financial commitment you will need to make and do not forget the time it is going to take to set up your own business – time which will be spent away from your desk. You cannot be earning whilst liaising with other professionals, interviewing staff and shopping for fixtures and fittings. See 'Setting up your own business' later in this section.

Teaching or training

Teaching for further education colleges and private training centres

Further education (FE) colleges will usually ask for a minimum of 3 years industrial experience within the nail industry from those who wish to teach, in addition to holding the qualification they wish to teach, an Assessors Award D32/33 (to be replaced by the A Units, see page 361), and also a Further Education Teaching Certificate. Private training centres may ask for some of these qualifications, but it is unlikely as they usually use staff trained in-house. A good nail technician with excellent skills may not necessarily be a good teacher and the reverse is also true. To be a good teacher you need to have a good thorough knowledge of the nail industry as a whole, including a range of technical skills over all three nail systems, their maintenance, product chemistry, knowledge of relevant Health and Safety issues and the ability to be able to motivate and pass on this information to students. The standard of training centres can vary, but those that take all the above points into consideration rather than prioritising class numbers or product sales will be the better ones. This subject will be covered in more depth in Chapter 9.

As an educator or trainer for a product company

You will find that most product companies have their own in-house trainers who have a good, thorough knowledge of the company's systems, products and procedures. It also means that the companies can keep abreast of who is training who, which helps with product sales. Good companies will make sure that their trainers are constantly updated every year – not only on new products, new procedures and new skills but also on their theoretical knowledge and presentation skills. You will find that the most successful companies in today's nail industry are those that have the best trainers networking with their students to impart knowledge and skills – not just product sales. Education is the key to success for a company and can enhance product sales. If a nail technician is taught well he or she will be able to establish a thriving business and require more training, more staff, more support and, lastly, more products.

Sales representative

As a sales demonstrator for product companies at trade shows

Companies that exhibit and attend trade shows need demonstrators to show off their products at their best and also to talk to potential clients about the features and benefits of their product ranges. These demonstrators must be highly skilled professionals with a thorough knowledge of their products. There is nothing worse than visiting a trade stand and having a demonstrator put on a nail that is of poor quality, or asking a representative a question and not getting an informative answer. It is in the interests of a product company to make sure staff are chosen carefully for this job. You should consider whether you have most of the following attributes when applying for this type of work:

- enthusiasm for the products you will be working with
- a thorough knowledge of the products
- the technical skills that can create the most beautiful nails
- good people skills
- the ability to work under pressure in crowded conditions
- the personality to work as a valuable team member
- the capacity to stand for long hours with no breaks
- the skills required to defuse confrontational situations

Most product companies will pay a daily rate, either in the form of products or financial remuneration, plus expenses to and from the show. Make sure these terms are agreed before you commit yourself. The company will also want to know your availability throughout the year, as there are now many trade shows and exhibitions.

As a sales representative on the road

You will need to have transport for this work, whether it be your own or a company vehicle. Establish at the outset the cost to you if a company wants you to use your own car and make sure you are reimbursed for petrol and mileage. Tax laws on company cars can affect your financial tax position and you should seek out professional advice if necessary. Remember that it could take you hours to reach a particular salon, so plan your day carefully, working out which salons you will be visiting. Try to focus on all of the salons in one area at a time. Some companies pay a basic wage plus commission, others may pay just a wage or commission only. Work out whether the job is financially viable before you start as you do not want to be out of pocket. Product companies should give you some form of training before sending you out on the road and may even want to test your practical skills for demonstration purposes before they take you on. You will usually find that a company employing you as a sales representative will expect you to have a few years experience within the industry before they send you out to customers as it is difficult for a novice to talk to an experienced salon owner on the same level. The safety rules which apply to travelling sales work are the same as those for mobile technicians, see Section 3 of this chapter for more information.

Training, skills and qualifications

Knowing yourself will help to determine the type of training which is most appropriate for you. There are many options available, but finding the right one can be difficult and costly mistakes can be made. The first considerations should be your budget, your circumstances, any time constraints and other possible commitments.

The three main providers of nail courses are:

1   further education colleges
2   private schools and training centres
3   manufacturers or product companies

Before choosing your training provider shop around to see what each one offers. You will need to look at areas such as:

● the cost
● the length of the course

- the number of hours per week and the days on which the course runs
- the credentials of the person teaching the course
- the course details, i.e. what is covered
- the qualification which you will gain, i.e. whether the course leads to a professional qualification or just a product certificate
- whether any support is available once you have finished training
- whether any further training or advanced classes are available
- the location of the courses
- the size of the classes
- whether you need to provide products and models
- whether any government grants are available

Once you have gathered together all this information, it may be a good idea to ask someone you know within the industry, even if it is your own technician, if they could help you to go through and consider what will best suit you. If you do not know anyone who works in the profession then telephone a Nail Association for independent advice on how to go about choosing the right course for you. They should be able to advise you or put you in touch with a professional who can guide you through this decision.

Further education colleges

You will find that most further education (FE) colleges will offer a nail qualification that leads to a professional certificate which is not linked to a product company. Obviously you will need to use someone's products whilst you do your classes but your trainer should let you have details of other product companies in your area, with contact numbers. In some cases you will find that the product company will also issue a certificate for their product training in addition to your professional certificate. College courses are usually much cheaper than private courses but are spread over a longer period of time and this can have disadvantages and advantages.

The advantages are:

- longer periods to practise your skills between classes
- more time to absorb all the necessary theory
- more hands-on practice
- you will get the opportunity to work over a greater range of nail skills and clients
- the chance to interact with other class members

- the opportunity to complete more treatments in a supervised environment

The disadvantages are:

- you need to be motivated to work at home between classes
- it can be difficult to find models for classes
- it takes longer to recoup money spent on nail kits
- there can be a delay before you can start working on clients at home as you need to wait several weeks before producing a new set of nails from start to finish
- classes are usually quite large, allowing less time to be spent with your tutor.

Private schools and training centres

Private schools do not usually receive government funding so their classes are usually more expensive but there are still a number of advantages:

- much smaller classes
- quality attention from your tutor
- the quality of handouts is usually better
- there is normally a good support system

You need to shop around to see what is available in your area and, if there is nothing suitable, you may have to be prepared to travel a bit further afield. We cannot stress how important it is to make sure that your first introduction into the nail industry is a good one. Make sure that your course covers the following areas:

- health and safety
- safe working practices and how to avoid overexposure
- anatomy and physiology of the hand, arm and nail
- chemistry
- application
- manicure
- client consultation
- aftercare
- finishing techniques
- maintenance techniques

If you want to check that the quality of the training centre is high, ask if you might visit whilst a class is in progress or if the centre can give you details of other technicians who have trained there and been happy with their course. You could also ask for an interview with the trainer to check that they are approachable and to ask whether they feel this course will suit you.

Manufacturers and product companies

The advantages of training with a product company are that you can be confident that the trainers will be very knowledgeable about the products they use in their teaching and that they will have good technical skills to pass on to you. You will find that the classes are usually smaller than at a college and the focus will be very hands-on. The training will take place over a shorter period of time, but will not necessarily require fewer hours. The advantage of this is that you can move on to building a clientele quicker. With the better companies, you will also benefit from a good support system for both techniques and products. They will also inform you of any new products or training courses that may be planned in the near future. Another plus factor is that there are people you can talk to at the end of the phone if you have any problems after your training is complete.

The disadvantages can be that a poorer quality company will be primarily interested in product sales and the training and back-up facilities will also be of poorer quality. When enquiring about courses make sure you ask questions that will shed light on these areas and make your judgement accordingly. It would be sensible to ask for a representative to visit you, or for you to visit the product company, and ask for a demonstration on yourself. This way, after a few weeks, you will be able to judge whether the product looks as good as when it was put on and ensure that the skill of the trainer has avoided any damage to your natural nail.

You will find that some manufacturers or product companies, albeit the minority, link their training to a professional qualification and if you can find one that does this, it is certainly worth considering. However, most companies will only provide you with a product certificate, so check with your local authority that they will accept this and will not require a professional qualification. You don't want to finish your course and then find that you cannot work, so spend some time investigating this.

Getting a job

The first step to getting a job is to have a good quality curriculum vitae (CV). You should update this each year to include any additional qualifications or experience that you have gained. A good CV should be:

Technical Tip

There are a very few professional 'nail only' qualifications available at present but this is changing. If you want further information on what professional qualifications you can achieve, information is available from our Nail Association or the NTO (National Training Organisation) that sets qualification standards in health and beauty or from HABIA (the Hairdressing and Beauty Industry Authority).

- well presented
- comprehensive
- clear and informative
- accurate
- typed or word-processed

When applying for a job, a potential employer is looking for details of your educational background, any work experience you have and also evidence of your skill level.

There are specialist professionals who can write your CV for you, but obviously there will be a cost involved. However, it could be worthwhile if the job you are applying for is high level or important to you. An example of a basic CV is shown below.

Example CV

CURRICULUM VITAE

Name:	Nancy Nails
Date of Birth:	1.1.1974
Address:	5 Nail Road
	Nail Town
	England
	123 ABC
Telephone Number:	01111 222222
Marital Status:	Single
Car Driver:	Full driving licence
School/College:	Nail Town Comprehensive
	September 1985–1990
	Fingers FE College
	September 1990-1993
Qualifications:	GSCE: Maths
	English
	Biology
	Art
	Science
	A Levels: English
	Art
Further Qualifications:	City and Guilds Beauty Therapy II
	Unit 19 Nail Extensions
	Nail Art Diploma
Work Experience:	2 weeks work experience in Talons Nail Salon
	Employment in Beauty Spot for 6 months
Hobbies:	Reading, swimming, art classes
References:	Mrs Hand, Manager
	Talons Nail Salon
	Mrs Arm
	Lecturer at Fingers FE College

Your CV can make the difference between you getting an interview or being rejected straight away. Once you've been called for an interview, it's up to you. Make sure all the spellings and details of the person to whom you are applying are correct and that your CV and letter or application form are sent in good condition, with the correct postage. Always keep a few copies of your CV on file in case you need to hand one out at a moment's notice.

Professional associations

There are very few 'nail only' associations. Some are more active than others and offer far more benefits to their members. If you are going to part with hard-earned cash, make sure you are clear on the details of these benefits before joining as a member. The benefits that an association should be offering you are:

- a discounted group insurance scheme
- monthly newsletters
- 'nail only' magazines, preferably monthly
- an advisory service
- reduced subscriptions to professional magazines
- meetings to update members on all issues to do with the nail industry
- members' badge and certificate for salon wall
- tiered membership to allow for the identification of qualifications and experience
- links with awarding bodies to offer professional qualifications

It is worthwhile joining an association as it will make you part of a bigger group of professionals who link up through meetings, articles in trade magazines and at shows. Membership of an association gives you the trade mark of a professional and a stamp of approval for the public and the industry and is a useful item to include on your CV or application for a job.

Setting up your own business

Professional advisers

When starting out in any business you will need help from other people. Even if you are considering the apparently simple option of working at home you may need help from a Nail Association on issues such as insurance or product

Technical Tip

The main two Nail Associations are INA (International Nail Association) and ANT (Association of Nail Technicians).

suppliers. If you are opening a salon, you will probably need professional advisers such as solicitors, surveyors, accountants, bookkeepers and possibly even a bank manager to help finance the business.

Try and use professionals who have been recommended to you by friends or someone in the industry and always check their prices before committing yourself to expensive costs.

Financing your business

You need to decide first which area of the nail industry you will be working in and then work out what this will cost you. If you are going to be working at home then the cost will be lowest – the expenditure will be on furniture, insurance and products. If you decide to work as a mobile technician then while you may not need to invest in so much furniture, you will have to look at a reliable form of transport, products, insurance and a mobile phone. Obviously the set-up costs for a salon can be vast and you might need to borrow the money from a lender – this could be a bank, building society or a member of your family. You could also consider a partnership.

Banks and building societies now offer not just loans but also sound financial advice on a whole variety of issues from lending to pensions. Most banks will help you with a start-up package giving excellent guidelines on starting a small business. They will also usually offer free banking for the first year of business.

If you are borrowing money from a building society or bank they may want to see a business plan and discuss how you will be repaying the loan. The following are the main points to consider when preparing your business plan:

- your financial situation
- your plans for the future and the development of your business
- any financial security you may have
- the nature of the business
- what premises you wish to lease or buy
- your career and the experience you already have
- the amount of money you need to borrow
- the support structure for the business

If you are going to borrow money from a family member make sure that you have a written agreement covering a final settlement date, i.e. when it has to be paid back, any interest they want to charge and how often they want repayments. This is an excellent way of starting a business as a family member may be willing to allow you some time to get the business up and running before you have to start making repayments. However, there have been many family splits over business and finance so you do need to have an agreement *in writing* to avoid any arguments arising that might split the family in two.

A partnership also has advantages and disadvantages and you need to consider all points before committing yourself to business with another person. Again, you must make sure before signing any contract that you have discussed and agreed all the issues.

The advantages of a partnership are:

- shared workload and responsibilities
- shared costs
- illness and holiday cover
- working with someone who has the same level of commitment to building a healthy business as yourself
- a partner may bring complementary skills to add to your own

The disadvantages are:

- having to share the profits
- additional overheads
- each partner is responsible for the other's debts
- individual ideas may vary, possibly leading to confrontation

If you decide that you wish to share your business with another person, or other people, look at their personal qualities and think about what these can bring to the business rather than just considering the financial input they can make. You need to know that you can trust and work with your partner. Ideally their skills, whether they be technical or people skills, should complement yours.

Some time after your business has become established you might consider forming a limited company as this is a good way to protect your other assets, such as your home. A limited company describes the situation where two or more people wish to own the company and they will ultimately be the shareholders. A limited company can be either private or public (PLC). A limited company has to be registered with Companies House and your accountant can arrange this for you. In the case of a private limited company the shares are not sold to the general public, whereas a PLC has to offer shares to the public on the stock market.

Insurance

There are three main types of insurance that must be considered when you are starting out in your career:

1 public liability insurance
2 product liability insurance
3 employers' liability insurance

Public liability insurance

If a member of the public or a visitor to your premises has an accident or is injured in any way, this insurance will protect you.

Product liability insurance

This is usually included with your public liability insurance, but you should check with your insurance company rather than leave it to chance. Product liability insurance will protect you against claims arising from products that are not necessarily the manufacturer's responsibility and which could be traced back to you. Every person who has used that particular product could potentially be involved in a claim, which is why product liability insurance is vital to protect the nail technician. It will also protect those who are retailing items.

Employers' liability insurance

This insurance will protect the employer against any claims made by their employees arising from negligence or injuries sustained at work. It is a legal requirement to display an employers' liability insurance certificate in the salon and a salon owner could face a fine if he or she has failed to do so (see Chapter 2).

There are other types of insurance that may be considered, but these are optional and not mandatory. For example:

- contents insurance for the salon, car or your home
- sickness or personal injury cover
- personal protection – you can insure your hands against damage

Although at the outset of your career these insurance policies may seem expensive and out of reach, it is worthwhile investing to protect yourself, your staff and your business as you need to be covered for every eventuality. Check that your policy is index-linked. If you have a 'new for old' policy you will be covered for the replacement costs of expensive articles rather than just the amount they are now worth.

Insurance companies will usually allow you to pay premiums monthly and also by direct debit. Always get several quotes before deciding which policy best suits your circumstances and your budget.

Advertising

When starting out in any business the cost of advertising can seem outrageous. Look at all of your options before deciding how much you are going to invest in your advertising budget. You will also need to look at the area you are working in and consider what works best for that area. Here are a few ways that you can advertise your salon or services:

- word of mouth from satisfied clients
- leaflet drops
- posters in waiting rooms – e.g. dentists', doctors', in fact anywhere where people sit and wait
- parish magazines
- local newspapers
- postcards in local shops or newsagents
- leaving business cards in hotels, banks and local offices
- price lists in bridal shops and boutiques
- getting hairdressers and other professionals to wear your nails – give them a discount or commission for every client they pass on to you
- local radio
- Thomson Directories and Yellow Pages – you are entitled to free line space in both of these; however a box will cost you and, if you approach them, beware their hard-selling techniques
- giving nail parties or wine and cheese evenings
- donating gift vouchers to local charities or school raffles
- visiting local WI and other organisations to give talks on what you do
- helping at local fashion shows

Try to monitor where your clients heard of your services. This will give you a good idea as to which form of advertising is the most effective. Do not spend a fortune on advertising at the beginning, even a small advert in Yellow

Pages is worthwhile, you can always have a bigger one next year. Look at the name of your business and remember that people will look through advertising directories alphabetically for names of salons or services.

Employing other professionals

The government has very strict guidelines on the employment of staff and you will need to familiarise yourself with all the legislation once you start to take on employees. If you contact your local tax office they will send you a new employers starter pack; alternatively you may find your accountant will guide you through all you need to know. As an employer you will become responsible for PAYE and National Insurance Contributions. A bookkeeper can prove invaluable, because they can do in an hour what would take most nail technicians three hours.

- Consider asking a bookkeeper or accountant to set up a system for you if you do not wish to use their services on a monthly basis.
- Invest in a good computer system such as SAGE.
- NEVER put off till tomorrow what you can do today.
- Always keep a record of wage slips and staff transactions.
- Give your employees a copy of all information that has been sent to the tax office by you on their behalf.

You will need to keep a personal file on each employee with up-to-date information such as:

- name and address
- home telephone number
- two emergency contacts with telephone numbers
- doctor's address and telephone number
- date they started employment
- P45 from previous employer and National Insurance number
- any sick leave that has been taken
- annual leave entitlement and dates taken
- contract – renewable and signed every year
- job description
- any disciplinary procedures taken and all relevant paperwork
- termination of contract, leaving date and reason for doing so
- references from previous employers or referees

- copy of CV
- copy of any professional or trade certificates
- job appraisal reviews
- rates of pay
- notes of any complaints or contentious issues during period of employment

Some of the above are a legal requirement for all employers but it is a good idea to keep a record of them all so that you can protect yourself whatever situation arises. Good record keeping will keep your business healthy in the same way you do for clients at a consultation.

Salon layout and environment

Learning objectives

In this section you will learn about:

- **salon size and layout**

- **different areas, such as staff room, stockroom, reception area**

- **how to create the environment you want within your salon**

- **decor**

- **salon equipment**

- **the exterior image of the salon**

When thinking about opening a salon you will need to consider the points in the list above very carefully. It is extremely expensive to open a salon with no clients and it may be sensible to build a mobile clientele first before investing a lot of money in premises, equipment and staff. It is difficult to do all the necessary jobs yourself and employing staff will be one of your biggest outgoings.

The factors listed above are also important if you are going to be self-employed in an existing salon as they could directly affect your income.

Location is a key factor in the success of any business. Look at a number of locations before deciding which will suit you best. Positions on main roads or high streets will be much more expensive and not necessarily more successful. Remember that clients will come to you anywhere if you are good at what you do. Convenient parking for your clients is one of the biggest considerations when looking for premises. Your clients want to come to you for a relaxing hour or two and will not want to battle with a lot of shoppers or have to park a mile away.

Look at the size of the premises and the length of the lease you are being asked to sign. If you think you will outgrow the premises within a year then do not sign a three- or four-year lease unless you can negotiate a get-out clause after a set period.

Size of the salon

You will have to decide how many nail stations you intend to have and then look at premises that will accommodate that number. When looking at the size, don't forget to consider the space you will need for other things as well as nail stations, like a stockroom, a staff room, etc. If you find premises that are likely to have spare rooms, you could rent these out to beauty therapists or similar professionals, or even turn the space into a tanning studio. Here is a list of factors to take into account when looking at premises:

- How many nail stations do you need?
- Is there room for staff facilities such as a washroom, toilet, lockers and staff room?
- Is there room for a stockroom, stock cupboard or storage facilities for products?
- Is a beauty room required?
- Can you have a separate reception area?
- Do the plumbing, electric sockets and lighting match your needs, as it can be expensive to change them?

Planning areas

Before you commit yourself to premises by signing a contract you should have a pretty good idea of how you want to set it out. Here are a few elements to be considered when planning different working areas:

- washing facilities are essential for both clients and staff
- toilet facilities should be available on the premises and suitable for both sexes
- there will need to be somewhere other than the working area for staff to eat and drink, as this cannot be done at a nail station

- you will have to designate an area for reception and to store staff and clients' coats
- lockers are a good idea for staff possessions
- a retail area or shelving is useful to display retail items
- music can create a particular atmosphere or mood

A most important area of the salon is your reception area as this is the part of the salon the client will first walk into. However you should also take into consideration the atmosphere of the whole salon. Client comfort is vitally important but you and your staff also need a pleasant environment to work in. Hopefully you will all be working long hours and comfortable surroundings will increase your efficiency.

Layout of a salon

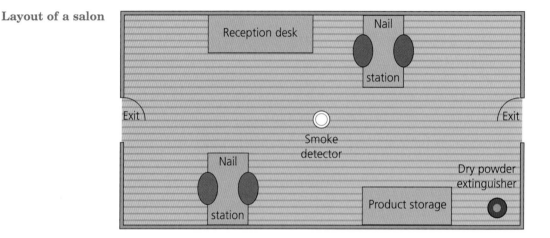

Environment

Lighting and heating

If the premises you choose have central heating already installed then it would be expensive to change this. If there is no heating then you need to look at the various options available to you. Your final choice may depend on the services connected to the premises and cost, for example there may no access to a gas supply. It is a Health and Safety requirement to provide a comfortable temperature for your staff to work in. Never use a heating system that requires a naked flame. If you have no windows, and there are plenty of salons that do not, you need to think about the temperature in the summer as well as the winter. If the salon gets too hot this can also contravene Health and Safety regulations and you may need to consider air conditioning. This may adversely affect some of the products you will be using, so you may need to seek the advice of a heating/cooling specialist before investing a lot of money. It is a salon owner's duty, under the Health and Safety Act, to provide adequate lighting in all areas of the salon including hall, stairs and passageways. You will find that most salons also provide a lamp on the nail station and, ideally, you should choose one that does not give off a lot of heat. Heat can not only affect the products you are working with but also cause headaches.

Ventilation

Beauty salons do not need to have ventilation installed but for nail technicians who work mainly with chemicals this is an important issue to consider.

Extraction is the most effective form of ventilation, taking stale air out and allowing it to be replaced with clean air. This subject is covered in greater detail in Chapter 2.

Decor

How you decide to decorate the salon needs to be given careful thought as once it has been completed you will have to live with it – or incur large and unnecessary costs. Consider not only your taste in colour but also that of your staff and the effect the colour scheme will have on your clientele. Crazy, bright colours will look lively but this might not be the atmosphere you wish to create. Choose colours that will complement one another and that will not be out of date within 6 months. On average a salon is decorated every 3 years. You may find that it is a condition of your lease that you have to redecorate or upgrade the interior of the salon every few years. Make sure this is something your solicitor clarifies before you sign the contract.

Painted walls are easier to maintain as they can be washed down – remember that we work with dust! It is also easier to repaint than it is to renew wallpaper. You could choose a main colour that will easily match a change of colour in accessories, allowing you to update the salon without having to completely redecorate. Here are a few items that may be colour matched to your decor:

- towels
- soft furnishings
- staff uniforms
- rugs and carpets
- blinds and curtains
- picture/certificate frames
- posters and advertising materials

Consider whether the salon is designed to encourage male and female clients and whether pink is really suitable for a male clientele. If your salon is south facing and gets a lot of sunshine then you may want to consider pale blues, lavenders or pale greens. If it is north facing and quite cold then you may want to use warm colours such as pinks, peaches, creams, lemons, etc.

Image is everything and clients will appreciate the thought and care that has gone into making the salon a special place for them to visit. Think of a theme and carry that theme through the decor, furniture, fixtures and fittings. Whatever your chosen style – modern or old-fashioned, Greek or minimalist – you must be comfortable with the one you have chosen.

Equipment

When choosing equipment for the salon it is really important to collect as many catalogues as possible and spend some time thinking about what will suit you and which pieces are in your price range. Trade shows are an easy way of looking at equipment as everything is gathered together under one roof, and there are at least five trade shows throughout the year. You may find that some companies will have special deals, sale items or start-up packages at the shows.

The most expensive pieces of equipment will probably be the nail stations and chairs. Nail stations or desks can be relatively cheap or very expensive. Look carefully at what your needs are, how many stations you need and how long you want them to last. Make sure when choosing a technician's chair that it is comfortable and gives good back

A selection of desks

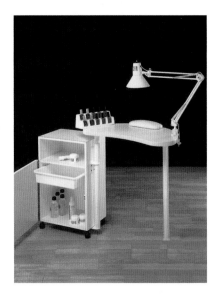

Courtesy of REM (UK) Ltd

Courtesy of REM (UK) Ltd

A selection of chairs

support. A nail technician can potentially sit in one position for more than eight hours a day and the chair therefore needs to be ergonomically designed to provide comfort and support over a long period of time.

Nail stations could be cheap computer desks from a DIY store or a marble-effect design, purpose-built by a local carpenter or purchased from a specialist supplier. However, the important factors are that the desk is not too wide to work over and that it is the correct height to work at. To ignore these two factors could, over time, cause serious back injuries. Do not be tempted to spend a large amount of money on glossy desks if your budget is tight. Superior furniture can be purchased later when a good clientele has been established.

Allow some space in the salon for retail and product storage. You may have cupboards already installed in the salon, but if these are in the kitchen area do not be tempted to use them to store nail products as they should not be anywhere near food or drink. Make sure the stock cupboard can be locked and is not near a heat source. Retail items should not be kept where heat can damage or destroy them, i.e. near a radiator or in direct sunlight. These items should be in the reception area where they can be viewed by clients, but if you have no room for free-standing shelving consider wall-mounted units.

If you cannot afford an electric till make sure you have a good cash box and a secure means of keeping a record of transaction and how it was paid. You will also need a system for recording each treatment and who performed it.

Check that all fire and safety equipment are in place and maintained regularly. These items are mandatory; see Chapter 2 for more information.

Display

A telephone with an answering machine is essential. Make sure that you have good battery back-up in case of electrical failure. Record your message, greeting the caller, listing your opening times and then ask them to leave their name and phone number. If your answer machine does not automatically record the time of calls, ask the caller to leave this information as well. Hands free telephones are excellent if you are a small salon and do not have a receptionist, but take care that clients' treatments are not interrupted too often, otherwise they will have good cause to complain.

Always make sure that you can quickly access the phone numbers of suppliers of electrical equipment. When choosing suppliers, try to use those who offer immediate replacement if there is a break down, or who will loan you equipment for a few days while yours is being repaired.

Till

The salon exterior

The exterior of your salon has the potential to either attract or put off possible clients. It can be expensive to paint the outside of a building and you will need to get a number of quotes from various contractors before making any decisions. You will also need to check that the building is not listed – if it is you will have to get permission from the local authority if you want to change the colour, put up a canopy, change the sign or improve the windows.

It is quite easy to brighten up the exterior with pot plants and hanging baskets but make sure these do not obstruct other businesses or pedestrians. You could find yourself facing a lawsuit if a member of the public trips over one of your pots.

If you are going to change the sign or put up a new one consider incorporating the following:

- salon name
- proprietor's name
- salon telephone number
- salon logo

Before you sign the lease, make sure you ask your solicitor to check it for any conditions referring to the upkeep of the exterior of the building. If you are sharing a building, find out what your responsibilities are and how they are shared with the occupants. You may also need to seek the permission of the landlord before undertaking any alterations inside or outside.

The layout of your salon will depend entirely on your budget and your taste, but you must remember that the salon is not just about what you like and dislike. Always remember that to attract as many people as possible into your salon, it should offer a clean, safe and pleasing environment for both clients and staff.

Salon security and staff safety

Learning objectives

In this section you will learn about:

- **personal safety and ways to protect yourself**
- **the safety of colleagues**
- **salon security**
- **telephone abuse**
- **outside of work and banking safety**
- **mobile technicians**

Safety and security is the responsibility of both employers and employees. It is the responsibility of every employee to maintain the safe and secure environment provided by his or her employer.

As nail technicians we come into close contact, day and night, with the general public. A large number of salons stay open until late in the evening and some premises might be in secluded locations. It is not only our responsibility but it is also common sense to take precautions for our own safety and that of our employees, colleagues and clients. There are many ways to do this and we will consider a variety of methods in this section. It is becoming much more common to hear of assaults, robberies and theft and we all need to take precautions to help prevent these happening. There is no guarantee that we can prevent all types of crime, but we can make it more difficult for these things to occur.

Personal safety

There are many ways that we can protect ourselves from harm and we need to be aware of potential sources of danger. It is good to be able to trust people but, unfortunately, we live in a society where we need to be aware that not everyone is worthy of our trust. Here are three areas to consider when thinking about harm.

Mental

Harm can be the result of intimidation, bullying, gossip, verbal abuse or jealousy. Mental abuse can come in all of these forms and from many people around you, such as clients, colleagues, managers and even strangers. Depending on an individual's personality, mental abuse can have an adverse affect on a person's self-esteem and even influence the way they work. Anyone who finds themselves in such a situation should seek help and advice from someone they trust. On too many occasions people leave their jobs without fighting for their rights. People who are being bullied usually feel very alone and inadequate and sometimes do not have the courage to ask for help, while the people around them can see what is going on but do not like to interfere. Always have the courage to stand up for yourself and always treat others as you would like to be treated.

Physical

Harm can also result from petty theft, burglary, sexual harassment, drug or alcohol abuse, physical violence on or off the premises or other threatening behaviour. Physical abuse can also come in many forms and from a variety of situations. It can be something as minor as a colleague taking your lunch or a major assault such as a sexual attack. There are ways to protect yourself inside the salon and also when you are travelling to and from work. Be sensible and be aware of your environment.

Verbal

Finally, harm can be as simple as someone shouting at you, screaming, swearing or issuing verbal threats. Verbal abuse can also come from a variety of sources whether it be from a client in the reception area or a supplier on the telephone. It may even occur inside the salon in the form of aggressive poaching of clients by a jealous colleague.

Ways to protect yourself

Personal protection is very much about common sense and is not generally something that can be taught. You should be aware of what is going on around you at all times; never take anything for granted. If a situation arises where you find you have to face an angry person, try to defuse the situation rather than inflame it with your own anger. Think ahead so that you never put yourself into a situation that has the potential to turn dangerous or costly.

Safety of colleagues

When working as part of a team it is everyone's responsibility not only to look out for themselves but also to be aware of their colleagues' safety. If the whole team is aware of each other's background – such as where they live, marital status and working hours – each member can offer support to one another inside and outside of work. For instance, if it is very late colleagues can leave work together to walk to a car park or even share lifts home. If a colleague is working alone late at night do not leave without checking that he or she has a key and locks the door from the inside after you leave. If any member of staff has an abusive or difficult client then the others should support him or her and not leave the area until the situation has been dealt with.

Salon security

There are many ways for a salon to be physically protected against theft or break-ins. With continual advances in technology there is no excuse for a salon not taking adequate precautions. Here are just a few suggestions:

- the reception desk should be behind or away from the door
- a five-bar lock should be fitted – this is also an insurance requirement
- depending on the area, metal shutters can be fitted to front windows and doors
- a closed circuit TV system can be installed
- movement and sensor alarms can be fitted
- coded alarm systems – these may be linked to a local police station
- you should register the key-holder with the local police station
- when the salon is closed, leave the till drawer open and empty
- do not leave cash in the salon overnight
- charity boxes should be hidden at night
- install security lighting

If you are thinking of opening a salon and have found suitable premises it would be a good idea to contact your local police station and ask to speak to the Crime Prevention Officer (CPO). A CPO will be able to give you advice on types of security and also advise on window, door and structural defence. He or she will also be able to provide contact numbers for relevant organisations – such as BSIA – who will then put you in contact with reputable advisers and installers of alarm systems. This advice from the police is available free of charge.

Keeping the reception area safe

Salon reception areas are usually very busy and it is easy to allow them to become cluttered. However, this offers potential thieves the opportunity to walk off with handbags and other valuable items. The receptionist – and staff in general – should be aware of the safety measures that can be taken to reduce the risk of theft:

- handbags and clients' personal belongings should remain with clients at all times
- coats should be hung in a place where they are visible and supervised by a member of staff
- retail items should not be placed near the door – preferably they should be in a display cabinet with doors

- the reception desk should be wide and have a high shelf so that clients cannot see into the till or view the appointment book
- if a panic button has been installed it should be out of sight of clients
- signs indicating that you take cheques and credit cards will suggest that you keep little cash on the premises
- it is a good idea to install a payphone for clients' use rather than let them use the one on your reception desk
- keep as little cash as possible in the till – there is nothing more tempting for an opportunist thief than seeing a till drawer open and overflowing with cash
- the till should never be emptied when clients are around
- counting money at the reception desk not only looks unprofessional but is also an opportunity for theft

The reception area should be visible from other parts of the salon and ideally should always have someone in attendance. If there is only one member of staff on the premises, say for instance during the lunch hour, then the salon door should be locked from from inside with the key left in the door – assuming, of course, that the client is a regular and not of the opposite sex. The reception area is one of the busiest in the salon and is the easiest for potential thieves to target.

Telephone abuse

It is easier to deal with someone who is being abusive over the telephone than someone who is standing in front of you, as you can simply put the phone down. However, if you are concerned about repeated abuse from the same person then it should be reported to the police.

Consider who it is that you are most likely to get abuse from and this will help you to take preventative measures:

- unhappy or dissatisfied clients
- family of staff members, i.e. angry wives or husbands
- ex-members of staff with a grievance
- sexual harassment – from acquaintances and strangers

Outside of work and banking safety

It is possible to make the salon environment safe and secure with all the latest technology, but there is little to be done outside the salon other than be sensible and take care. It is important that family members know what time you start and finish work and that colleagues are aware if you are taking any time off. There is nothing worse than being absent when other people are expecting you and have no idea where you are. It is unnecessary and discourteous – your colleagues will be relying on you to come in to do the work scheduled for that day, but they will also be able to check that you are safe or raise the alarm in an emergency if you are normally reliable. Here are a few precautions you can take when outside the salon:

- when banking takings use a special case and do not draw attention to the fact you are carrying money
- only the proprietor or manager should have responsibility for taking money to and from the bank
- always bank during office hours
- try to bank at different times each week
- consider having accounts at different banks
- bank every day in busy periods, such as around Christmas
- carry a personal alarm
- be aware of your surroundings and the people you normally meet
- if you think that you may be being followed, cross the road and head for a busy area
- if anyone attempts to attack you, shout for someone to ring the police or/and use your personal alarm

All of the above points refer to a small salon or individual technician. If you work in a larger salon, there will be strict guidelines laid down by your insurance company and the legislation in the Health and Safety Act 1974 to take into account.

Mobile technicians

If you are a mobile technician you will have to be extra careful about where you are going, who you are visiting and how much cash you are carrying. It would be sensible to let someone know what your movements are going to be each day and alert them if these are going to change. A mobile phone is essential so that you can contact someone quickly. Keep all the windows and doors of your vehicle locked, especially if you are in an area that you have never been to before. Always try to ask someone in advance what the area is like, if only to check on the availability of parking and the quality of lighting. Do not stop if you see an accident when you are on your own in the car. Have an up-to-date membership of the RAC, AA or equivalent. You must always take care to keep your kit and any valuable items out of sight when your car is parked. Ensure that you have a decent map or good directions from the client you will be visiting and let him or her know what time to expect you.

Reception

Learning objectives

In this section you will learn about:

- **the role and skills required of a receptionist**
- **acquiring an appropriate telephone manner**
- **how to keep an appointment book**
- **handling cash transactions**
- **the reception area**
- **keeping records**
- **client confidentiality**
- **acts relating to the sale and supply of goods and services**

The role of the receptionist

Some small salons do not employ a receptionist; they rely on one of the nail technicians answering the phone when they do not have a client. Remember that the client is paying for the nail technician's time – it would be very rude to take a call during that client's allocated time. If all of the staff in the salon deal with the phone and the appointment book, then they must be trained in customer care so that the telephone and appointment book are handled correctly and consistently or this could lose you clients. In larger salons, juniors are often expected to take turns fulfilling this role.

If an answer phone is used frequently, prospective clients may not bother leaving a message and may phone the next salon in the directory instead. A high percentage of the prospective clients who use a telephone directory to find a salon are not aware of the reputation of a particular salon nor have they been recommended by another client; this person will just move down the list in the phone book looking for a positive result in the form of a person who can book them an appointment rather than an answer phone service.

The salon's regular clients may leave a message but would not be sure their enquiry had been dealt with if they are aware that more than one person operates the phone lines. On many occasions messages might not reach the intended nail technician. This could lead to possible double-bookings or leave the client feeling dissatisfied with the service or the salon. A receptionist's voice at the end of the phone can prevent this situation. You should try to consider these situations from a client's point of view.

The skills of the receptionist

Most of the larger salons will employ a receptionist to aid the smooth running of the salon. The choice of receptionist is one of the most important decisions you are likely to make. The wrong choice can lead to your business suffering, while the correct choice will improve your customer service so your business will grow and flourish.

The salon needs to make the correct impression when a visitor enters the salon for the first time, as you may not get a second chance. The receptionist plays a key role here: with a smile, a pleasant greeting and a helpful, attentive attitude. The client should not be left standing around waiting for the receptionist or left to wander around the salon looking for the nail technician.

The receptionist's job involves considerably more than just pointing the client in the right direction for treatment and answering the telephone. A good receptionist should have a variety of skills, including the following.

A smart and tidy appearance

A receptionist should be clean, tidy and have a smart appearance as they represent the salon and first impressions are important.

A good telephone voice and manner

A clear, audible, polite voice on the phone is important to avoid misunderstandings over times and treatments. We will look at this skill in more detail below.

Excellent communication skills

As the receptionist welcomes all clients and visitors into the salon and liaises between the clients and the technicians, good manners and good communication skills are very important.

A receptionist who has some customer care experience is also an advantage as, sometimes, clients will have a grievance or complaint. Such occasions must be handled in the correct manner. Initially, listening skills are very important. The client should be taken to a quiet area or office and seated. The appropriate staff should be informed and the receptionist should be able to cope with this situation in a caring and supportive way without compromising either the client or the salon.

Good organisational skills and efficiency

An experienced receptionist should have acquired effective working practices and be able to keep the whole salon organised. This is the key to efficiency. Many jobs need to be done on a daily basis and establishing a good routine and procedure is the only way to ensure these are carried out effectively.

Be capable of working on his or her own initiative

A receptionist needs to develop initiative. This means starting something that needs to be done and following it up rather than waiting to be told to do something. Embarrassing situations and potential booking mishaps can thus be avoided.

Clear handwriting

Legible handwriting is important so that anybody can pick up the appointment book or notes and can read and understand them without having to ask for a translation of the writing. Printing rather than scribbling is often one way to achieve this.

Keyboard skills

In today's modern salons a computer is often a standard piece of equipment, so good keyboard skills can be a big advantage and an asset to the salon. If appointments or records are kept on the computer good organisation skills are required of the receptionist.

Team skills

In the salon environment everybody must be a team player.

Useful Tip

Keeping a message board is a good way of avoiding bits of paper building up all over the reception area. Each member of staff must get into the habit of checking it regularly.

All members of staff must know and understand their job and take full responsibility for their actions. The manager should not need to keep checking everyone's work as this is time consuming and can lead to an unpleasant atmosphere in the salon.

Other members of salon staff can lean heavily on the receptionist to make, change or move appointments in a crisis. They rely on the correct time being booked for appointments so that they are neither rushed nor have unnecessary periods without a client.

If any member of staff is running late the receptionist is the first person to offer an apology to the client and to help smooth over any problems. This is a vital role as sometimes the receptionist is the only member of staff visible in the reception area.

Telephone manner

The telephone is often the first point of contact with the client so the greeting should be pleasant and friendly. For example, you might say something similar to the following:

> Good morning. Thank you for calling Beautiful Nails. Rachel speaking, how can I help you?

It is important then to listen and give the client time to speak. That way the request may be dealt with efficiently.

The receptionist should end the telephone conversation after booking all appointments by confirming the:

- name
- appointment time
- treatment
- phone number – work and home if necessary

The receptionist should then thank the client for calling, using his or her name.

Appointment book

An organised receptionist will make a list of the treatments performed in the salon. The treatment times of all members of staff should also be noted as:

- staff changes can be frequent in the salon
- a new member of staff may need time to adjust to products or treatments

Technical Tip

The receptionist should be knowledgeable about the treatments offered by the salon and the timings of treatments, but should not enter into a consultation over the phone. They should record the client's name, phone number and, if necessary, ask a qualified member of staff to ring back at a convenient time or book a client consultation so that the client's questions can be answered and the suitability of specific treatments can be discussed confidentially.

- some members of staff may be training
- times will improve (shorten) with experience
- some staff may have problems with particular treatments
- lunch times and breaks need to be considered
- holidays and sick days must be recorded

Appointment book

	KIM	TRACY	MICHELLE	SOPHY
9.00	MRS WILLIAMS		SONIA GREEN	
9.15	0101 694 283		0101 694 732	
9.30	NEW SET	SUE PARKER	REBALANCE	
9.45	OF NAIL	0101 694 439	& BACKFILL	STARTS WORK AT 12 NOON
10.00	EXTENSIONS	NATURAL NAIL		
10.15	ACRYLIC	MANICURE		
10.30	ANN HARVEY	KELLY WATTS	CHANTAL HAYES	
10.45	0101 694 681	0101 782 3400 2 NAILS	0101 734 6011	
11.00	REBALANCE	MRS SMITH	NAT NAIL	
11.15	ACRYLIC	NEW SET	MANICURE	
11.30		OF NAIL	ROXY IRWIN	
11.45	LUNCH	EXTENSIONS	0101 691 0234	
12.00		ACRYLIC	NEW SET	ELLEN CLAYTON
12.15	PAM HUGHES	0101 694 1011	NAIL EXTENSION	0101 928 6400
12.30	0101 694 782	LUNCH	FIBREGLASS	NEW SET
12.45	PEDICURE			NAIL
13.00		MS HARRIS	JANINE HUNT	EXTENSIONS
13.15	JESS WAITES	REBALANCE	0101 462 891	AND
13.30	0101 694 700	ACRYLIC	PEDICURE	AIRBRUSH
13.45	NATURAL	0101 782 6059	AND	DESIGN
14.00	NAIL OVERLAY		NAIL ART	ROSE COLLIER
14.15	DENTIST	JILL POTTS		NAT NAIL
14.30	APPOINTMENT	REBALANCE	LUNCH	MANICURE
14.45		ACRYLIC		0101 969 4801

C	Cancellation	NS	No show	✕	Client has had treatment

Handling money

Cash, cheques and card transactions

Only authorised personnel should handle cash and its equivalents. It is often the receptionist who has this responsibility. The less access that members of staff have to the till the better, as this can greatly reduce errors.

In some salons a supervisor will be responsible for cashing up at the end of the day. This is when the cumulative and cash totals are recorded and book keeping entries are made.

Cash errors can occur for any of the following reasons:

- incorrect price charged for a service
- products priced incorrectly
- cash draw left open
- staff not trained properly
- incorrect change given

The following measures can help to prevent problems at the cash desk:

- a strict training programme for all relevant staff
- removing cash from the premises over night
- never leaving the payment point unattended
- only designated staff using the till
- implementing a system for recording all transactions
- using a modern till to record all purchases
- implementing a designated staff authorisation system for cheques and credit card transactions
- establishing a salon policy for dealing with fraudulent monetary transactions

Many of the tills available today will:

- give you daily totals broken down into a number of different transactions
- work out the change for the till operator
- identify the total takings for each staff member in the salon
- give you VAT totals
- separate product totals from service totals
- incorporate a lockable draw for when personnel are not present

Most of the major banks will rent out to you on a monthly basis a machine for credit and debit card transactions. These

Technical Tip

If you join the Federation of Small Businesses this will automatically reduce your monthly machine rental payment, lower your switch (debit) charges and also reduce the percentage payable on credit card transactions.

Federation of Small Businesses, Whittle Way, Blackpool Business Park, Blackpool, Lancashire FY4 2FE.
Tel: 01253-336000

Part of the receptionist's job involves preventing visitors from casually walking around the salon, including paying customers and cold callers such as sales representatives or tradesmen.

The reception area is the ideal place for a salon stylebook showing the latest trends in shapes, colours or nail art.

machines deposit all card transactions directly into your bank account. They also have a training facility for use by the supervisor when training new employees. All of the card machine companies offer staff training when they install the machine and have a helpline for any subsequent enquiries.

The reception area

The reception area is the first part of your salon that a client will see and it is the area which will have the greatest impact on visitors. It must be a welcoming, clean, friendly and comfortable place as clients must never feel intimidated or embarrassed to ask questions.

Not all salons will have the space available to set aside a large area, but you should try to make provision for a desk, a telephone, the appointment book and comfortable seating away from the busy salon area.

Many of the following items can usefully be included in your reception area:

- A *salon price list* should be displayed to avoid any misunderstandings over prices.
- *Salon promotional information* on treatments can be made available – check with your product suppliers, many of whom produce beautiful leaflets precisely for this purpose which will save you time and expense.
- *Aftercare leaflets* are also produced by many manufacturers for sale to salons, recommending the correct aftercare products and such leaflets serve to back up the **aftercare advice** given by the nail technician.
- *Comfortable seating* for clients while they are waiting is important as they must not be allowed to interrupt other customers' treatments.
- The *magazines* in your reception area say a lot about the type of image you are trying to create; they should be in good condition and preferably not months out of date.
- Some salons like to offer *tea, coffee or soft drinks*, but do make sure there are no dirty cups left around, always clear them away immediately.
- The reception area should stock the *retail products* that the nail technicians recommend as aftercare products. If these products are not available in the salon, clients will buy them in the high street, leading to lost revenue for the salon and the possibility of the client not carrying out the aftercare correctly by using the wrong products.

Keeping records

All client consultation forms and client record cards are confidential and should therefore be locked in an appropriate cabinet. No one – without exception – should have access to this information apart from authorised personnel or the individual client. Under no circumstances may phone numbers or other personal details be passed on to a third party. If client details are kept on a computer you must also comply with the Data Protection Act.

Client confidentiality

All conversations and discussions with your client about their treatment are private and should remain so. Some of the day-to-day conversations held with a client during treatment are also in confidence and should not be repeated. Staff must observe the strict rules of the salon and all junior staff members must be made aware of the importance of confidentiality.

Acts relating to the sale and supply of goods and services

All salons should be aware of the legislation relating to the sale of goods and services. Staff should be informed of their responsibilities in this respect, and kept up to date on any changes in the legislation. In what follows we briefly consider six acts which will affect you as a nail technician. Health and Safety legislation is covered in greater detail in Chapter 2.

The Sale of Goods Act 1979

This requires goods to be accurately described without misleading the customer in any way. The law takes into account:

- suitability of the goods for a particular purpose
- their quality
- description of the goods

The Supply of Goods and Services Act 1982

This act went further than the 1979 act to include standards of service, which should be:

- of reasonable quality
- described accurately
- fit for the intended purpose

The act also requires that the service provided to a customer should be:

- carried out with reasonable skill and care
- within a reasonable time
- for a reasonable cost

The Sale and Supply of Goods Act 1994

This act amended all previous acts by introducing guidelines on defining the quality of service.

The Consumer Protection Act 1987

This piece of European Community (now European Union (EU)) legislation provides consumers with protection when buying any goods or services to ensure that all the products used on a client during the treatment, in addition to service or retail products sold to the client, are safe.

Trades Description Act 1968 (revised 1972)

This act protects customers from misleading descriptions or claims relating to treatments and retail products. For example, a statement such as 'This is a miracle cure, which will prevent you needing to maintain your nail extensions' is not likely to be true and would therefore be regarded as misleading.

Data Protection Act 1984

The Data Protection Act requires businesses to be registered and comply with the rules for the storage and security of all data relating to clients' records and maintaining client confidentiality. In today's market, many salons rely on the use of computers to control stock and to record client information. The Data Protection Act serves to protect clients' personal information. The act requires that all businesses using computers in this way ensure that the following controls are put in place:

- only relevant information should be stored
- there is only authorised access to this information
- individuals are allowed to access the information that is held on them
- reasonable precautions must be taken to prevent unauthorised access to any information stored

However you decide to record and store your clients' information, a client should never under any circumstances be able to look at or read another client's record card. Never leave a client consultation or record card out on a desk. Records must be returned to their file, desk or draw immediately after treatment. Remember that all information is strictly private. If a salon does not set clear standards of professionalism and maintain them the clients will notice and quite probably take their custom elsewhere.

Effective stock control

Learning objectives

In this section you will learn about:

- **the utility or opportunity value of stock**
- **terminology**
- **planning stock levels**
- **stock control**
- **storage**
- **stock rotation**

It is a crucial part of any business that the management is aware of the amount invested in stock, what products and retail are held in stock and ways of effectively rotating stock. A failure to organise these matters could result in loss of business and revenue, and give the salon a bad reputation because technicians are unable to do their jobs properly. Eventually clients will find other retail outlets for the services and products they require.

Utility or opportunity value

All stock has value which can be categorised in two ways:

- all items in stock have a utility or opportunity value – they will make money from being used or sold
- all items have a monetary value, as they all cost something to buy

Potential clients may ask for either a product or a service and if the necessary products are not available to sell or be used to perform the treatment the client will have three options:

- to accept an alternative treatment or product, perhaps after some persuasion
- to find another salon or retail outlet which can provide what they want
- to wait until the item or service is available

The last two options could involve a considerable financial loss to the salon in the long term, not only from that particular customer but also from other potential customers – friends, relatives, colleagues and acquaintances who might follow your last customer's recommendation and go to a rival salon.

Terminology

Stock is a term used in business to encompass all the items kept by the salon to be either used or sold. Stock can take many forms depending on the type of salon and the services it provides, but usually falls into the following main categories:

- *Stock in trade* refers to items that are ready to sell and have been bought into the salon for retail, e.g. consumables such as polish remover, polish, files, buffers and cuticle oil.
- *Raw materials and components* are the products used by the nail technician to produce the end result, including hand creams, oils, files, tips and adhesives, etc.
- *Finished goods* are what the nail technician has produced at the end of the service, e.g. a set of sculptured nails.
- *Spare parts* are items that wear out or break down in the salon, such as manicure bowls, pump dispensers, brushes and tools.
- *Consumables* are small and inexpensive items that are used daily and need to be replenished frequently, such as till rolls, cotton wool, cleaning materials. Any item which does not come into any other category will fall into the consumables category.

There are two main pieces of documentation which deal with stock:

- An *invoice* is a document that records the fact that ownership of goods has passed from a supplier to a customer. It will tell the customer how much is owed

NAILS R US

2a Smith Street
London
W1 4GF
Tel: 0x0 9876 5432
Fax: 0x0 9876 5431
email: payment@nails.co.uk
website: www.nails.co.uk
VAT Reg.No.000 000

Account Number:	101-1001
Salon Name:	All Nails
Contact Name:	Michelle Jones
Address:	14 High Street
	London
	SW17 8YH
Telephone:	0x0 1234 5678
Fax:	0x0 1234 5679
Statement Date:	3-Jul-2001
Due Date:	10-Jul-2001

ACCOUNT STATEMENT

Code	Description	Unit Price	Quantity	Total Price
692	White Towel	£5.00	1	£5.00
5600	Nail Brush	£0.50	6	£3.00
609	Hand Cream	£5.99	2	£11.98
150	Nail Varnish Remover	£2.00	10	£20.00

Payment terms are strictly 30 days from invoice date	
Please make cheques payable to NAILS R US	
Credit & Debit cards accepted, please have your card details ready when you call	

Sub Total	£39.98
Postage	£4.50
VAT	£7.78
Total to date	£52.26

and what VAT is due, if any. Invoices should be carefully filed away after being paid for future inspection by accountants, tax or VAT inspectors. They are tax input documents for VAT as well as records of expenditure. Each business expenditure needs to be accounted for by the production of a receipt or receipted invoice.

- A *credit note* is the reverse of an invoice. It is a note which shows that a supplier owes a customer money for any one of the following reasons:

  1 goods supplied were damaged
  2 goods were not received
  3 overcharging by the supplier
  4 returned goods

Planning stock levels

Salon stock control is a very important part of your business, especially if your turnover in retail products is very small. In such cases a large investment in stock would be foolish without some kind of promotional plan being put in place to improve the situation.

Bearing in mind the value of stock, the size of your stock should represent your turnover in both retail items and products for treatments. Too much stock on the shelves could cause you a financial problem, especially if you are borrowing money to finance your business as you will be paying interest on your loan.

Some shops and salons like to use a just-in-time method for ordering goods in. This works by minimising the investment and amount of stock the salon holds and relies on manufacturers being able to deliver within 24 hours of ordering. To make this system work you will need to check that the supplier holds adequate stock levels and can guarantee delivery within 24 hours.

Stock control

There are two basic systems of maintaining stock control and collating all the information required:

- manual
- computerised

If the salon computer is used for stock control, it can help to reduce errors, especially if you set minimum and maximum stock levels. The computer will flag up all the products that need to be reordered.

Manual systems require greater discipline and rely on every member of staff following the rules and keeping the information on the stock record cards up to date, preferably after each sale. When the minimum stock level is reached a new purchase order is raised.

Maintaining stock records should not be complicated or time consuming otherwise staff will put this job off and find themselves trying to remember at the end of the day what they have sold leading to errors and incorrect stock levels.

The following checklist will help you control your stock by maintaining accurate stock records.

- Regular stock checks must be done, not just at the end of the year. It should be possible for the stock keeper to see all stock levels at a glance.
- Identify one member of staff as a stock keeper with responsibility for controlling the situation and who should be aware of the following elements:

NO	PRODUCT CODE	PRODUCT	BASE STOCK	DATE: 29/2/93							DATE: 7/3/93						
				Counter stock	Stockroom stock	Total stock (i)	Order	Received	Total stock (ii)	Sold	Counter stock	Stockroom stock	Total stock (i)	Order	Received	Total stock (ii)	Sold
1	00191	Nail Polishes	10	6	2	8	2	/	8	2	4	2	6	/	2	8	/
2	00192	Nail Polish Remover	10	4	2	6	4	/	6	/	4	2	6	/	4	10	2
3	00193	Cuticle Oil	10	4	2	6	4	/	6	4	2	/	2	4	4	6	1
4	00194	Hand Lotions	6	4	/	4	2	/	4	1	3	/	3	1	2	5	2
5	00195	Nail Soak	5	2	2	4	1	/	4	2	2	/	2	2	1	3	2
6	00196	Acrylic Powder	5	2	/	2	3	/	2	/	2	/	2	/	3	5	1
7	00197	Sculpting Forms	8	4	2	6	2	/	6	4	2	/	2	4	2	4	1
8	00198	UV Gel	8	5	/	5	3	/	5	1	4	/	4	1	3	7	2
9	00199	Fibreglass	5	2	1	3	/	2	5	1	3	1	4	1	/	4	2
10	00200	Base Coat	5	3	1	4	1	/	4	3	1	/	1	3	1	2	/
11	00201	Top Coat	4	2	1	3	1	/	4	3	1	/	1	3	1	4	2
12	00202	Nail Art Paints	6	3	/	3	3	/	3	2	1	/	1	2	3	4	1
13	00203	Rhinestones	6	2	3	5	1	1	6	2	3	1	4	2	1	5	/
14	00204	Couch Roll	6	4	/	4	2	/	4	2	2	/	2	2	2	4	1
15	00205	Cotton Wool	6	2	/	3	2	1	4	/	3	1	4	/	/	4	2

STOCK SHEET

Stock record sheet

1 location of all stock
2 quantities of all products held
3 tracking system, i.e. where stock has gone, whether to the salon or retail
4 the point at which stock must be reordered

- Consider all forthcoming promotions and plan in advance.
- Keep a book to list all products that are running low and are in need of ordering.
- Set minimum and maximum stock levels.
- Check delivery times and order accordingly.
- Try to place one large order regularly rather than lots of smaller orders which could incur higher delivery costs.
- All deliveries must be checked against the delivery note or invoice for errors, and any mistakes must be reported immediately to the supplier.

- Never assume someone else has dealt with a shortage; check that the item has been added to the shortage list or that the stock keeper has been informed.

Storage

All products must be stored correctly and safely. It could be costly for the salon if a member of staff has an accident or if damaged stock has to be replaced. The following points should be considered when setting out your stock area:

- it should have a lockable door
- one person should be responsible for stock
- an up-to-date stock list is kept
- the stockroom has a controlled temperature
- appropriate fire precautions are taken for products being stored
- COSHH (Control of Substances Hazardous to Health) information is readily to hand
- protective clothing is available, if required
- there should be strong, safe shelving with heavy items kept at a lower height
- stock should be kept away from sunlight
- chemicals are to be stored correctly in the recommended containers
- all products should be in their original containers
- labels should be clear and undamaged
- contact details of suppliers should be kept centrally and be easily accessible
- emergency and First Aid information should always be to hand
- any relevant Health and Safety literature should also be available

All members of the salon's staff should be aware of these guidelines relating to the storage of stock, not just the stock keeper.

Stock rotation

All stock has a 'shelf life', that is a period of time after which it is not going to work effectively or may even be unsafe to use. It is the salon's responsibility to know how long each item can be kept in the stockroom or on the shelves. The 'first in first out' rule should always apply without exception – you should always use the oldest stock first. The following points will help you to plan stock rotation effectively:

- restock shelves from the back so that older items are pushed forwards
- packaging can change, so check with the suppliers before you order a large amount that this is not going to happen in the near future
- if using natural products check carefully as they often have a much more limited shelf life
- if stock is out of date it should be disposed of
- for stock that is not selling consider putting it on special offer
- look regularly at your best and worst sellers and reorder accordingly
- plan ahead for seasonal changes such as Valentine's Day and Christmas
- presentation is one of the keys to good sales – make sure shelves are well stocked and look attractive as this will encourage a quicker turnover

Managing stock is essentially about monitoring product quality, quantity and security whilst taking into account supply and demand.

Chapter summary

This chapter has touched on the areas of stock control and reception skills but its main aim has been to identify the range of areas that each potential professional nail technician needs to consider before embarking on their nail career. Becoming a professional nail technician is not just about performing nail treatments; technicians are business people as well and this chapter covers the main areas of knowledge needed to run a business as easily and effectively as possible. It identifies the various career paths every technician may choose to follow and the advantages and disadvantages of each.

Working safely

Our work as professional nail technicians means that we use specific work practices, chemicals and equipment that are subject to certain Health and Safety Regulations and we need to have a sound knowledge of those that apply to the nail industry in general. We endeavour to cover as much as we can in the space available here and intend the information to be up to date at the time of writing. All Health and Safety Regulations are subject to change over a period of time due to national legislation and the influence of the European Union. It is your duty to yourself, your colleagues and your clients to keep yourself up to date on any new legislation that is introduced. In this chapter we will look at cross infection and how to avoid it by implementing rules for keeping your working environment clean and as germ free as possible. We touch our clients every hour of our working life and need to be aware of the precautions we should be taking to inhibit the spread of any disease-causing organisms. Overexposure is another vital area to consider and this chapter also covers the main ways in which chemicals can be misused and the consequences of ignoring important safety rules.

In this chapter we will consider the following aspects:

- **Health and Safety legislation**
- **overexposure**
- **cross infection and salon hygiene**

Health and Safety legislation

Learning objectives

In this section you will learn about:

- **the Health and Safety Act 1974 and other relevant acts**

- **Control of Substances Hazardous to Health (COSHH)**

- **First Aid at work**

- **risk assessment**

- **fire regulations**

- **electricity at work**

Because it is such an important issue, there is a great deal of legislation relating to health and safety. Within the service industry, we are legally obliged to provide a safe and hygienic working environment, paying careful attention to health, safety and security.

Health and Safety at Work Act 1974 (revised 1994)

Health and safety at work relates to the measures designed to protect the health and safety of people while they are at work and also to protect members of the public visiting the workplace – whether they are paying customers or simply passers-by. Most countries in the western world have developed legislation to protect the health and safety of their workforce and in Britain employers must take reasonable care to protect their employees from the risk of disease, injury or death. Employers have a responsibility to protect themselves and those around them from the same risks.

It is a legal requirement for employers either to display an approved Health and Safety poster or to supply employees with an equivalent leaflet. This material is updated from time to time in line with changes in legislation.

The factors that affect health and safety can be divided into three main groups:

1 *occupational factors* – people could be at risk from illness or injury from the work they do, e.g. asthma from paint spraying

2 *environmental factors* – the conditions in which people

Courtesy of HSE

Health and Safety poster

work may cause problems, e.g. noisy environments can cause deafness

3 *human factors* – poor behaviour and bad attitudes can contribute to accidents, e.g. lack of concentration, carelessness and rushing jobs

Your employer has a duty under the law to protect, as far as is reasonably practicable, your health, safety and welfare at work. The Health and Safety at Work Act added further regulations to existing legislation. The Health and Safety Executive (HSE) appoints inspectors to do ensure that employers comply with the act. Local authorities are responsible for business premises and shops and they enforce the requirements of the act. In general, employers' duties include making the workplace safe and reducing risks to health by providing proper supervision and training.

The Health and Safety Act 1974 incorporates a variety of legislation and regulations as discussed below.

The Management of Health and Safety at Work Regulations 1992

This act requires a salon owner, for example, to make formal arrangements for maintaining and improving safe working conditions and practices. These arrangements should include providing training for all employees and monitoring working risks. This latter point is known as **risk assessment**.

The Personal Protective Equipment (PPE) at Work Regulations 1992

Through the process of risk assessment, managers should identify activities that require special protective clothing or equipment to be worn. These articles should then be made available to all staff and a good supply kept on the premises at all times.

The Workplace (Health and Safety and Welfare) Regulations 1992

This act provides the employer with a code of practice that can help them to maintain a safe and secure working environment. These regulations cover the legal requirements that relate to the following aspects of the working environment:

- ventilation
- safe and secure salon layout
- sanitary conveniences

- safe flooring, easy access and traffic routes
- drinking and washing facilities
- changing facilities
- staff room facilities
- handling of waste materials
- maintenance and upkeep of windows, doors and walls
- cleanliness of the working environment
- maintenance of all equipment
- maintenance of the workplace in general

The Manual Handling Operation Regulations 1992

A risk assessment should be carried out by an employer of any activities undertaken by employees which involve manual lifting. Evidence should be provided that the following have been considered:

- the capabilities of each individual worker
- any potential risk of injury
- the manual movement involved in the lifting activity
- any action needed to minimise potential risks

The Provision and Use of Work Equipment Regulations (PUWER) 1992

This act requires the identification of any new and old equipment that is used. Specific regulations address the dangers and potential risk of injury that could occur during the operation of certain equipment. They state the duties of the employer, employees and the self-employed. It also identifies the requirement to select suitable equipment and attend to its maintenance. Equipment manufacturers also have a responsibility to provide information on any specific training needed to operate the equipment.

Employers' Liability (compulsory insurance) Act 1969

Employers are responsible for the health and safety of their employees while at work. Employees may be injured while at work, and former employees may be eligible to make a claim if they become ill as a result of the work they did whilst in your employment. Both groups may try to claim compensation from you if they believe you are responsible.

The Employer's Liability (compulsory insurance) Act 1969 ensures that employers have at least the minimum level of insurance cover against any such claims.

An HSE inspector can check that you have employer's liability insurance with an approved insurer for at least £5m. The inspector can ask to see your certificate and other details and you can be fined up to £2500 for any day you are without suitable insurance cover. If the certificate is not displayed and it is not produced on demand, you could be fined up to £1000. Employers should keep all insurance certificates that have been issued.

Technical Tip

Don't forget about public and product liability insurance. See Chapter 1.

The Offices, Shops and Railway Premises Act 1963

This addresses the minimum standards required in the following areas for premises to operate:

- sanitation
- cleanliness
- ventilation
- lighting
- overcrowding

This act is linked to the Health and Safety at Work Act. Note that new EU directives will affect this act. It covers each part of shop premises from the shop to the showroom, hall, stair and passageways. Premises are required to have appropriate fire fighting equipment and clean staff toilets and washroom facilities which are easily accessible and suitably lit and ventilated. Halls, floors, passageways and stairs should be properly constructed, free from obstructions and properly maintained. There should also be an area where staff can hang clothing.

Control of Substances Hazardous to Health (COSHH)

Using chemicals or other hazardous substances at work could put people's health at risk. Therefore employers are required by law to control exposure to hazardous chemicals and substances to prevent ill health. Employers have a duty to protect employees and any visitors who may be exposed. All employers must comply with the Control of Substances Hazardous to Health Regulations 1999, but it is a good management tool as it sets out basic steps. If an employer fails to meet the required standards by not adequately controlling hazardous substances or chemicals they can

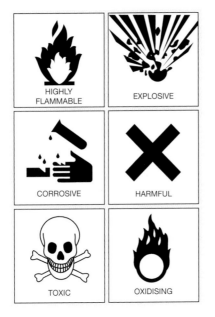

COSHH warning signs

be prosecuted. Adverse effects can range from mild eye irritation to chronic lung disease. Understanding and following the rules of COSHH can not only lead to safer working conditions, but can also improve employees' morale and subsequently raise productivity in the workplace.

The next seven stages will help to guide you through COSHH regulations.

Stage one

Carry out a risk assessment to assess any hazardous substances that may give cause for concern in your workplace.

Stage two

When the risks have been identified, record them and decide what action and precautions – if any – are to be taken. Check with product manufacturers for COSHH or material safety data sheets (MSDSs). You should read and understand all the information you are giving. If you do not, you must ask questions. Ignorance would not be an acceptable excuse if there is a problem.

Remember to check that any systems you introduce work effectively. Nail technicians should be aware of the **routes of entry** into the body. The products that are used in the nail industry can be absorbed through the skin if not used correctly. Checks must be made and regular training put in place to prevent mistakes being made.

Stage three

Under the COSHH regulations there must be adequate control of chemical usage to prevent overexposure. In the nail industry exposure can be greatly reduced by good housekeeping and regularly updated training.

Stage four

Training should be monitored to make sure employees are adopting the techniques they have been taught, and all comments should be recorded.

Stage five

Monitor the exposure level if necessary. Nail technicians must know how to recognise overexposure symptoms and what to do in an emergency. All symptoms should be recorded.

Stage six

Carry out appropriate health surveillance if COSHH regulations have set specific requirements.

Stage seven

Ensure all employees are fully trained, informed about procedures, kept up to date and supervised.

Disposal of chemicals

All chemicals and substances identified in stage one of the risk assessment must have a designated means of disposal. The manufacturers keep COSHH or MSDS sheets and they will normally be happy to supply you with the relevant information if requested. The activity box will help you to establish good working practices for the disposal of chemicals.

A COSHH or MSDS will give you information about:

- any hazardous ingredients
- safe exposure levels
- possible routes of entry into the body
- emergency First Aid advice
- fire precautions and appropriate fire equipment
- safe working practices and safety precautions
- early warning signs of overexposure

First Aid and accidents

Whenever an illness or injury occurs wherever it may be and whatever its cause, it is imperative that the correct action is quickly taken. The First Aid Regulations 1981 require employers to provide appropriate and adequate equipment and to inform employees of all First Aid arrangements.

Signs should be placed telling staff who the first aider (or appointed person) is and where the First Aid box is kept. There is legislation relating to how many first aiders or appointed persons there must be, according to the type of business and number of employees. The appointed person is someone who can take charge if an injury occurs or if someone falls ill at work. One of this person's duties is to take responsibility for the First Aid box and this includes stocking it and replacing any item that may be used. This person should be available at all times but may not necessarily be a qualified first aider. The first aider is a

Activity

- Contact the manufacturer for COSHH or MSDS sheets.
- Draw up a chart listing all chemicals used in the salon.
- List all safety equipment required and precautions which should be taken.
- List the requirements for disposal of all chemicals in the salon.
- Set and record acceptable standards of safety within the salon.
- Ensure all staff are trained to the required level.
- Record all accidents and their details.
- Review procedures on a regular basis.

person who has been trained in the administration of First Aid and who holds a current First Aid certificate. Their training must be approved by the HSE. A first aider can also take the responsibilities of an appointed person.

It is not a nail technician's responsibility to treat an injury or condition. This should be left to a professional such as a doctor or nurse. But it is, however, the nail technician's responsibility to see that help is called and only to apply First Aid if he or she holds a current certificate. Although it is not a legal requirement for nail technicians to have a First Aid certificate it is a good idea for all individuals to gain this qualification. The three main organisations that offer certified training are St John Ambulance (in England and Wales), the British Red Cross and the St Andrews Ambulance Association (in Scotland).

First Aid kit

There is no standard list of items that should be kept in a First Aid box. If there are no special risks in the working environment, the size and contents of a First Aid box can vary according to the number of employees and the nature of the business.

The following is only a list of suggested items:

- First Aid booklet or leaflet giving general advice
- sterile eye dressings
- individually wrapped triangular bandages
- packet of individually wrapped sterile adhesive dressings in assorted sizes
- medium-sized (12 cm × 12 cm) sterile, individually wrapped, non-medicated wound dressings
- large (18 cm × 18 cm) sterile, individually wrapped, non-medicated wound dressings
- safety pins
- disposable gloves

Consider also the following points:

- Because of the nature of the nail business, the kit should also include eye wash and an eye bath.
- Tablets and medicines should *not* be kept in the First Aid box.
- COSHH and MSDS sheets should be available in case of accidents.

Activity

- Locate the First Aid kit and the accident book.
- Check who is the first aider or the appointed person responsible for the kit.

Reporting accidents

Accident book

The reporting of all accidents and near misses must be recorded in the accident book which should be kept with the First Aid kit. Note that all accidents should be recorded, no matter how minor. The following information is required:

- the full name and address of the person/s involved in the accident
- date, time and place of the accident
- circumstances of the accident
- all details of what may have contributed to the accident
- any witness accounts of events
- witness's name and address
- action that was taken, e.g. First Aid, ambulance, etc.

Reporting of Injuries, Diseases and Dangerous Occurrences Regulations 1995 (RIDDOR 95)

Under RIDDOR 95, employers are legally required to report certain injuries, diseases and near misses at work. The information helps the Health and Safety Executive and local authorities to identify how and where risk occurs. This information assists them in their investigations of serious accidents.

Death or major injury

This category includes any accident connected with work, including physical violence. If an employee, visitor or self-employed person working on the premises suffers illness or injury which is work-related and affects the person over a three-day period a fully completed accident form (F2508) must be sent to the enforcing authority within ten days.

Disease

If a doctor reports to you that an employee is suffering from a reportable work-related disease you must complete form F2508 A and forward it to the enforcing authority. Reportable diseases include certain poisonings, some skin diseases such as occupational dermatitis, skin cancer, chrome ulcer and oil folliculitis/acne. Lung diseases including occupational asthma, hepatitis, anthrax and tuberculosis are also notifiable.

Definition of major injuries, dangerous occurrences and disease

Reportable major injuries are any fracture other than to fingers, thumbs, or toes; the dislocation of the hip, knee, shoulder, or spine; amputation; loss of sight – temporary or permanent; a chemical or hot injury to the eye or any permanent injury to the eye; any injury resulting in an electric shock or electric burn leading to unconsciousness or that requires resuscitation or admittance to hospital for more than 24 hours; unconsciousness caused by asphyxia or exposure to a harmful substance or biological agent; acute illness requiring medical treatment, or loss of consciousness arising from absorption of any substance by inhalation, or ingestion through the skin; acute illness requiring medical treatment where there is reason to believe that this resulted from exposure to a biological agent or its toxins or to infected material.

For further information see the HSE leaflet, RIDDOR Explained, or consult http://www.hse.gov.uk/riddor

Risk assessment

There are two types or **risk assessment**. The first is one which we all do every day of our lives, such as when crossing the road. We stop, look, listen and assess the speed of oncoming traffic; we look at weather conditions and consider if we should be crossing at a zebra or pelican crossing. We then assess the overall risk of crossing at that particular spot and how long we have to do it. This is called an *informal risk assessment*.

The second type is known as a *formal risk assessment* and should be carried out in every workplace where there are people employed or working as self-employed. They are usually carried out by a trained member of staff who is familiar with the task being performed and is aware of the relevant safety issues. External consultants can be employed to conduct a risk assessment for a company which does not have the time or the resources to carry out an assessment. These consultants will usually liaise with managers, supervisors, or other members of staff to help in the writing of the risk assessment.

A risk assessment is the process by which staff, supervisors and managers are asked to identify potential risks in the workplace and find ways by which accidents, problems and potential ill health can be prevented. A risk assessment is a legal requirement but can also be useful for companies as it can help to identify problem areas, decide on priorities, highlight staff training needs and help with quality assurance programmes.

It is an examination of the hazards that cause harm to people in your working environment. Once this has been achieved you can ascertain whether your precautions are adequate, or whether more can be done to prevent injury and harm. The object of this section is to guide you through the assessment of the risk in your own business.

What is a hazard?

A hazard is anything that has the potential to cause harm. For example:

- damaged flooring
- damaged equipment
- harmful substances
- sharp tools
- fire
- bad lighting
- noise levels
- inadequate ventilation

What is a risk?

Risk is the likelihood that a hazard could cause harm or injury and can be affected by a variety of factors. For instance, if a salon has a carpet that has a tear or an edge curling up, the risk factors could be:

- the level of lighting in that area
- how bad the damage to the carpet is
- how many people walk over it
- what type of shoes those people wear

Control measures

A control measure can be either an action or an item that will help to remove or reduce a potential risk. Hazards should be removed if possible. If they cannot be removed, then it is important to reduce the risk by making staff and clients aware of the potential problem. In the example of the carpet above, put a barrier or warning sign over it.

Your workplace should be carefully examined for potential hazards, some of which will be very obvious, such as trailing flexes from lamps, and others which are not so obvious, such as dust that could be inhaled. Once all the risks have been identified you can consider the consequences of injury or harm in the long term. Look at the likeliest scenarios first

Activity

Look at the potential hazards in your place of work. Concentrate on significant hazards, things that could cause harm or injury. Ask questions of your employees to check that all risks have been considered. This information should be recorded, given to all staff and a record kept on site.

and the less likely ones afterwards, but always remedy *all* potential risks. You may decide to introduce some personal protective equipment into the salon, but if you do not then you should consider the long-term risk of not doing so on yourself, your staff and your business.

Whatever control measures you put in place, they must be checked on a regular basis to make sure they continue to work efficiently.

Risk assessments themselves should be reviewed at least every six months or when new techniques, products, or equipment are introduced into the salon. If a risk is identified records should be updated immediately.

Decide exactly who is at risk from which hazards, for example new personnel, young trainees, visitors, members of the public, etc.

Evaluate all the risks and decide if the precautions are adequate or whether new procedures need to be put in place. Consider what the law says you must do to limit the risk. Have you put the industry standards in place? The law says you must do what is reasonably practicable to keep your workplace safe. Decide whether you can remove the hazard, and if not what will be the best way to control the hazard and make conditions as safe as possible. In the nail industry chemicals and solvents are used, so these need to be assessed and the necessary precautions taken, including the control of substances hazardous to health regulations (COSHH). Staff must be trained in the use, application, and transportation of products or hazardous substances.

All of the comments and findings derived from the assessment must be recorded. Any changes made should also be recorded. If you have less than five employees, you are not required by law to write anything down. However, the fact that you have less than five employees does not mean there are no risks and it is useful to keep a record. It will show that checks have been made and that precautions are in place. Such information could be invaluable when training new personnel. Your findings should always be shared with your employees.

Review all the information you have gathered on a regular basis. If any new substances or machinery are introduced then they should also be considered. It is also a good idea to check regularly that any precautionary measures remain in place and are still working properly.

The following pages show two styles of form which could be used when conducting a risk assessment.

SUGGESTED FORM FOR RISK ASSESSMENT 1

NAME OF SALON Nails R Us
COMPANY ADDRESS 1 High Street
Anytown
POSTCODE AN1 2YT

DATE 02 January 2002
REVIEW DATE 02 April 2002

LIST HAZARDS	PEOPLE AT RISK	CONTROLS IN PLACE	ACTION TAKEN
- Wires in a heavy traffic area	- Clients, staff and all visitors	- Technician was responsible for removal of gel machine when not in use	- Trunking placed and wires organised. Technician reprimanded
- Boxes in front of Fire Exit	- Clients, staff and all visitors	- Manager in charge of keeping fire routes clear	- Boxes removed to store room and 'KEEP CLEAR' notice placed. Staff trained and Manager cautioned
- Fire extinguishers not in high-risk areas, such as the chemical store, by the fire exit.	- Clients, staff and all visitors	- Annual check on all fire extinguishers and placement	- Advice was sought on correct placement.
- One fire extinguisher not serviced for the past two years.	- Clients, staff and all visitors	- 1 new extinguisher was acquired after service visit and therefore placed in an unsuitable position	- Fire extinguisher contractor was called in to carry out a service
- Lose carpet tile	- Clients, staff and all visitors	- None	- Door was dragging up carpet tile. Door was rehung and new carpet tiles were fitted.
- Waste bin overflowing causing a problem with vapours	- Clients and staff	- Each technician is responsible for correct disposal of his or her own waste.	- A larger metal bins provided. Technician reprimanded.

NOTES
- Tracey had complained about tripping over wires and loose carpet tiles (pleased with the repairs and actions taken)
- Risk assessor picked up on the fire escape routes being blocked and extinguishers out of service date

NAME *Claudine Rowley* SIGNED *CERowley* DATE *02.01.02*

Risk assessment form

SUGGESTED FORM FOR FIRE RISK ASSESSMENT

NAME OF SALON Nails R Us
COMPANY ADDRESS 1 High Street
Anytown
POSTCODE AN1 2YT

DATE 10 January 2002
REVIEW DATE 10 April 2002

LIST HAZARDS	PEOPLE AT RISK	CONTROLS IN PLACE	ACTION TAKEN
- Roller shutters on metal cabinets where chemicals are stored were not locked down at night	- Staff	- Manager to close up all cabinets on a nightly basis	- Manager cautioned
- Bins need to be metal	- Staff and Clients	- Technicians responsible for own waste and correct disposal of.	- 6 metal pedal bins purchased
- Incorrect extinguisher for chemical and electrical fires	- Staff, clients and visitors	- Inherited from previous tenant	- New extinguisher
- Fire exit doors need new signs	- Staff, clients and visitors	- Inherited from previous tenant	- New exit and fire door signs purchased and placed
- One fire exit blocked by stock boxes	- Staff, clients and visitors	- Manager to have removed all stock items to designated stock room	- Manager cautioned

NOTES
- We have replaced one incorrect extinguisher, total present in salon is now 3 – all are suitable for electrical and chemical fires
- Managers Comments: Salon had been very busy at the time of a delivery and driver placed boxes in front of the fire exit

NAME *Claudine Rowley*   SIGNED *CERowley*   DATE *10.01.02*

Fire Risk assessment form

The Fire Regulations and the Fire Protection Act 1971

All workplaces should have or make arrangements for detecting a fire. If smoke alarms are used they must conform to British Standard 5446: part 1. Another option is smoke detectors, but you must make sure they are designed for the purpose, as those used for the domestic market are manufactured to a different standard than those for automatic detection in business premises. Smoke alarms tend to be more sensitive than smoke detectors, thus sometimes causing unwanted fire alerts. Ensure that what you use is suitable for the situation, for example a heat detector may perform better than a smoke detector in a fume-laden or dusty environment, but may not be appropriate for the rest of the premises.

Flammable liquids can present a significant risk of fire. Vapours are usually heavier than air and can travel long distances, so are more likely to reach an ignition source. Fire extinguishers can be purchased from local DIY stores, but in order for insurance policies to be valid they must be annually serviced and maintained. Fire extinguishers can last for several years and some are guaranteed for up to ten years but the correct maintenance is essential.

Fire extinguishers are available for different types of fire. The type required for your business will depend on the risk classification and the kind of fire to which your business is vulnerable. Fire extinguishers should normally be located in conspicuous positions on escape routes, preferably near exit doors. If for any reason this is not possible, Health and Safety (Signs and Signals) Regulations 1996, require that their location must be indicated by signs and where possible directional arrows.

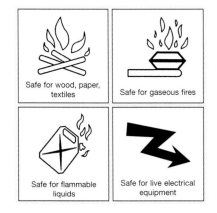

Safe for wood, paper, textiles	Safe for gaseous fires
Safe for flammable liquids	Safe for live electrical equipment

Fire extinguisher symbols

Fire drill training

The fire training given to your employees should be specific to your workplace. You must make provision to explain emergency procedures to all staff and personnel; information should be clear and understood by all your employees. Take into account the findings of the risk assessment and the work activities, duties and responsibilities of employees. Training should include practical fire drills, arrangements for calling the fire brigade and evacuation of the premises.

Fire precaution legislation deals with general fire precautions. These include:

- means of protection and how to give warning in case of fire

- the provision of means of escape
- ways of fighting fire
- the training of staff in fire safety
- how to raise the alarm

Fire regulations include a requirement to undertake an assessment of the fire risks on your premises. This is to include the risk of a fire occurring and the risk to people in the event of fire. Before starting your risk assessment check if there are any existing arrangements. Your risk assessment could identify additional requirements that need to be addressed. If you have any doubts or queries about the regulations or how they apply to your business contact the local fire authority for advice.

A fire risk assessment can be carried out independently or as part of the general risk assessment process. Using the form shown earlier, draw a floor plan marking doors, windows, fire extinguishers and other exits. This will help you to identify any obstacles in the event of evacuation and allow you to pinpoint problem areas. After completing the floor plan the risk assessment can be conducted in the following way:

- identify all ignition sources and any fire hazards

This is the most vital step. Once complete you should next check:

- the location of people who are likely to be in danger in the event of a fire occurring
- that any existing fire precautions are adequate
- that all ignition sources are controlled
- that fire detection warnings are in place
- that the means of fighting fire are in place
- the maintenance and testing procedures of all existing fire precautions
- that the means of escape are unobstructed and clearly marked

Safety Tip

Fire fighting should only be undertaken if it represents no risk to the individual.

Finally, put the following procedures in place:

- staff fire training for all employees
- record all comments from employees and the findings of the assessment; draw up a plan of action; inform, train, and give feedback to all those concerned
- revise your assessment and procedures if any changes occur; set a date for the next review

The Electricity at Work Regulations 1992

All the electrical equipment that is used in the salon should be tested once a year by a qualified electrician. This is sometimes called PAT (Portable Appliance Testing). Care should be taken when using all electrical equipment and staff must be fully trained. Although it is the responsibility of the owner or supervisor of the salon to ensure the equipment is safe to use and is maintained, it is also the duty of staff to check the equipment is safe to use.

The following precautions should be taken:

- keep written test sheets (the HSE can ask to see these)
- check electrical flexes for signs of wear or damage
- check the date of last PAT test
- all appliances must be switched off and unplugged at the end of the day
- all electrical appliances should be kept away from sources of water
- when not in use all appliances should be placed in a cupboard with the flex secured around the appliance
- if there is a problem with an appliance it should be removed from use and labelled
- electrical appliances should only be used by trained personnel
- all broken, loose or worn plugs or sockets should be replaced
- do not overload sockets with too many plugs

The main causes of hazards in the case of electrical appliances are:

- inadequate or non-existent earthing
- incorrect fuses being fitted
- inadequate maintenance of equipment
- incorrect or bad wiring of plugs or equipment

Activity

- Design a written test sheet.
- Identify a training programme for all appliances if none is in place.
- Identify a person to take responsibility for electrical appliances.
- Draw up a list of all electrical appliances in the salon.
- Design a chart to record:
  - the appliance serial number
  - the date when the appliance was last tested
  - whether the appliance is working or not working
  - the fault
  - the date the appliance was withdrawn
  - the date the appliance was repaired

Overexposure

Learning objectives

In this section you will learn about:

- **overexposure and how to avoid it, including good housekeeping and ventilation**

- **routes of entry into the body**

- **personal protection**

It is possible for an **allergic reaction** to occur with any of the professional treatments clients receive in the salon environment, for example, hair, beauty, nails and massage with aromatherapy oils. This can be a real problem for a sensitive client. Fortunately the majority of problems which are related to the fingernails can be avoided through good education as supplied by manufacturers on their beginners and foundation courses, and by practising safe techniques with an understanding of overexposure.

Overexposure

For every chemical there is a limit to the level of exposure which is safe. When the safe level is exceeded, the body reacts, so any early warning signs should not be ignored. If the same treatment or procedure is repeated in the same way on a regular basis under such conditions, it is very likely to lead to a major allergic reaction. Both clients and technicians are susceptible to reactions to certain substances.

When a person experiences an allergic reaction to a substance or chemical, it is necessary to remove the product or irritant from the body. Medical advice should then be sought. Many technicians wear thin rubber gloves to work in if they have an allergic reaction to a product. However, if the skin is broken the technician will often experience a further irritation and subsequently become allergic to the rubber or latex gloves. The only real solution is to withdraw from the substance or product and recover.

There will usually be clear warning signs that the nail technician, or client, is becoming sensitive to a product or substance. Watch out for:

- localised skin or **cuticles** that become sensitive to pressure or that itch
- redness or sores for a while after application

Safety Tip

Remember, an allergic reaction will not happen overnight. It is repeated or prolonged contact with chemicals over a period of time that causes this unpleasant experience – usually four to six months.

Safety Tip

Roughing up, over-filing or over-buffing the natural nail plate is not necessary with modern nail products. It is very destructive and causes the nail plate to become porous. Consequently, products can be absorbed through to the nail plate and into the **nail bed** much more easily.

Safety Tip

Changing products at times of sensitivity is not a wise move. No other product should be applied at this time as there is a real chance that the person could become sensitive to the new product. This is because the **histamine** level in their body will have risen through the initial chemical exposure. The skin and the histamine levels must return to normal before a new system is applied, or a further reaction may result.

Safety Tip

Set your standards and then maintain them. Your income, health and the establishment of a good clientele all depend on this.

Although this discomfort may only be temporary and will usually subside after a few hours, it could be an early warning sign and must not be ignored.

Once a person develops an allergy to a product, or an ingredient of it, they will always be allergic to it in varying degrees. Each time they are exposed to it, the reaction becomes more violent and there is no alternative to the decision to stop using the product. In reality, this will mean a loss of income for the nail technician and a period of recuperation without nail extensions for the client.

With knowledge and understanding of how the body becomes sensitive to a product, or substance, most allergy problems can be avoided. A body can react to all nail product systems – **UV acrylic, UV gel**, acrylics and other **wrap** systems.

At the first indication of overexposure, you should check your application techniques around the cuticles and sidewalls. If you continue the application in the same way, an allergic reaction will result. The **nail plate** can become overexposed due to the acrylic having a consistency which is too wet. This can result in the nail plate becoming very white in colour.

If a client has become allergic to an acrylic system, even if their skin has returned to normal, they would not be a good candidate to wear a gel system. Gel is an **acrylate** that is also likely to cause an allergic reaction to a sensitised client, especially if the gel is not applied properly. The only real alternative system for this client is a **fibreglass** system.

We have a responsibility not to put ourselves, work colleagues and clients at risk through overexposure. It is possible to work safely with chemicals and products, but there are strict rules and guidelines to follow. It would be very foolish not to learn these rules as the practice of using safe techniques is paramount to a long career in the nail industry.

Routes of entry into the body

The three main ways that substances are taken into the body are:

1 **inhalation** – breathing fine dust particles or vapours
2 **absorption** – through the skin, or through cuts and abrasions
3 **ingestion** – by consuming chemicals accidentally

These are known as **routes of entry** to the body.

Inhalation

Nail technicians need to take great care to maintain the quality of the air in their salon or work area. **Vapours**, which are formed when a gas or liquid evaporates into the air, and dust resulting from filing are the two key dangers.

The lowest level that an ingredient or odour can be detected in the air is one ppm (part per million). When researching the safe limits for **ethyl methacrylate**, the latest recommendation by the Cosmetic Ingredient Review Panel (CIR) – an independent review panel comprising toxicologists, dermatologists and medical doctors from the United States of America – is that the conservative safe limit for continuous long-term occupational exposure is 100 ppm. In salons the average measured value is one-fifth this level.

In addition to overexposure, prolonged or repeated inhalation of products may cause other problems such as

- headaches
- sickness
- dizziness or fainting
- fatigue
- coughing or irritation to the respiratory system

If these problems occur, the person should be moved outside into the fresh air until he or she stabilises.

Preventing inhalation

A controlled approach to product application, good housekeeping including the correct disposal of waste and proper **ventilation** all contribute to good air quality and help to prevent overexposure through inhalation.

Controlled approach to application

- When using a liquid and powder system, it is good technique to pick up the *correct* **mix ratio** every time. This avoids the need to constantly wipe the excess **monomer** onto a paper towel, indirectly extending the surface area of product evaporating into the atmosphere. This also makes commercial sense – consider the amount of monomer that is absorbed onto a paper towel and disposed of each day by a careless nail technician.
- Use accelerator or setting sprays sparingly and at a downward angle to reduce the risk of inhalation. Again, this procedure is also more cost effective.

Dappen dishes

Metal bin

Technical Tip

The rate of evaporation of products and chemicals used in nail treatments is affected by temperature so this must be monitored when handling volatile chemicals.

Ventilation unit

Good housekeeping

- Keep all products tightly capped until required. Recap as soon as possible. Limiting exposure just to the application time greatly reduces both evaporation and contamination.
- Decant monomer into small containers for use. Dappen dishes are ideal as they are stable and reduce the evaporation by limiting the exposed surface area of the product.
- Put all items away after use.
- Use metal containers for chemical and product storage.
- Use suitable waste bins. They need to be of metal construction with close-fitting metal lids. Plastic bins, or bags, are not suitable as they allow vapours to escape and contaminate the breathing zone. Remove waste before bins become full to prevent lids being wedged open and vapours escaping into your breathing zone.

Ventilation

Overexposure through inhalation is a real hazard. There is a 60 centimetre sphere around our heads from which all the air we inhale is drawn, known as the **breathing zone**, and this must be kept as free as possible from vapours and dust to prevent overexposure by inhalation.

Nail technicians working from home need to look at ventilation issues carefully and seek professional advice from their product supplier or local air extraction supplier. Problems with ventilation are less likely in the salon environment where there should be a greater awareness of ventilation and of the side effects of overexposure through continuity of product training.

Adequate ventilation is a necessity. Although a number of options exist, as the air needs to be changed regularly (this varies on the size of the salon and the number of technicians) the only real solution is an extraction unit.

Ventilation/extraction unit

A professional fitter of ventilation systems will measure your working area, note the number of nail stations and advise on a suitable extraction unit, and where it would be best fitted. This is usually to an outside wall or window.

Advice should also be sought on the airflow in the salon as the air cannot just be extracted without being replaced. There needs to be an air inlet so the new extraction unit can work efficiently. This is normally achieved by an additional vent lower in the wall or window.

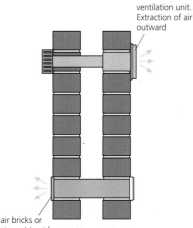

ventilation unit.
Extraction of air
outward

air bricks or
air vent to aid
influx of air

Airflow

You should also consider a control switch for the extraction unit, as it may not be required all of the time. To keep the cost down some companies suggest wiring this into the light switch so that if you always have the lights on when you are open the extractor is running. You may also need to update your heating system if the extraction unit is high on the wall or window and heat rises.

Local exhaust

Local **exhaust** methods of ventilation can work efficiently if some simple rules are followed. The hose must be placed to the side of the nail station so that the source of vapours are pulled away from the nail technician and client. If the hose or canopy is placed above the nail station, all the vapours are pulled up through the breathing zone, increasing the risk of overexposure through inhalation.

Control switch for extraction system

Charcoal filters

There are some desks available on the market with a filter and a fan fitted into the table top directly under the work area. There are also charcoal filters available which can either be in a desk or free standing. The filters need to be changed each week, however, which can make them very expensive.

These units work by the activated charcoal absorbing the vapours like a sponge, but some of the filters are very light. This form of protection can prove ineffective for monomer vapours which are not easily absorbed by activated charcoal. The filters very quickly become saturated with vapour and dust rendering them ineffective.

Safety Tip

Don't be fooled into thinking that 'odourless' products are free from vapours. They are still present, just harder to detect, and need the same precautions. The amount of vapour in the air is not determined by the **odour**, it is controlled by the evaporation rate.

Fans

Fans only serve to circulate air that is already contaminated by simply moving the vapours around. Opening a window would not be sufficient to extract unclean air and may cause another set of problems such as the nail products not setting correctly. Some products crystallise at low temperatures and many products set too fast at high temperatures, sometimes before the application is complete, making the finishing very difficult. **Primer** freezes at approximately 11°C or 52°F. Some UV gels set if used in a warm, bright environment such as a conservatory or even by a south-facing window on a very bright day. Many nail technicians have unintentionally cured a pot of gel!

Personal protection

Inhalation

As a nail technician, you will be working with the substances discussed in this chapter all day. You should always take sensible precautions to prevent overexposure to yourself. However, you must also act to protect your client.

Dust masks are an option to prevent unnecessary inhalation when filing, especially if using drills. Drills create very fine airborne dust particles that are easily inhaled so dust masks and efficient extraction systems should be high on your priority list. Dust generated by hand filing produces much larger particles and the majority of these will fall to the table and can be collected on a paper towel for disposal.

Absorption

Absorption of chemicals is through the skin or nail plate. Prolonged or repeated contact is usually required to cause an allergic reaction, the symptoms of which include:

- redness
- swelling
- sores
- rashes
- itchiness
- blisters to the local area of contact

The corrective action is to remove the product as soon as possible and refer your client to his or her GP for expert advice and treatment. Products can be absorbed through the skin by failing to take the correct precautions when applying or dispensing them, or through bad housekeeping.

Preventing absorption

Application

You can help prevent absorption by the correct and safe application of chemicals.

- Cover all cuts and abrasions on both the nail technician and client before commencing any nail treatment.
- Leave a tiny free margin (1 mm) around the cuticle line when applying any type of nail **overlays**. No product should touch the skin under any

---

Safety Tip

Air fresheners do not improve air quality. They only mask odours for a short period of time.

Dust masks

circumstances. Do not use your finger or thumb to clean around the client's cuticle area when too much product has been applied to the nail plate. Avoid touching the cuticle with either product or brush.

- Avoid back brushing the **smile line**. The monomer that is still in the brush can cause the nail plate to become wet with monomer which could affect the mix of the next bead that is applied, making the bead too wet.

- Any excess monomer that is on the natural nail can be absorbed by the nail plate, which could lead to a possible overexposure problem. Too wet a mix may also cause the overlay to pop in the centre of the stress area.

- Never apply monomer to the nail bed without the **polymer powder**. Some nail technicians wrongly believe that this procedure increases **adhesion**. In fact, the only result is that the client will have a reaction over a period of time as the nail plate will absorb the excess monomer.

- It is common practice in some salons to add more monomer to a too dry mix to make it easier to work with. This will not change the mix ratio of the product as **polymerisation** has already started to take place. All that will happen is that since it cannot be absorbed by the powder, the excess monomer will flood onto the surrounding skin or cuticle and lead to overexposure.

- Keep the nail plate clean and dry when applying a product.

- Spray accelerator at the manufacturer's recommended distance to avoid burning and thinning of the nail plate.

- Never intentionally touch the skin with any nail product during application regardless of the system being used.

- Good aftercare advice to clients is also a requirement, as a small minority of clients actually overexpose themselves by continually gluing nails back on after letting the maintenance appointments slide for a week or two.

- Avoid applying a 'wet mix' of liquid and powder to the nail plate.

- Use the appropriate size of brush when applying a liquid and powder. A large brush will hold more liquid or product in the belly of the brush, thus affecting the mix ratio.

- Apply gels in thin layers to aid **curing** of the product.

Safety Tip

Some of the **adhesives** that clients purchase from other retail sources are not the correct product for the intended purpose. Some are not hypoallergenic or are not intended for nails. Clients often overexpose themselves by using this type of product.

- Apply fibreglass **resin** in a thin controlled manner.
- UV gel can also cause overexposure problems. If the nail technician touches the skin with gel before the curing process has taken place this could cause a reaction to take place on the skin over a period of time. If the gel product is applied in thicker layers, the UV rays cannot penetrate the gel and will leave uncured gel on the natural nail. This is a very common reason why clients can become overexposed to the UV gel systems. If the bulbs in the UV lamp are in continuous use, they should be changed every four to six months. The UV bulb can wear out, resulting in cold spots and inefficient curing. This will leave uncured gel on the nail plate and may result in overexposure. Also if the product is applied too thickly the client may complain of burning; the cause of this is that some gels shrink by up to 25 per cent during the curing process – it can feel like the natural nail plate is being pulled back with it. The remedy is to apply thin layers, then the gel will be fully cured.

Good practice

- Change towels after filing. If you don't, there is a danger that you will end up leaning in the dust which will cause a skin reaction over a period of time.
- Do not wipe your brush on a paper towel during application. There is a danger that you will end up resting your hand or arm on it during the filing and buffing stages.
- Clean your brush properly – even during application. Do not use your finger and thumb! If your brush handle gets dirty during application, stop and clean it. Monomer and gel can be very sticky substances and should be removed from the fingers and hands immediately.

Decanting chemicals

One of the main times when nail technicians can expose themselves to product absorption is while handling and decanting **chemicals**. Product suppliers usually discount bulk chemical supplies, but these then need to be decanted into more manageable containers. Always follow health and safety regulations and don't get lazy. Follow the correct procedures on the manufacturers' labels and use the correct equipment, for example:

- disposable gloves
- a dust or vapour mask
- safety glasses

Keep the area used for decanting well ventilated. Follow this process when decanting any chemical – even when using a pipette to decant small amounts of liquids into dappen dishes – or when cleaning up any spillage.

Ingestion

Although it goes without saying that you would never consciously ingest the chemicals you use as a nail technician, bad practice can lead to inadvertent ingestion, for example since vapours are attracted to hot drinks, a nail technician (and their client) could be drinking their products every time they have a hot drink which could add up to a large amount of ingested chemicals over time.

Preventing ingestion

Safety Tip

Banging hands down onto a dirty towel will release dust into your breathing zone and the use of drills will cause finer dust particles that are more easily ingested.

- Wash your hands before consuming any food, from a casual sweet to lunch.
- Do not store food in the same place as products.
- Use cups or containers with lids for drinks in the working area.
- Do not consume food at the nail station.
- Always use clean tissues and towels for clients.

As the nail technician, it is you who should be aware of the dangers and who has access to suppliers' information. Be aware that most clients – and possibly even other staff in your immediate working environment – may not have access to or completely understand this information. Consider the following people, for example:

- receptionist
- beauty staff
- members of your family, if working from home

Knowledge of chemicals is the best defence against overexposure and good practices are a necessity not a luxury!

Ways to protect the individual

There are rich rewards to be made from the nail industry today, especially if you are proficient and adaptable to the

Useful Tip

Ignorance is not a valid excuse against overexposure.

Activity

- Find out about the salon safety procedures that are in place regarding storage and transportation of products.

- Is the equipment used in the salon to the required standard?

- Does the safety equipment offer maximum protection?

- Are the procedures suitable and adequate for the task?

- Has a risk assessment been completed or updated?

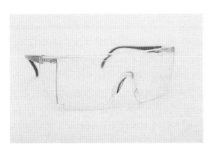

Safety glasses

clients' needs. A good nail technician will always be in great demand and have a thriving clientele. Their earning capacity is vast and a nail technician's working career could span 20–30 years. To maintain this, an awareness and understanding of all the chemicals and their specific use in the salon is needed.

Many of the best nail technicians overexpose themselves in the early stages of their career when they are still learning their craft. This is the time when they start to sensitise themselves. An understanding of overexposure is of great importance. If you ignore the signs you could one day find you have lost your livelihood or business. Look for an alternative system that you are proficient in and prefer to use.

Prevention is the best course of action rather than the cure. Personal protection in the salon is really important for ourselves, our colleagues and our clients.

Eye protection

The wearing of safety glasses is a precaution and you should offer a pair to your client. If a client asks why, be honest with them and they will respect you for your honesty. Take the opportunity to explain proper precautions. Clients will probably enquire why some of the other salons do not offer them a pair.

A nail technician should not wear contact lenses in the salon environment for the following reasons:

- although safety glasses offer good protection against accidental splashing they offer no protection against vapours or airborne dust

- vapours can collect behind the contact lens and etch the eye, leading to permanent damage to the eyesight

- soft lenses can absorb the vapours also causing etching of the eye

- if any solvent or chemical is accidentally splashed into the eye, cleaning can prove very difficult – consider how a solvent or chemical degrades a plastic surface or workstation

Good practice

To work safely, you need to understand:

- sanitation, disinfection and sterilisation (see next section)

- ventilation and extraction

- the advantages and disadvantages of your chosen system
- possible routes of entry and overexposure issues
- the consequences of ignoring dust control
- the effects of temperature on nail service
- storage and waste and disposal
- odourless products
- the effects of fans and draughts on products

Good practice includes

- reading all labels and seeking advice from your trainer or manufacturer if you are in any doubt
- taking personal protection seriously – use gloves, masks and eye protection. Remember, there are two types of face mask – one for vapours and one for dust – and don't forget to renew your mask every few days
- using a covered dappen dish for monomer

Cross infection and salon hygiene

Learning objectives

In this section you will learn about:

- **how to protect yourself and your clients**
- **pathogens – bacteria and viruses**
- **decontamination – sanitation, disinfection and sterilisation**
- **hygiene procedures**

When you work as a nail technician you will come into contact with members of the public and perform treatments on nails – on both hands and feet. There is always a risk to you of injury or infection when working on your clients. Every surface from our hands to desk tops, door handles, floors and tools can potentially carry microscopic **pathogens**, that is disease-causing organisms. It is our duty as professionals to be able to recognise these and control them. We do this by decontamination which comes in three stages: **sanitation**, **disinfection** and **sterilisation**.

Pathogens

Disease can be spread through direct contact with the source of infection. This includes direct contact with bodily fluids, whether from coughing, sneezing, direct contact with contaminated blood, pus, sores, cuts or grazes. All cuts on the hands must be covered with sticking plaster or suitable dressing to prevent a secondary infection.

Bacteria

Bacteria are either pathogenic or non-pathogenic. Non-pathogenic bacteria are not harmful to human beings, in fact they are often beneficial, for example they aid the digestive system. However, pathogenic bacteria – which probably constitute less that 30 per cent of all bacteria – are undesirable in the salon environment. They are sometimes referred to as germs.

The growth pattern of bacteria

Bacteria multiply and thrive in warm, dark, unsanitary places and conditions. Each **cell** of bacteria has the ability to grow and, when mature, the cell divides. In turn, these two cells grow and divide, and so the pattern continues. You can therefore see how important it is to control pathogenic bacteria, as in a matter hours millions of bacteria can be present on implements or surfaces.

Different types of bacteria

- *Spirilla* are spiral shaped. This type of bacteria causes syphilis.
- *Diplococci* grow in pairs. This type of bacteria is responsible for pneumonia.
- *Bacilli* grow in rod shapes. This type of bacteria is responsible for tetanus, typhoid, influenza, diphtheria and tuberculosis.
- *Cocci* can grow in groups or singularly. This type of bacteria produces pus.
- *Staphylococci* bacteria grow in clusters. Infections are usually inflamed, causing pustules, boils and abscesses.
- *Streptococci* is the form of bacteria responsible for strep throat infections, rheumatic fever and blood poisoning.

How bacteria spread

Bacteria can be transmitted through direct and indirect contact. They are airborne and can also spread in water. Spirilla and bacilli are capable of propelling themselves in liquid.

SPHERICAL BACTERIA (COCCI)

Diplococcus
(pneumonia)

Staphylococcus
(pustules, boils, etc.)

Streptococcus
(sore throats)

ROD-LIKE BACTERIA (BACILLI)

Bacillus tuberculosis
(tuberculosis)

Clostridium tetani
(tetanus)

Bacillus typhosus
(typhoid fever)

SPIRAL FORMS (SPIRILLA)

Spirillum

Treponema pallida
(syphilis)

Different types of bacteria

Viruses

Viruses are also pathogenic but are much smaller than bacteria. These often spread by coming in contact with an infected person. Viruses are responsible for chicken pox, measles, mumps, influenza, colds or coughs. The following precautions should be taken to prevent cross infection:

● Change workstation and washroom towels regularly.
● Use paper towels where possible.
● Wash and sanitise hands before and after each client. This is very reassuring for the client to see.

AIDS and Hepatitis B

AIDS (Acquired Immune Deficiency Syndrome) is the most serious result of infection by a virus known as HIV. People with this virus in their bloodstream are said to be HIV Positive. Not all HIV Positive people develop AIDS – some stay well with no indication at all that they are carrying HIV.

HIV can disrupt the body's normal defences against disease and leave the body open to infections that would not normally occur. HIV is quite easily destroyed outside of the human body. Once any blood has dried – which can take a matter of seconds – the virus particles cannot survive. That is why HIV can only be spread by contact involving the direct transfer of blood or serum from one infected person to another. To date there are no reported cases of anyone catching the HIV virus through any nail or beauty treatments. If all sanitary procedures are followed it would be practically impossible for this to happen.

Hepatitis B causes inflammation of the liver leading to severe illness and usually jaundice. This disease can be fatal. It is transmitted by blood and serum from an infected person to another. Once a person has had this virus it can remain in his or her bloodstream for many years making the person in question a carrier of the disease. Adequate precautions should be taken in the salon to prevent the transmission of this disease. It is an employer's responsibility to advise their staff to have a vaccination against Hepatitis B and also to make sure they are correctly trained in the disposal of contaminated waste.

Decontamination

Decontamination by sanitation, disinfection and sterilisation minimises the risk of cross infection. All nail technicians should be aware of the guidelines laid down by the Local Government Miscellaneous Provisions Act. Guidelines on the following areas are available from your local authority:

- personal hygiene and working practices
- cleaning and sterilising of implements
- salon cleaning to a high standard

Sanitation

Sanitation will reduce the number of pathogenic bacteria on a surface. This is the lowest form of decontamination and should be carried out before disinfection and sterilisation. Simply washing hands and tools will remove most harmful bacteria and control the spread of disease. Washing in soapy water can remove dirt, oil and other product residues and is essential, for instance, before immersing tools in a steriliser to allow the full decontamination to take place.

Your clients will appreciate cleanliness in all its forms and sanitation will prove how seriously you take their custom, welfare and health.

Safety Tip

- Cover all cuts and abrasions with dressings or plasters.
- Wash hands in soapy water before and after each client.
- Do not use sharp or pointed instruments near any obvious infected areas of skin.
- If the nail technician is cut he or she must hold the cut under running water until the blood flow has stopped; then apply a dressing or plaster before resuming work.
- If you come into contact with another person's blood or bodily fluids the area must be washed with soap and hot water as soon as possible.

The following points should be taken into account when carrying out your sanitation procedures for the working area or salon environment:

- always try to provide hot and cold running water
- change towels in the washroom/kitchen regularly
- use and provide liquid soap, preferably with anti-bacterial ingredients
- both the client and technician should wash their hands before *and* after each treatment
- there should be a separate sink for clients to wash their hands – never have a bowl full of cups under the tap when washing hands, this contravenes Health and Safety regulations
- toilet tissue and paper towels must be provided at all times
- clean uniforms should be worn every day
- hair should be tied back
- wedding band and small earrings only to be worn when working
- avoid touching your face whilst working and warn the client of this too
- all consumables should be removed and put into the proper waste bin
- bins should be emptied regularly and not allowed to overflow
- remember to clean door handles when cleaning other surfaces
- no eating, drinking or smoking in the salon
- food should not be kept in the same storage facility as nail products – this includes the fridge as well as cupboards
- soiled and dusty towels and linen should be removed and kept in a lined bin
- all laundry should be washed at the correct temperature
- floors, walls and other surfaces must be constantly dusted and wiped clean
- children should not be allowed in the salon, but if this is unavoidable then it is the parent's responsibility to control them; make sure they are aware of this
- pets should not be allowed in the working environment under any circumstances, with the exception of guide dogs for the blind or disabled
- when cleaning the top of a desk make sure all the containers are wiped as well

Safety Tip

Sanitation processes are vital and must not be ignored.

- do not place any tools or implements in your pockets, behind your ears or in your mouth

There are many ways to ensure that your working environment is clean and as dust-free as possible. Make sure you make time for *good housekeeping*.

Sanitation sprays are normally available from your product manufacturer for use on files, buffers and workstations. Some manufacturers recommend hand sanitisers which are available in the form of soap, a spray, cream or a gel.

Disinfection

This is the second stage of decontamination and greatly reduces the pathogenic bacteria on a non-living surface. This method is not suitable for the hair, skin or nails. Disinfection is used for the following:

- floors
- walls
- workstations
- chairs
- pedicure and manicure bowls

Note: This process does not remove **bacterial spores**.

When using disinfectant it is important to follow the manufacturer's instructions and dilute to the correct level. If the concentration is too weak, the disinfectant may be inadequate to remove the pathogenic bacteria and may possibly act only as a sanitiser.

Disinfection is almost as thorough as sterilisation and can be used quite effectively in the salon. Disinfectants are designed to remove pathogens and some are very strong, so should be used with care. However, they can be an **irritant** to skin tissue and can be dangerous if the manufacturer's instructions are not followed properly. Always make sure you read all instructions and keep disinfectants out of the reach of children. All disinfectant manufacturers are legally bound to give you a list of ingredients and directions for safe use. They must also advise you which pathogens the product is able to control.

There are many disinfectant solutions on the market today and it is up to you which one you use. Before investing in a disinfection system look at what is available, what they are designed to do and your requirements for your work environment. It is a good idea to review your system every year, see if there are any new products on the market, if your salon requirements have changed and, lastly, whether what you are using is still performing properly.

All disinfectants should be able to kill a variety of pathogens and the following must all be covered by your disinfection system:

- bactericides
- fungicides
- viricides

There are two main methods of disinfection within the salon:

- heat treatment
- chemical treatment

Heat treatment could be applied, for example, by a steam cabinet. This is a dangerous item and the siting of such a machine needs careful consideration. The ideal would be to place it in a separate room or kitchen as it is not a suitable piece of equipment to have within the salon itself. When using any type of steam or boiling water the implements need to be washed first to eliminate any dust and **contamination**. This method can only be used on metal tools. All employees must be trained in the proper use of the equipment.

For chemical disinfectants to be effective tools need to be immersed for longer than 15 minutes and not just wiped over. Alcohol will erode and blunt, possibly even rust, metal tools and should be used carefully. Alcohol can also be used as an antiseptic on the skin.

There are many chemical solutions available as disinfectants. If using these make sure they have a rust inhibitor such as sodium nitrate, otherwise you may find your expensive nippers will be useless after a few weeks.

Sterilisation

Sterilisation is the total destruction of all living organisms on an object. The word sterilisation is often misused, for example living tissue cannot be sterilised. You cannot sterilise a cuticle, nail plate, skin or hair. The salon's hard surfaces, for example floors, walls and nail stations, can be disinfected or sanitised – complete sterilisation would be impossible to achieve.

Items that can be sterilised are

- all metal tools and implements
- plastic tools

All tools must be washed in warm soapy water then rinsed and thoroughly dried before proceeding to one of the following methods of sterilisation.

Chemical sterilisation

Chemical sterilisation is the most popular and effective way of maintaining the hygiene of tools and implements. After washing tools in hot soapy water, they should be rinsed and then thoroughly dried. The tools should be completely immersed in a chemical solution for a period of 20 minutes. All chemical agents must be diluted according to the manufacturer's instructions. Diluted solutions must be changed on a regular basis, as recommended by the manufacturer. If the solution is diluted too much it acts only as a disinfectant or sanitiser and is ineffective as a sterilising agent.

Sterilisation should be carried out in a deep container with a close-fitting lid. It is advisable to have an inner perforated tray with handles which will allow the tools to be lowered into the solution. If the solution becomes cloudy change it immediately. In a busy salon you could consider having two sets of tools.

Some of the main sterilising agents on the market are:

- alcohol
- gluteraldehyde
- quaternary ammonium compound (QAUTS)

The autoclave

An autoclave is suitable for small metal implements. An autoclave is a metal container that is specifically designed

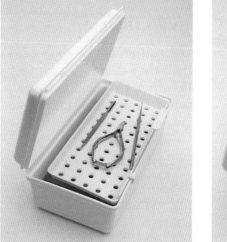

Sterilisation tray

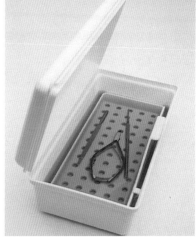

Sterilisation tray with liquid

Autoclave

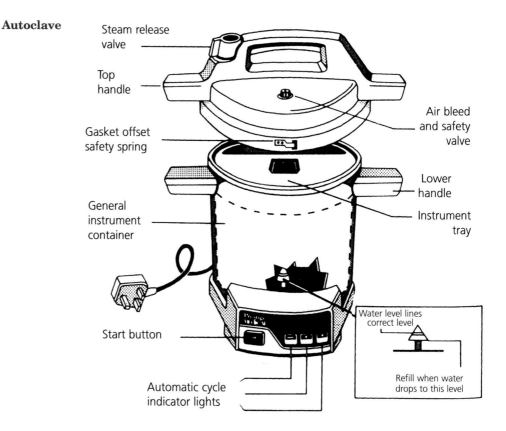

Steam release valve

Top handle

Gasket offset safety spring

General instrument container

Start button

Automatic cycle indicator lights

Air bleed and safety valve

Lower handle

Instrument tray

Water level lines correct level

Refill when water drops to this level

Technical Tip

Remember that all chemicals are subject to COSHH regulations.

to create and withstand heat and pressure. It uses high pressure steam at a temperature of 126°C. The only type of autoclave that can be used effectively and safely within the salon environment is an electrical one that has an automatic cycle. A measured amount of water is placed into the autoclave and pre-washed tools are put onto a rack above the water so that the steam can circulate freely around them, ensuring all surfaces are sterilised. The lid must be closed and locked before the machine is switched on. Pressure builds up inside the unit and causes the temperature to rise. After the programme is complete you must ensure that the pressure has returned to normal before trying to remove the lid.

Any equipment or tools that are removed will be sterile only until they come into contact with other items, fingers or the air which can hold pathogens. It is a good idea to have a sealed, clean container to keep sterilised implements in until they are needed.

Glass bead steriliser

Glass bead sterilisers are not suitable for the salon environment due to the high temperature dry heat they use. There is a high risk of burns if used by untrained staff.

This type of steriliser is used for small regularly shaped objects which have little surface detail, as only the surface area that is in contact with the glass beads can be considered to have been sterilised. The irregular shape of a pair of nail clippers would not be deemed sterile because the entire surface area could not possibly be in contact with the glass beads. Also the high temperatures used may affect the metal and cause sharp edges to become blunt.

Ultra violet cabinet

Ultra violet light has limited use as a sterilisation method due to the fact that tools would have to be turned to expose all surfaces to the UV rays. However, if the tools are already sterilised a UV cabinet can provide a germ-free environment for storing implements.

Hygiene procedures

Good **hygiene** procedures prevent the spread of infection. Aim to make the following points part of everyone's working day in the salon:

- Sterilise all metal tools.
- Disinfect all work surfaces.
- The technician and client wash their hands before commencing any consultation or treatment.
- Cover any cuts or abrasions.
- Sanitise hands and clients' hands.
- Sanitise all files and buffers in the presence of clients.
- Use clean towels and disposable paper towels.
- Use pump dispensers instead of open containers.
- Replace all lids and caps on containers immediately.
- Only have out on the nail station the items or products required to perform the treatment. They should then be put away.

Dispensing creams and lotions

If possible choose pumps or sprays as containers for creams and lotions, as these are more hygienic. If your chosen hand cream is only available in a tub or a pot you should always use a disposable spatula. Never use your fingers, as you will add bacteria to the cream, and those bacteria will multiply and could infect your next client.

If a client with an obvious infection has been worked on with cuticle creams, polishes or other such products these should then be disposed of and not used on any other clients.

Washing towels

Towels should be laundered in hot soapy water at a minimum of 60°C. The towels should be washed on their own not with any other household laundry. Each client should have a clean towel for their treatment, to prevent the build-up of dust and reduce the risk of cross infection from the previous client. If you are faced with a high towel rotation rate in a busy salon, use thin towels. They are quicker and cheaper to dry.

Files and buffers

Cost often dictates that files and buffers are used for more than one client before disposal. This requires them to be sanitised before and after use. At the end of each day use a small nail brush to scrub the files and buffers that are not being disposed of with anti-bacterial soap. Should a client suffer a cut or abrasion to the skin during the treatment, then the file or buffer must be disposed of immediately on completing the service. This action is taken to avoid cross infection. An alternative is for the client to purchase their own. This should be sanitised before treatment, then washed after treatment and placed in a clean envelope and attached with a safety clip to the client's record card.

The nail desk

Do not use the workstation surface as a storage area as the nail desk must remain clear and uncluttered to enable thorough disinfection practices between client treatments. This will promote clean and tidy work habits. To give the client confidence in your hygiene standards, sanitise the work surface in the client's presence. Tools should, if possible, be removed from the sterilisation unit only as required or stored in a UV cabinet.

Chapter summary

We owe it to ourselves and our clients to work in a safe and hygienic way, using all the rules laid down by our product companies, local councils and the Health and Safety Executive. The current situation has been covered in this chapter, but we do advise you to check on all issues at least every 6–12 months. The modern professional nail technician has no reason not to follow the rules and regulations that have been identified within this chapter.

Remember that health and safety regulations address potential hazards and have all been laid down for the benefit of yourselves, your colleagues and your clients.

Consultation and communication

This chapter helps you through the skills required for communication with your colleagues and clients. Some people are natural communicators, others are not, and it is important to acquire a range of different communication skills. There is more to communication than just verbal exchanges and sometimes there are unpleasant aspects to deal with. We identify a range of areas, techniques and situations you may encounter. It is important to understand how effective communication skills help when carrying out a client **consultation**. The best way to carry out an in-depth consultation and the consequences of not doing this effectively are also covered. Every professional nail technician should be aware of how important their dress code and their personal hygiene are when working with the public. Earlier chapters have covered general points about protecting yourself and your client in terms of correct seating, proper furniture and the right equipment. Every professional industry has a code of conduct and ethics and the nail industry is no different. You are representing a whole industry when you work with your clients, not just yourself, and this chapter takes you through the various areas you need to consider in order to present the right image of professional conduct.

In this chapter we will consider the following aspects:

- **communication skills, personal appearance and conduct**

- **consultation techniques**

- **ergonomics**

Communication skills, personal appearance and conduct

Learning objectives

In this section you will learn about:

- **the basic principles of effective communication**
- **types of communication with others**
- **listening skills**
- **questioning techniques**
- **professional behaviour**
- **industry code of ethics**
- **correct uniform and dress code**
- **hygiene rules**

Right now, whilst you are studying, people all over the world are communicating by writing, sending e-mails and faxes, reading letters, answering phones, making appointments, chatting with clients and talking with colleagues. Most people take communication for granted – we communicate in various ways throughout our lives without ever really thinking about it, yet communication is the lifeblood of all businesses.

Although we communicate all the time we don't always use our skills effectively. How many times do you hear phrases such as: 'I'm sorry I misunderstood', or 'I thought you meant...', or 'What did you really mean by...?' Each of these phrases indicates mis-communication. Between client and technician this could be disastrous; between colleagues it could cause damage to working relationships. Effective communication is essential to any business and it cannot be ignored.

Basic principles of communication

Effective communication depends on three basic principles:

1   establishing and maintaining relationships
2   decision making
3   practising all communication skills

How you communicate affects every relationship you have with other people and how that relationship is maintained. When you communicate, think of the type of relationship you wish to have with that person. You establish relationships for the short term and maintain them over the long term. Even if you know a client will only visit you once (for example, because they are from abroad), you still need to establish an effective working relationship with that client. There are always consequences to your business from treating people badly or in a positive way. Think how you would feel if:

- you had been made to wait 30 minutes beyond your appointment time
- your technician insisted you had only booked for a polish instead of a rebalance
- you had to wait for your technician to finish her telephone call to a friend before acknowledging you
- your technician chewed gum all the way through your treatment

You have the power to make people feel good or bad – not just by performing a good treatment but also by the way you communicate with your client the whole time he or she is with you. Remember that frustrated or angry clients share their experiences with other potential clients. Unhappy employees complain to each other and cause a bad atmosphere. Always treat others the way you would like to be treated.

Look at the different styles of communication and how these affect your working relationships. Always ask yourself questions: Who are you communicating with? Look at the various ways you can use communication as a tool to build a good business.

Types of communication

The two main types of communication are verbal and non-verbal. However, there are many different ways and messages we can communicate through these channels.

Verbal communication

The most common verbal communication is talking. When a person talks, however, it is not just their words that communicate a message. Silence, listening and non-verbal aspects, such as tone and manner, are often more important that the words themselves.

We are lucky in our industry that one of the first things we do when we have a new client – before we even start the treatment – is to fill out a client profile/treatment card. This is a great opportunity to start building a foundation for good two-way communication with the client. During this initial communication, you will share information with your client about prices, timings, products, retail, homecare and return visits and they will share some very personal details with you about their age, lifestyle, health and background. Access to this type of information about your client helps you decide on the words and the tone you will use.

You might find that some clients are very sensitive to divulging their age or health issues. Be encouraging – try sharing some of your own experiences to put them at ease. Know when to talk and when to listen. Remember body language can be the key to starting a successful relationship with a client. Effective communicators reflect on a situation and make appropriate decisions before they communicate.

The two most important areas for good communication skills are:

- active listening
- questioning techniques

Active listening

As a nail technician it is really important to know how to be a good listener. Confidentiality is also paramount – clients may tell you things about their lives that they have never told anyone else.

Good listening skills include:

- smiling
- making eye contact
- having good body language (no crossed arms, nodding to agree, etc.)
- actually listening to what is being said so you can reply naturally
- being honest or not commenting
- asking the client to clarify if you are unsure, i.e. 'so what you want is...?'

Listening attentively will allow and encourage your client to talk openly. It will make them feel able to describe what they really want and allow you to make a professional judgement on the service needed. It is easy to pick up on whether or not someone is really listening – remember your clients will feel

Useful Tip

Musicians need to practise their skills even with a natural gift. The same goes for those who use communication skills. As a nail technician good skills are required to ask clients for the important personal information which is needed to perform an effective treatment.

valued if you are attentive, they will enjoy their treatments and are more likely to return than if you appear to be bored by their conversation.

Questioning techniques

It is impossible to perform any nail treatment without asking your client some questions. Your questions should relate to the treatment and not be misleading. The questions you ask your clients should make them feel valued and respected and demonstrate that your prime interest is the way their hands will look. You need to be aware of the types of questions you should and should not ask. A closed question will usually get a one-word reply from a client, whereas an open question will elicit much more information and ultimately result in a better treatment for the client.

Example of a closed question

> 'Are your nails flaky and brittle?'
> *Answer*: 'Yes.'

Example of an open question

> 'Do you take any precautions or use any products when doing housework?'
> *Answer*: 'I wear rubber gloves and always use hand cream.'

Non-verbal communication

Non-verbal communication is critical to the success of a salon and of a nail technician. Everything that clients see and experience while receiving their treatment communicates an important message which will contribute positively or negatively to both your personal success or the salon's success.

Some of the key areas to pay attention to are:

- Maintain a good appointment system. Being kept waiting or turning up to an appointment to find that an error has been made and that the technician is double-booked sends out the wrong message.
- Invest in attractive stationery. The design of your appointment cards and price lists speaks volumes about your professionalism.
- Sending clients birthday and/or Christmas cards

makes them feel valued and may just nudge them into making a return visit.

- Discount or loyalty cards tell your clients how much you appreciate them.
- Your **body language** should make your client feel that he or she is the centre of attention and that you are enjoying performing the treatment.
- Your appearance is often the only information a potential client can use to make a judgement about your skills. Your uniform and appearance should be both clean and neat (see the section on personal appearance below).
- Make sure the salon is clean.
- An attractive retail area will boost your professional image as well as resulting in link sales.
- Out-of-date magazines should be avoided at all costs.
- Offering tea- or coffee-making facilities demonstrates that you are concerned about your clients' comfort while they are in your salon.

Useful Tip

Use every opportunity to communicate something positive about yourself and your salon.

Personal appearance and hygiene

As a nail technician you need to set a good example in terms of grooming. The more professional you look, the more confidence your client will have in you. The first impression made is often the one that lasts, especially if a potential client just popped into the salon to check availability or prices.

Uniform and dress code

 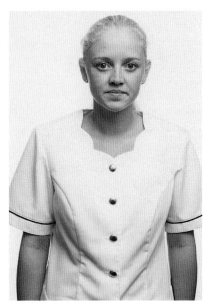

Whites

The ideal outfit is a white dress, uniform jacket, shirt or tabard, which should be neat, clean and pressed. This item should be changed daily.

Skirt or trousers

Wear a suitable skirt or trousers. Trousers should not be tight, as most of the day will be spent sitting at a nail station. Skirts should be a sensible length.

Footwear

Wear sensible low-heeled shoes and natural-coloured tights.

Jewellery

Jewellery should be kept to a minimum. Small stud earrings and a wedding band can be worn. Anything with large stones may trap bacteria between the stones, and dust can act as an irritant if caught under jewellery.

Hair

Hair should be clean, neat and tidy. Long hair must be tied back away from the face as long hair may touch the client while you are working or fall into any open products.

Skin

Your skin must be kept in good condition. Make-up should be minimal and not overdone.

Cleanliness

Shower or take a bath every morning. This is especially important in the summer or when the weather is hot. It can be a very unpleasant experience for a client if the nail technician is suffering from body odour.

Use an effective combined deodorant and antiperspirant. A good antiperspirant will minimise perspiration and a deodorant will help to reduce the breakdown of sweat that causes an unpleasant body odour. All deodorants and antiperspirants will be more effective on clean, hairless skin. A bad odour and the build-up of bacteria occur when secondary perspiration is secreted onto the first layer of perspiration.

Cover any cuts on the hands and fingers of the client or nail technician with plasters. Nail technicians should avoid strong perfume and wash their hands before and after any treatment.

Technical Tip

Black and navy blue are not good colours for a nail technician to wear as they show all the dust. If these colours are part of your uniform, place a towel over your lap to collect filing debris.

Useful Tip

Some clients may feel intimidated by a heavily made-up therapist or nail technician. All clients should be made to feel at ease.

Technical Tip

Ask your client to wash his or her hands before polishing nails. This will remove any dust and oil might otherwise spoil the polish.

Oral hygiene

Keep teeth and gums healthy with regular visits to the dentist. This will help to keep your breath fresh. Do not eat spicy food before performing a treatment and never chew gum when treating a client.

Nails

Nails should be in good condition at all times, after all *you are your own best advertisement.*

Professional conduct

The impression you make on people, however, is not just based on how you look. Every nail technician needs to know how to conduct themselves in the salon environment and in front of clients. Naturally, you should treat clients in the way you would expect to be treated if you were paying for a personal service. You must never behave in any way that could compromise the client's opinion of you or your colleagues as professionals. You should treat all the salon's clients with respect at all times and it is also important to gain your clients' respect. You can only do this by acting in a professional manner at all times.

Here are a few points to take into consideration when you are starting your career:

- Be willing to learn and keep on learning throughout your career.
- Be open to constructive criticism from colleagues or mentors who have more experience in the nail industry or with the public in general.
- Know your products and keep constantly up-to-date.
- Always show a cheerful and courteous manner to clients and colleagues.
- Be honest about everything that you do, lies will find you out.
- Do not hide mistakes.
- Be willing to listen and be objective with your clients.
- Never argue with clients.
- Be careful of becoming too familiar with clients.
- Do not take your clientele for granted. Remember the client is paying for your time – make them feel important, treat them with respect and do not rush them. Clients always have a choice.
- Be efficient and a good timekeeper.

- Respect your colleagues and other technicians around you. Do not gossip about other clients or members of staff.
- If you have nothing positive to say about another nail technician, salon or product then make no comment at all. If a client is complaining try to change the subject diplomatically.
- Follow all Health and Safety regulations.
- Make sure your hands and nails reflect your profession.
- Be loyal and never complain, especially in front of clients. They do not need to listen about your bad day or how badly things are going for you, but you should always listen to what they have to say.

Useful Tip

Remember, high standards earn you an excellent reputation.

Professional ethics

Nail technicians should be aware of how to conduct themselves in front of their clients and colleagues and be able to work effectively as part of a team of professionals.

- Take pride in your work – being a professional means that you are part of a bigger team of people – even if you work alone, you represent the nail industry.
- Know your subject thoroughly – always keep up-to-date on new products, techniques and legislation.
- Be proud of your reputation – you will start without one and build a good foundation over a period of time.
- Keep your word – do not make false claims that you cannot achieve and that you know are not possible.
- Always fulfil your obligations – if you have told a client you will be somewhere or a colleague that you will do something do not let them down.
- Be loyal to employers, employees and colleagues – be open and truthful. If you are unhappy, discuss the issue with the person concerned in private, but if this is impossible talk to your manager.
- Remember that gossip always collects 'add on' facts. Your opinions should be kept to yourself.

Consultation techniques

Learning objectives

The **consultation** is one of the most successful tools you can use to enhance your business. A good consultation technique will provide an opportunity to meet and welcome potential clients into your salon and allows you to put them at ease. Remember to listen to the client and watch their body language – your aim is to put them at ease.

In this section you will learn about:

- **the aims of consultation**
- **the information that is needed on the client consultation or record card and why it is required**
- **the importance of assessing your client's needs**
- **treatment recommendations**
- **maintenance, aftercare and home care advice**
- **maintaining client records**

A successful consultation requires the nail technician to listen carefully and question clients in a sensitive manner. Remember the client is an individual and each treatment is adapted to meet the client's unique set of circumstances. Respect for the individual client must be maintained at all times – never assume you can become over-familiar with the clientele.

Aims of consultation

The client consultation record can be an extremely powerful tool if designed correctly. It can guide and prompt the nail technician to ask for and record the correct information in a logical order with the minimum amount of fuss and time. It will allow this information to be understood by the staff in the salon, which is useful if, for some reason, the client sees another nail technician in the salon on a future visit.

A good consultation record will also help to prevent any possible misunderstanding that could arise between the client and the nail technician. It will help you to assess the client's needs, provide an opportunity to discuss their requirements and expectations and allow you to make recommendations for treatment. You must include aftercare advice and give the client an aftercare leaflet. You should make a note of this on the record card. Both the client and nail technician should sign the client record card, as it is a legal document that an insurance company would want to see if any problems arose.

Remember what was said about communication skills in the previous section. Use open questions, look at the client when asking questions, and carefully record the information. Try not to keep your head bowed over all the time when writing down the answers.

Information required for a client record card

Client consultation and record cards

Beautiful Nails

Nail Application Analysis

CLIENT PROFILE		HANDS & NAILS	
Client Name :	Maxine Gregory	Date :	10 March '02
Occupation :	Teacher	Skin type :	<u>Dry</u> - Normal - Sensitive
Sports :	Golf, Gym	Cuticle :	Norm - Dry - <u>O'grown</u> - N/Btr
Hobbies :	Travel	Nail Length :	<u>Short</u> - Medium - Long
Freq of nl/serv :	<u>1st time</u> - Infreq - Reg	Nail Shape :	Rnd - Ovl - Sq - <u>Sq/Rnd</u>
Reason for nail extns :	Holiday	Condition :	N/Btr - <u>Dam'd</u> - Oily - <u>Dry</u>

MEDICAL HISTORY		DOCTOR	
Diabetic / Asthmatic :	Yes - <u>No</u>	Doctor's Name :	Dr. Forster
Hypersensitive Skin :	Yes - <u>No</u>	Address :	The Surgery Blakelands Milton Keynes
Contact lenses :	Yes - <u>No</u>		
Allergies :	<u>No</u>	Telephone no :	12345-987 654
Contra-indications :	<u>No</u>		

CLIENT'S EXPECTATIONS		TREATMENT RECOMMENDATIONS	
Nail Length :	Short - <u>Medium</u> - Long	System :	<u>Ld/Pdr</u> - Fibgls - Silk - Other
Nail Shape :	Rnd - Oval - Sq - <u>Sq/Rnd</u>	Nail Length :	Short - <u>Medium</u> - Long
Nail Finish :	Natural - Polish - <u>Fr/Tips</u>	Nail Shape :	Rnd - Oval - Sq - <u>Sq/Rnd</u>
Polish shade(s) :		Nail Finish :	Natural - Polish - <u>Fr/Tips</u>

AFTERCARE TREATMENT PLAN

Rebalance Frequency: 1 - 1.5 - <u>2</u> - 2.5 - 3wks Homecare Advice : * Rubber Gloves * Non-acetone polish remover

Retail : Oil & Polish Remover * Nail removal advice * Regular use of Solar Oil

Client Signature : *M. Gregory* The Nail treatment & aftercare plans have been explained to me. Client data is recorded here with the consent of the Client for the sole purpose of producing a client record card. (DP Act)

Name : Maxine Gregory
Address : x Fox Milne, Milton Keynes, Bucks, MKx xAA
Tel : (h) 12345-678 900
(w) 98765-432 100 (adv) Yell.Pgs

Beautiful Nails

Nail Perfect Record Card

RIGHT hand					LEFT hand					Date	Tech	Polish	Comments
8	6	5	6	1	2	7	6	7	9	10Mar	KS	None	French Manicure tips-pink/white
\	\	\	R	\	\	\	\	\	\	23Mar	KS	None	1x Repair, left hand
\	\	N	\	\	\	\	\	\	\	05Apl	AS	177	1x New Nail, left hand
\	\	\	R	\	\	\	\	\	\	19Apl	KS	None	Backfills - pink & white powder
\	\	\	R	\	\	\	\	\	\	30Apl	KS	None	1x Repair, left hand

The following information is required on the client consultation or record card.

Name

It is very pleasing for a client to be greeted at the reception desk by the nail technician with a smile and being called by their name. It is an obvious way to identify clients' cards and it also means that colleagues can access clients' details in cases of sickness or holiday.

Address

The client's address is needed for the following reasons:

- in case of emergencies, such as a client becoming ill and needing to be taken home, or to contact relatives
- in case of GP referral
- in case of salon relocation
- some salons like to send information on special offers, open evenings or new treatments that are available

Phone numbers

Work, mobile and home telephone numbers should be recorded. There are many reasons you may have to call a client, for example in case of illness or if the nail technician is running late.

Gift voucher and flowers

Age range or date of birth

Not all salons ask their clients for their date of birth. Some prefer to use an age range system – 18–30, then 31–45, then 46 or above – to prevent embarrassment. This information is valuable when drawing up a profile of your clientele and can help you to target your advertising more effectively. Recording dates of birth allows you to reward regular clients by sending a gift voucher, birthday card or bouquet.

Source of recommendation or advertisement

Make sure you ask every client who receives a treatment who it was who recommended you or where they saw your advertisement. Record this information – it is a good way to find out what form of advertising works best, for example client referral, small ads in a local newspaper, leaflet drops or Yellow Pages.

Reason for treatment

The following list shows some of the many reasons why a

client may visit you for a treatment. Make sure this information is entered onto the client record card – it can be used to identify the best times of year, venues or groups of people to target with your advertising.

- weddings
- holidays
- Christmas parties
- Valentine's Day
- anniversaries
- nail biters
- people with thin, split or flaky nails
- professionals who require low maintenance
- art and air brushing enthusiasts

Occupation, sports, hobbies

These are the areas of your clients' lives that can affect their hands and nails. For example:

- occupation – cook, outdoor worker, receptionist, acupuncturist
- hobbies – amateur dramatics, woodwork, pottery
- sports activities – swimming, rock climbing, volleyball
- whether they have young children

All of these factors will influence the client's treatment with regard to length, shape and products. If the client is, for example, a busy mother or works in a factory environment, the length of their nail enhancements will be affected. It is important to understand that the busier your client's lifestyle, the greater is the likelihood of stress being put on the nails and damage being caused to the natural nail if you have allowed the client to wear the wrong length nails. Some guidance on safe lengths is given below.

Medical history

Record the client's doctor's name, address and phone number in case you need to obtain permission for treatment to be carried out. Remember, if you are not comfortable or you are in any doubt about an injury or a condition you do not recognise, seek professional medical advice before performing the treatment.

Whether the skin is hypersensitive

The skin may react if the client is very hypersensitive.

Safety Tip

As a general rule for applying nails to a safe length, always be guided by the size of the natural nail bed.

Technical Tip

Ask GPs to confirm *in writing* if treatment can be performed. This letter must remain on file. If permission is required, do not proceed until it is received. Failure to follow this procedure may invalidate your insurance.

Check the hands and cuticles for any obvious signs yourself and question the client before proceeding with any treatment. Signs to look for include

- redness
- sores or broken skin
- rashes
- inflammation

Record this information carefully on the client's consultation card.

Allergies to products or chemicals

Ask if a client has worn nail **extensions** before. If the answer is yes, find out if they experienced any problems in the past and what system they were wearing. Make sure any comments are recorded on the client record card.

Contact lenses

It is good practice to ask if the client wears contact lenses. It is worth noting because the client might ask you to make the nails shorter on the fingers that are used to insert and remove their lenses.

Contra indications

All **contra indications** should be noted, and the client should be referred to their GP if necessary. If none are present, this should also be recorded on the client consultation or record card.

Note: See Chapter 4 for a full list of contra indications.

Condition of hands and nails

Information acquired in this section is very valuable, especially if the client's skin or nails are in a poor condition or damaged. Here are a few important points that need to be recorded on the client consultation card:

- whether the client picks or bites his or her nails
- any accidental damage
- whether the client has come from another salon
- whether the client has changed nail technicians

A client changing from one nail technician or salon to another runs the risk of having different products and levels of expertise used on them. It is imperative that this is pointed out at your initial consultation, and the client must be aware that your products may not be compatible with those of a previous technician or salon. You must get the client to sign that they take full responsibility for any problems that may occur as a result.

The following illustrates the wording you could use on your record card:

> Beautiful Nails cannot take responsibility for any work that has been done previously on your nails by another salon or technician and you should be aware that there are risks to using another salon's products and services. Your technician will talk you through these and you will have to sign your agreement before we can proceed with any treatment.

Taking care to have this information recorded in writing is important in case a complaint arises. The process gives the client the opportunity to witness the information being recorded and to comment before signing the record card.

Skin type

Different people have different skin types and you need to be aware that this may affect a nail enhancement treatment. If, for instance, a client has clammy hands or excessively oily skin it may indicate that nail enhancements could be prone to **lifting**. Any extra action taken, such as using products to counteract the oiliness, must be recorded. You may need to check with your product supplier if they have any products designed for this situation or perhaps an advanced technique that they could pass on.

Condition of cuticle

Assess and record the condition of the client's **cuticles**, for example whether they are dry, normal or overgrown and whether the client is a nail biter. This will determine how much cuticle preparation you will need to do before a nail enhancement treatment or, if performing a manicure, whether you would recommend a hot oil or specialised treatment to help the problem. The condition of a client's cuticles affects not only any product application you may perform, but also the aftercare advice and the home care package recommended. If this is not done and noted on the client's record card and they return with problems, you will have no evidence of the advice you gave.

Natural nail length and shape

It is important to note this information as the natural nail length and shape will have a considerable bearing on the

---

Safety Tip

Always ensure your clients are aware of possible problems arising from a change of salon or technician. Make sure they sign a disclaimer or your insurance may be invalidated.

Technical Tip

If you have a client with severely overgrown cuticles they may need a manicure before attempting to wear nail enhancements successfully. You cannot do a water manicure before putting on nail enhancements as this will affect the product and the nails could come off prematurely. It is much better to perform the manicure on one day, advise the client on home care and how to look after the cuticles for one week and then let them return to the salon for the nail enhancement treatment.

recommendations and the successful outcome of the treatment.

Client's expectations of nail length, shape and finish

The client's required nail length, shape and finish should be recorded. It is very important to listen to all the client's requests for length, shape and finish before giving advice on any possible limitations to the successful outcome to the treatment.

Nail technician's treatment recommendations

This is the best opportunity the nail technician has to advise and record all the recommendations made. It is very important to do this with regard to length, shape and finish and any restrictions to the treatment should also be noted and clearly explained to the client. If there is a complaint this may be the only written evidence the nail technician has to prove what advice was given. The client may wish to ignore your advice and recommendations. In such circumstances, the importance of the client's signature is evident, as are the consequences of not obtaining the client's agreement to the treatment plan.

System recommendations

The system that is recommended should be recorded. The nail technician should advise the features and benefits of the chosen system. The three systems are:

- fibreglass system
- acrylic system
- gel system

Nail length recommendations

The nail length that you advise must be recorded. Remember, if there are breakages due to the client's request for a longer nail length, you will need a record of all your recommendations.

The rules for safe length are:

- The extension from the free edge to the tip would be considered long if it was the length of the natural nail bed.
- The extension from the free edge to the tip would be considered average if it was half the length of the natural nail bed.
- The extension from the free edge to the tip would be

considered short if it was a quarter or less of the natural nail bed.

Shape recommendations

Your recommendations for the shape should be recorded. You will choose the shape best suited to the client's natural nail shape, cuticle and arches, and it will also be the strongest shape if the nails are damaged, weak or very short. If the client requests something against your recommendations, this should also be recorded.

Aftercare advice and maintenance recommendations

A good client consultation record should also include the period until the client is advised to return for a maintenance appointment. It is a good idea to record all aftercare and home care advice given. You should also note all aftercare products recommended and what (and when) the client purchases. An aftercare booklet or leaflet should be handed to all clients on completion of their treatment and home care advice should be included in this.

Aftercare advice

With good **aftercare advice** on when to return for rebalance appointments the client will learn how to maximise his or her investment. The client should be made aware that a rebalance appointment is designed to prevent problems occurring. The client should be informed that if they let their rebalance appointment become overdue or postponed it may jeopardise the integrity of the natural nail. If nails have to be constantly repaired because a client goes too long between rebalance appointments, the natural nails will deteriorate over a period of time. This will lead to disappointment and dissatisfaction for the client, as he or she will find his or her nails constantly breaking.

Invariably, this type of client will blame the nail technician, so you can see the importance of good aftercare advice – and of good record keeping. This is a good point to remember if a client visits your salon complaining about another salon – try to look at the whole picture, and bear in mind that to some extent the client must accept responsibility for stretching out maintenance appointments after being given good advice. Many clients in this situation simply say they have not been given the relevant information. This is another good reason for handing them an aftercare leaflet and obtaining their signature. Occasionally nail technicians will have to ask themselves if they want to continue treating this type of client.

Technical Tip

If a client asks you not to shorten the length it very important to record this information, as the next time they return to the salon to maintain their nails they may have four weeks growth. This is considerably longer than you intended at your original consultation. If no records are kept the nail technician has no redress. The client will only remember they never had a problem before but that now they are suffering from breakages, damage and loss. The client will sometimes need to be reminded that it was they who changed the client agreement with the request for longer length.

Home care advice

Home care advice should include useful tips on avoiding damage to nail extensions and to the natural nails, for example:

- treat nails as jewels not tools
- beware when opening car doors and ring-pull cans
- do not pick or tear the nail extensions off
- have the extensions removed professionally
- follow the aftercare advice on rebalance appointments
- use only recommended products, for example non-acetone polish remover
- use the recommended oil two to three times a day

Maintaining client records

The client record card must be updated each time the client visits the salon for a treatment, no matter what service is provided, or how small the repair. There should be no exceptions to this rule. If any changes are made to the treatment plan they must be included on the record card. Any changes that have not been recorded will probably not be remembered by the nail technician two weeks later at the next maintenance appointment. Also, should any other nail technician in the salon have to perform the maintenance, he or she would have no prior knowledge of the client.

Ergonomics

Learning objectives

In this section you will learn about:

- **correct posture and why it is important**

- **RSI – what it is, how it is caused and how to prevent it**

- **the importance of a positive attitude**

- **choosing and using tools and furniture**

- **how to advise your client to look after their own hands and nails**

- **the importance of your health and how to maintain it**

Ergonomics is the science that studies the efficiency of people in their workplace. It deals with how we effectively use ourselves and our environment to get the maximum productivity out of every working day. To the manicurist or nail technician, this includes their posture, furniture and attitude as well as their tools, equipment and working methods.

Posture

Correct posture when sitting

Correct posture when lifting

Correct posture when carrying

Correct posture

As a nail technician you will spend long hours sitting in one position, repeating the same actions throughout the working day. Sitting down with your arms forward and head bent over can involve strain across the shoulders (the trapezius muscle), resulting in backache and headaches. Over time, the muscles can begin to tighten causing too much pressure on the nervous system. If this is ignored the symptoms worsen and may even result in a loss of sensation in the hands and arms (see repetitive strain injury).

One of the most important things in encouraging correct posture is to invest in the right chairs and desks (see below). To achieve the correct posture whilst sitting, you should:

- sit erect, with your weight evenly distributed
- place your lower back against the chair back
- keep your lower back slightly hollow or curved
- keep your shoulders back and head erect
- when leaning forward, keep your back straight
- ensure clients' hands are held at an easy angle and not stretched over the desk
- not put too much pressure on your elbows when leaning on the desk
- make sure you do some shoulder exercises at the end of the working day
- not sit cross legged as this position will twist your spine and give you a sore neck and shoulder problems
- keep your head straight and in line with your shoulders, not held to the side or constantly bent over

There are a number of measures which can be taken in order to alleviate problems associated with sitting in the same position for extended periods of time.

- Listen to what your body is telling you and do not repeatedly sit in painful positions.
- Stand up and stretch between each client treatment.

Poor posture is often a contributing factor to repetitive strain injury (RSI). RSI is an umbrella term used to refer to various kinds of work-related musculoskeletal injuries affecting the neck, shoulders, arms, wrists and hands. In some professions it can also affect the legs and feet.

Nail technicians run the risk of RSI through performing treatments using the same muscles all day. Every technician entering the nail industry should be made aware of the risks of RSI when they first learn how to treat nails.

RSI can cause serious pain and, if ignored over a period of time, could require surgery. It is a progressive condition starting with mild pain or tiredness in the hands, arms, etc. appearing throughout the working day but with total recovery overnight. Over time, the pain will start to persist overnight, but recovery can take place after a few days rest. However, if you continue to put yourself at risk, the result will be persistent pain which does not go away even after complete rest. The earlier treatment is begun, the better the chances of complete recovery. If left, complete recovery is not always possible although symptoms can be reduced with treatment.

The symptoms of RSI include tenderness and pain in the affected areas; swelling in the hands or forearms; tingling, numbness or loss of sensation; muscle spasms or weakness, including loss of strength in the grip and difficulty using the hands for everyday domestic, work and personal tasks.

It is easy to understand why a technician could suffer with hand, wrist and arm problems but you should be aware that you are also susceptible to injury in the shoulder, neck and back areas. Bad posture and poorly designed work stations are often to blame (see tips for choosing nail desks and chairs). However, all RSI injuries are avoidable with knowledge and application of the right techniques. It is every technician's responsibility to look after him- or herself – we are all guardians of our own bodies.

It is easier to prevent RSI if you understand the underlying structure of the affected parts of the body. One of the areas most commonly affected by RSI is the wrists. Two fibrous bands of tissue cross over the wrist and form a channel (the **carpal tunnel**). The nerves and tendons that control the wrist and hand pass through these bands. When an injury occurs in this area, the swelling pinches the nerves together, causing pain. If this is ignored the condition will worsen and

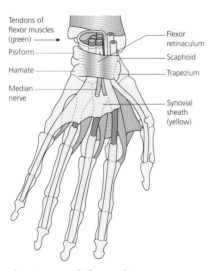

Tendons of flexor muscles (green)

Pisiform

Hamate

Median nerve

Flexor retinaculum

Scaphoid

Trapezium

Synovial sheath (yellow)

Anatomy of the wrist

become permanent. Pain is the body's way of telling you where the injury is located. Never ignore any pain in your body.

Good practice in working methods to avoid RSI

The following tips can help to prevent RSI problems arising.

- Use a softer touch with the file. A heavier touch will not speed up your finishing time, it will simply push the grit of the file further into the board instead of smoothing the nail surface and at the same time place more stress on your wrist.
- Use longer rather than shorter sweeps with your file and buffers. This will increase your speed as well as help to protect you.
- Do not use tools that vibrate excessively. Vibration will aggravate conditions such as carpal tunnel syndrome. If you are using a drill, make sure you have a good quality drill and have had thorough training in its use.
- Don't forget to check your sitting position.
- Use a wrist support for your client so that you are working in the correct position.
- Do not lean over your table, bring your client's hand nearer to you.
- Try to file with your arm and not just with your wrist. Hold your wrist straight whilst filing.
- Don't forget to take regular breaks and stretch out the back, shoulders and arms.
- Do not strain your neck or hang your head whilst working.
- Rotate your wrist and flex your fingers between client treatments. Shake your hands or perform a few simple exercises before sitting down to begin the next treatment.

Attitude

A positive attitude is essential to building a successful business and a happy clientele. As a nail technician, you must develop a good relationship with each client. There is nothing worse than working on someone towards whom you have a negative attitude. Your body will be tense and both

Safety Tip

If any pain or swelling occurs frequently in the hand or wrist area you should consult your doctor and be prepared for a period of rest. You should also analyse your techniques to see where improvements can be made.

Technical Tip

Here are two exercises that can be done throughout the working day to ease tension and loosen muscles:

1 Rotate the shoulders forwards three times and then backwards three times. Make sure the circles are as big as possible to get a good stretch.

2 Gently swing your arms in a circle forward three times and then backwards three times.

Hand exercises

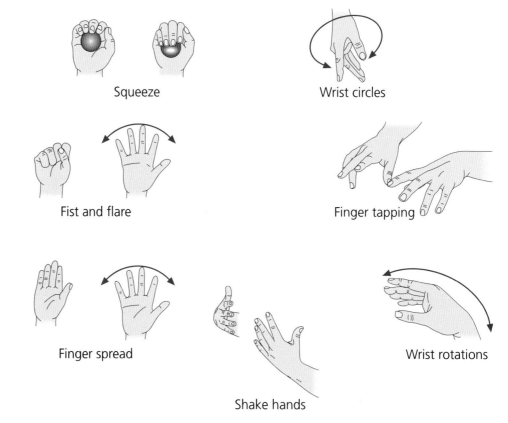

you and they will suffer. Every client wants to feel pampered and it will be impossible to achieve this if you are on edge and tense.

There are a number of techniques to encourage a good relationship with your clients whilst performing treatments, and they will also help you to enjoy the time you spend with your clients.

- Make sure you address them with the title they would like, this could be by their christian name or by title and surname.

- Make sure you have correctly identified their needs and they are getting exactly the service they want from you.

- Always make sure clients are warm and seated comfortably.

- Do not leave your client unless you need to get something for them.

- Do not cut corners or rush the treatment.

- Encourage your clients to talk – try not to use closed questions.

Technical Tip

Laughter is one of the best cures for stress.

Technical Tip

Invest in tools that will help you do your job more effectively and efficiently.

- Always let your client know they have your total confidentiality.
- Be a good listener.
- Use a soft tone of voice.
- Keep a smile in your hands as well as on your face.

Tools and furniture

When starting out it is not always possible to invest in the most up-to-date tools and equipment. However, there is some very good moderately priced equipment on the market. Look at the tools and equipment you will be using the most and decide where it would be best for you to invest your money. Remember those tools that will be used the most are likely to wear out or degrade quickly so quality might be more cost effective for these items.

Technician's chair

A manicurist or nail technician should invest in a good chair. A properly designed stool or operator's chair will make a significant difference to how you feel at the end of the day and even more of a difference at the end of a long, busy week. A good chair with back support or a special back chair with knee support will encourage good posture.

Suitable chairs

Courtesy of REM (UK) Ltd

The nail desk

The nail desk is a very important item for every nail technician and manicurist. It will not only make the difference between sitting comfortably or having to lean over and put unnecessary stress on the arms and the back, but it can also affect your image.

When choosing a nail desk, look at:

- the width – if it is too wide you will have to lean
- the height – your elbows and arms should rest on the desk's surface without having to stretch or hunch over
- the drawers – they should be easily accessible and suitable for storing chemicals and products; ideally, they should be on your dominant side
- arm rest – there should be an armrest for the client; this is not only more comfortable for them but safer for you in the long term

Suitable nail station desks

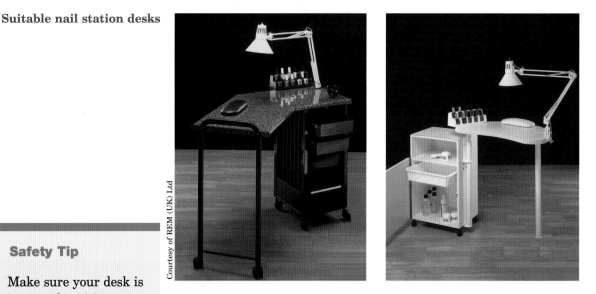

Courtesy of REM (UK) Ltd

Your desk should have as few products on the surface as possible so that it looks uncluttered. Have out only what you need at the time; it looks more professional and will also prevent accidents. This topic was also considered in Chapter 1 in the section on salon equipment.

Before purchasing an expensive item like a nail desk make sure you collect a number of equipment catalogues so that you can compare prices and what you are getting for your money.

General list of tools and equipment

You will need the following smaller items of equipment:

- tip cutters
- cuticle nippers
- toenail clippers
- files and buffers
- desk light
- towels

Safety Tip

- Make sure your desk is in a good position near to electricity points so that there are no trailing leads.
- Make sure the hand you are treating is presented at the right angle to avoid causing you any strain by using an armrest for your client.
- Your desk should be secure while you are working on it as this could cause accidents. If you have a desk on rollers make sure they are locked.

- scissors
- cuticle pusher
- disposables

Tip cutters

Maintenance: Tip cutters should be cleaned between each client. Do not leave them in the sterilisation unit for long periods of time as they can deteriorate or rust. Occasionally you may need to place some oil on the screw or spring to prevent any squeaking when you are using them. Check that the blade is sharp – these can normally be replaced, so check with your supplier before purchasing. Keep the cutting edge of the blade towards yourself when cutting or reducing the length of the **nail tip**, never towards the client as you may cut the top of the finger.

Cuticle nippers

Maintenance: Cuticle nippers should always be sterilised between clients. They must never be used for any other purpose than removing excess non-living tissue around the cuticle or **hang nails**, as this would render them useless, as the cutting blades would be blunt. Good quality cuticle nippers can be sharpened; check with the supplier before purchasing.

Toenail clippers

Maintenance: Toenail clippers should always be sterilised before and after use. To keep them in good order they must never be used for any other purpose than trimming or clipping toenails.

Scissors

Maintenance: Your scissors should be cleaned between clients. Do not leave them in the sterilisation unit for long periods of time. If using scissors to cut and shape tips they must be kept sharp, or they may crease the tip as well as cutting it and thus render it useless. If using scissors to cut and trim fibreglass or silk, you should have a pair which are used only for this purpose. This prevents the fibre from fraying or tearing because the scissors have become blunt. It is best to purchase separate pairs of scissors for each job that needs to be done rather than using one pair for all tasks.

Cuticle pusher

A metal cuticle pusher is the most hygienic to use. It should always be cleaned and sterilised before use, remembering not to leave tools in the sterilisation fluid for long periods of time, as some chemical solutions can rust and degrade metal tools. If using a plastic **hoof** pusher this should also be thoroughly cleaned before use. If a wooden orange stick is used, it must be disposed of immediately after use.

Files and buffers

Maintenance: Files and buffers must always be sanitised between clients and at the end of each day. Use a nail brush and anti-bacterial soap to wash and brush each file, allowing them to dry naturally. You can keep a file and buffer for each client in an envelope or container, filed under the client's name or kept with the client's record card. Some files cannot be sanitised because they deteriorate. If you use this type of file then you must dispose of them after use. Buffers last much longer if you use them without oil, so ask your clients to wash their hands before you buff their nails to a high gloss shine.

Desk light

You should take care when choosing a light for your nail station. It should be capable of standing on the nail station and have an adjustable arm to allow it to be moved to give the maximum light. Use a halogen bulb as this gives off less heat, also helps to reduces the possibility of headaches, as you are working with your head very close to the light source. Also any heat given off can have an adverse affect on the curing and setting of your products.

Towels

There should be a clean towel for each client. Towels should be washed on a hot wash of at least 60°C and should not be washed with any other laundry.

Disposables

Cotton wool, tissues, paper towels, lint-free pads and wooden orange sticks should be new for each client and disposed of after use.

Healthy hands for client and technician

As a manicurist or nail technician, your main concern is naturally your client's nails, but you should be able to give your clients general advice on how to keep their hands in good condition. Your clients will have more respect for you if they believe that you care about the well-being of their hands as a whole and can give them advice on how to keep them in good condition at any time.

Technical Tip

The higher the grit the softer the file. A 100 grit file will have 100 pieces of sand or grit per square inch or per square 2.54 centimetres. This grade is used for rough shaping on artificial nails only. A 240 grit file will have 240 pieces of grit so obviously the grit size must be much smaller to enable 240 pieces of grit to fit into the same area. This grade is used for initial buffing or on a natural nail.

Listen carefully when doing your initial consultation so you can learn about your client as a person, his or her work, home life and stress levels. These three factors affect every part of our body.

You will also want to keep your own hands looking and feeling good. They are the most important tools of your trade and hopefully will help you to grow a good business over time. Your hands will reflect your professionalism and say a lot about you. If your hands look awful, a client will not have a high level of confidence in your skills, whereas if they look beautiful you will find people are attracted to you because of them. Clients will also have more confidence in your retail products and will believe they work because they will assume they are one the reasons why your hands look great.

Here are some general tips for protecting you and your client's hands and nails:

- Use rubber gloves lined with cotton for protection when using harsh chemicals.
- Use mild soaps or hand cleansers, which will not dry out the skin.
- Always rinse hands thoroughly and dry properly with a soft towel.
- Always use hand cream or lotion after hands have been in water to rehydrate the skin and prevent any possible dryness.
- Remove rings before washing the hands to prevent a build-up of soap or detergent that could cause a reaction.
- Give the hands a good massage right to the fingertips when using hand cream.
- Use a good cuticle cream or oil daily to keep them soft.
- Always use a base coat if wearing enamel.
- Avoid the overuse of harsh enamel removers – once a week is usually enough.

The following tips help to maintain the strength and flexibility of the nail:

- If you get a split in a nail, mend it or cut it.
- Always use a file to neaten any rough edges rather than picking or biting, as this will tear nail plate layers.
- Use strengtheners or hardeners for short periods to help weak or thin nails.

- Buff nails to increase circulation and draw important nutrients to the area.
- The type of nails you have are hereditary but, although vitamins and minerals cannot help the state of the nail, they can help towards general good health.
- A balanced diet, including fruit and vegetables, will help your general health, maintaining the health of all of the body, including the hands.
- Don't allow the nails to become too long, the smaller the nail, the smaller the free edge.

Why are diet and nutrition important?

Your attention to your appearance cannot end at your hands and nails. In this industry, your clients expect you to look healthy, fit and well groomed. If your health lets you down, you will not only look and feel tired, but you will be prone to illness and infections from your clients. As well as being bad for your own health, this can be detrimental to your business as you will lose money if you are off work.

A client comes to you not only to have their hands treated but also to get away from their daily routine. They don't want to sit with someone who is constantly sniffing or coughing nor do they want to look at someone who has dark circles under their eyes, hasn't had the strength to tend to their hair or make-up or, even worse, who is moaning because they don't feel 100 per cent and shouldn't really be at work. Clients want to be with someone who is cheerful, will listen to their moans or swap happy news. Being treated by someone who looks healthy and well groomed makes customers feel more positive and happy to part with their hard-earned wages.

We live in a world today of so many fad diets that it is impossible to count them all. A diet simply means what we eat each day. In order to stay alive and for our body to work effectively we need certain daily nutrients. As manicurists and nail technicians we open ourselves to a constant invasion of germs by sitting opposite clients all day, and we therefore need to protect ourselves.

- Eat fresh instead of processed food.
- Eat foods high in vitamins and minerals – if you don't like certain foods and feel you lack certain minerals then take supplements.
- Eat as many raw foods as possible, especially vegetables, fruits and salads.

- Eat only when you are hungry.
- If you crave biscuits, chocolate and processed foods just take a nibble, that usually staves off a craving.
- Drink lots of fluids, especially water.

Did you know the following facts about the body?

- Around 69 per cent of our body is made up of water.
- We lose around 2 litres of water per day through evaporation and excretion.
- Diet will affect nail plate growth but not the structure, thickness or strength of the natural nail.
- Drinking a glass of tepid water when waking in the morning will help to rid the body of toxins.

Exercise for all

Our profession requires sitting in one position for long periods of time. Although this means we are not putting the systems of our body under pressure from exertion, our sedentary working habits can be just as bad.

Exercise is absolutely essential for the well-being of our bodies. It is vital for:

- maintaining muscular tone
- maintaining heart and lung capacity
- taking food and oxygen to all organs of the body

Ideally, we need to increase our heart rate every day for 10–15 minutes. This can be fitted into a daily work schedule. For example:

- run up and down the stairs for 5 minutes
- jog on the spot for a few minutes
- take a brisk walk down the road for a few minutes, breathing in deeply
- perform a few stretching exercises
- get a stimulating massage

If this is totally impossible, then make sure either before or after work you:

- take the dog for a long walk
- go swimming with the kids

Safety Tip

Every technician should have at least a 10–15 minute break between client treatments to allow them to stretch, take the pressure off nerves that are being compressed and get the blood flowing a little quicker to help circulation. If they don't do this, over a period of years they could suffer from joint and back problems.

- exercise at home or a gym
- go for a cycle ride
- walk home from work

Light

Studies have shown that people who work under artificial light can suffer from:

- skin problems
- hormone imbalances
- depression

It is imperative that you allow your eyes to be exposed to natural light for at least an hour each day. This can be very difficult in the winter when we go to and come home from work in the dark, but it is well worth allowing yourself at least a 30-minute lunch break to get some fresh air, to stretch and to allow the natural light to work on your body.

Chapter summary

You know yourself that when you meet someone for the first time, or visit premises you have never been to before, first impressions count. It is so easy, especially when first starting out in business, to forget the points we have covered in this chapter. Remember to smile, even if you feel as if everything is going wrong, always present a clean and tidy image, and take into account you and your client's comfort. Follow the points raised in this chapter and add your own personal identity and touches to your business. A productive consultation relies on good communication skills; paying attention to your personal appearance is part of conducting yourself professionally; remember that all the areas covered in this chapter depend on one another to work effectively.

Anatomy and physiology

4

It is important to understand how the body works and how we can affect the workings of the body with our treatments and products. In this chapter we cover all the major systems of the body and their functions. The structure of the skin and nails is also covered in depth and we will look at how we, as nail technicians, can enhance the appearance of both. Possible damage to the structures we work on could happen through lack of knowledge or improper techniques and it is important that we learn how to prevent this. Nail and skin disorders and diseases are also identified and explained. Every nail technician must be able to recognise the point at which they should refer a client to a GP and not try to make a diagnosis. We are representatives of our trade and as such we need to keep our hands and feet in top condition all the time. General advice on our own health are included in this chapter.

In this chapter we will consider the following aspects:

- **the systems of the body**

- **anatomy of the natural nail**

- **diseases of the skin and nails**

- **contra actions to nail treatments**

The systems of the body

Learning objectives

In this section you will learn about:

- **why it is so important for a nail technician to understand the workings of the human body**

- **the human cell and its structure**

- **the structure and functions of the skin**

- **the vascular system and its relationship to the lymphatic system**

- **the skeletal system**

- **the muscular system**

The importance of understanding the human body

As professionals we work on other people's bodies and for this reason we should be aware of the workings of those bodies. We not only need to know about diseases and disorders of the skin and nails, but also how the body works and how we as nail technicians can affect those functions. It is important to know that when we massage during a manicure or pedicure we are increasing the blood flow around the body and to be aware of the effects this will have on our clients.

It is up to you to learn enough about the functions of the body to be able to recognise when not to work on a client and also when a treatment can help a client's condition. You should *never* try to diagnose a condition. You should always ask your client to see their doctor if you are concerned about anything, do not recognise a condition or notice that something has changed since you last saw your client.

The body is a fabulous machine but it needs care and attention to help it to work properly. Nail treatments not only enhance the look of a client's hands but can also have a psychological benefit on your client's well-being.

The human cell and its structure

All the **cells** of the human body have the same basic structure, although they differ in their functions. A cell is usually made up of 70–80 per cent water, 15 per cent

Cell structure

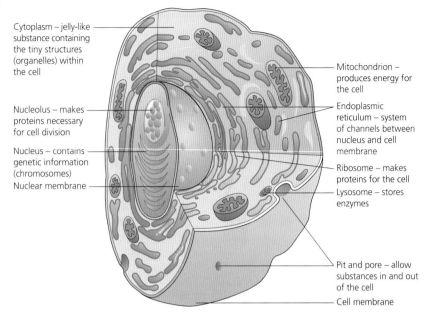

Cytoplasm – jelly-like substance containing the tiny structures (organelles) within the cell

Nucleolus – makes proteins necessary for cell division

Nucleus – contains genetic information (chromosomes)

Nuclear membrane

Mitochondrion – produces energy for the cell

Endoplasmic reticulum – system of channels between nucleus and cell membrane

Ribosome – makes proteins for the cell

Lysosome – stores enzymes

Pit and pore – allow substances in and out of the cell

Cell membrane

proteins, 1 per cent carbohydrates, 3 per cent lipids (otherwise known as fatty acids) and 1 per cent nucleic acids and minerals.

The outer layer of the cell is known as the *cell membrane* which acts as a sieve through which some substances are absorbed and others rejected. Nutrients can be transported across the cell membrane by chemical substances generally known as *carriers*. In the middle of the cell is the *nucleus* which is surrounded by its own *membrane*. This is the control centre of the cell and it plays a very important part in influencing reproduction and growth. The nucleus has a network of fibres known as *chromatin*. It is this part of the cell that contains *deoxyribonucleic acids*, commonly known as *DNA*. DNA is the genetically inherited information required for the maintenance of cells and their reproduction. When the cells reproduce the chromatin fibres assume the form of a twisted skein that divides into a number of 'V' shaped loops known as *chromosomes*. Every cell in the body has 46 chromosomes arranged in 23 pairs.

Genes are parts of the DNA molecule and every gene carries a specific hereditary trait. These traits could be physical – such as skin type or nail shape – biochemical or physiological. Genes determine the physical appearance of an individual and also their physiological make up, for example the individual's tendency to develop certain diseases. A new-born baby receiving DNA from its parents develops characteristics that reflect those of its parents, grandparents and other family members. As the child grows it is also affected by environmental factors such as diet and education.

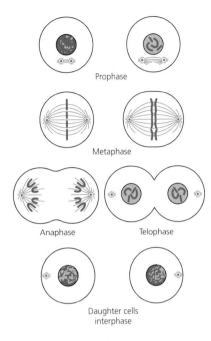

Prophase

Metaphase

Anaphase

Telophase

Daughter cells
interphase

Stages in mitosis

Cell division (mitosis)

The cells of the human body divide in a complicated manner called *mitosis*. This process takes place in a number of stages:

- *Prophase* – the centrosome divides into two parts, each with an individual centriole. Each centrosome moves to the opposite side of the cell whilst remaining connected by fine, thread-like fibres.

- *Metaphase* – the chromatin becomes more structured in its shape and forms longer rod-shaped structures. The chromosomes arrange themselves around the cell and the nuclear membrane begins to disperse. The chromosomes appear to be connected to the threads of centrosomes at either end of the cell.

- *Anaphase* – the chromosomes begin to divide equally lengthways. The two groups begin to pull away from each other to opposite ends of the cell and at this stage the threads start to break.

- *Telophase* – a constriction appears around the centre of the body of the cell. The threads disappear entirely as the nuclear membrane reappears. The constriction of the cytoplasm increases until the cell is divided, the chromosomes disappear and the filament-like structure chromatin is re-formed. This completes the cycle and the two cells that are formed are called 'daughter' cells. All cells grow and reproduce in this way.

Each cell goes through this activity of growth and reproduction. Cells continually grow until they are ready to reproduce by mitosis.

Cells receive nourishment from the bloodstream through the cell membranes. This process is either a chemical or a physical change which takes place in the cells and helps to create heat and energy. In turn, worn-out protoplasm is built up and repaired, and secretions or enzymes are generated. This is the process known as *metabolism*.

A cell is capable of movement and can respond to stimulus whether it be thermal, chemical or physical.

The structure of the skin

The skin is the largest organ of the body and covers a total area of between 1.3 and 2 square metres depending on the size of the person. The skin has to be tough enough to be able to withstand the knocks it receives in daily life and also sensitive enough to be able to send signals when we are in danger or are facing environmental changes such as heat and cold. The skin is constantly working even when we are asleep or relaxing on a beach. It helps to regulate other body processes and protects us from the following:

- allergens
- chemicals
- UV exposure
- micro-organisms

The skin needs to be kept in good condition at all times if it is to protect our bodies from harm. A closer look at the structure and functions of the skin will help you understand how we can help keep our clients' skin in good condition.

Structure of the skin

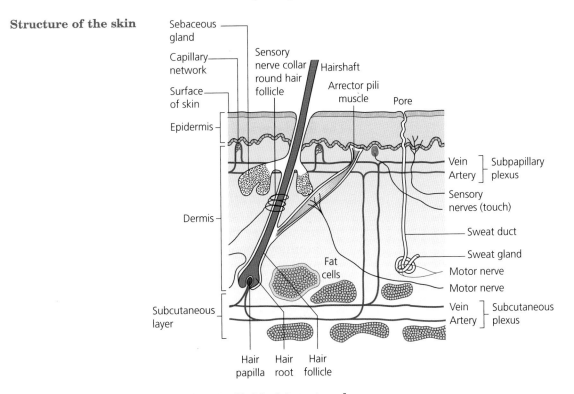

The skin is divided into two layers:

1 The **epidermis** – topmost layer
2 The **dermis** – basal layer

Below the dermis is subcutaneous tissue which serves to anchor the dermis.

The epidermis

The epidermis is made up of five layers of tissue that contain no blood vessels and very few nerves. It is pierced by hair follicles and the ducts of sweat and sebaceous glands.

Layers of the epidermis

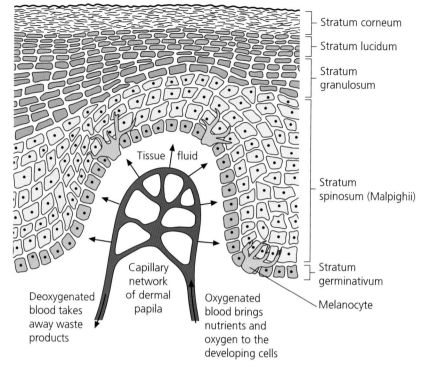

Stratum corneum

Stratum lucidum

Stratum granulosum

Stratum spinosum (Malpighii)

Tissue fluid

Stratum germinativum

Capillary network of dermal papila

Melanocyte

Deoxygenated blood takes away waste products

Oxygenated blood brings nutrients and oxygen to the developing cells

The five layers of the epidermal layer are:

1 *Stratum germinativum* (basal layer). These cells, packed tightly together and constantly being reproduced form the deepest stratum of the epidermal layer that rests on top of the dermis. As these cells are pushed towards the surface they become components of other layers. This cellullar regeneration can be increased or decreased by a number of factors including ill health or age. The colour of the skin is also determined by this layer as it contains pigment-bearing cells known as *melanocytes* which produce melanin.

2 *Stratum spinosum*. This layer is composed of several layers of cells that vary in size and shape. The upper portion of this layer is known as the prickle cell layer. The cells are linked by very fine threads which give them a spiky appearance.

3 *Stratum granulosum* (granular layer). As the cells from this layer rise to the surface they flatten and become progressively larger and accumulate granules containing keratohyalin which helps in the production of epidermal keratin. It has between one and four layers.

4 *Stratum lucidum*. This layer has no nuclei, is narrow, transparent and has little outline. The cells at this stage are nearly at the end of their life cycle and are becoming dehydrated. The keratohyalin granules that are present in the stratum granulosum are now being turned into keratin.

5 *Stratum corneum* (horny layer). This is the outermost layer of skin and is composed of several layers of flattened irregularly shaped cells. They assume this flattened form from the evaporation of their fluid content. This layer consists almost entirely of keratin. As the cells near the surface they are shed or rubbed off during normal daily routines. This layer protects the skin, preventing dehydration of the skin tissues. It can take 3–4 weeks for cells to activate in the stratum germinativum and rise through to the surface stratum corneum.

The dermis

This is called the 'true skin' and it lies immediately beneath the epidermis. This layer contains blood vessels, lymph vessels, nerves, sweat and sebaceous glands, hair follicles, arrector pili muscles and papillae. The dermis is comprised of two separate layers:

1 the papillary layer (pa-pil-ah-ry)
2 the reticular layer (re-tik-u-lar)

The papillary layer lies directly under the epidermis and contains the small cone-like projections that extend upwards into the epidermis, called *papillae*. Papillae contain small blood vessels or nerve endings. This layer can also contain some melanin.

The reticular layer is the lower area of the dermis where the blood and lymph vessels, sweat glands and sebaceous glands, hair follicles and the arrector pili muscles are situated. It also has a dense network of collagen fibres which run parallel to the surface. These fibres give the skin its elasticity and can be damaged by ultra violet light.

The subcutaneous tissue

The subcutaneous (sub-koo-tay-nee-us) layer is made up of fatty tissue more commonly known as adipose tissue. It is not technically skin, but anchors the skin and acts as a protective cushion for the body. It also stores fat to be burned for energy. It can vary greatly in thickness according to the age, sex and health of the body. Sitting beneath the dermis layer, it contains the following:

- *Blood supply*. There is a network of arteries that run parallel to the surface of the skin contained in the subcutaneous layer. These branch into smaller capillary networks around hair follicles, sebaceous and sweat glands. The capillary network is responsible for transporting vital food and oxygen to the living cells. The amount of blood flow to the surface is controlled by the nerve endings in the capillary walls.

- *Lymph*. The lymphatic capillaries drain away tissue fluid which contains waste products from cell activity and foreign bodies such as bacteria. This is part of a network of fine lymph vessels throughout the dermis.

The nerves

A nerve is made of fibres and sends messages from the organs of the body to the central nervous system. As the skin is an organ it is no exception and contains many nerve fibres. There are two types of nerves within the skin's structure:

1 motor nerves
2 sensory nerves

Four sensations can be experienced through the skin, these are:

1 pressure
2 touch
3 pain
4 temperature

All sensations are due to the network of sensory nerves and receptors within the skin. The majority of receptors lie deep within the dermis but those that register pain are to be found in the lower epidermis. All sensations are stimulated by influences external to the body, such as extreme heat or cold. This message is then taken along the central nervous system and the brain decides how to act on this information. If the brain decides that action is required, it will send a message along the motor nerves to the necessary organ or muscle. If the original message was, for example, that the skin was cold, the brain instructs the arrector pili muscle to contract and trap air next to the body for warmth, this is what we call 'goose-bumps'.

Other components of the skin

Hair follicle

This is a depression of epidermal cells pushed deep into the dermis responsible for the production of the keratinised structure called hair. The blood vessels in the dermal papillae supply the food and oxygen necessary for hair growth. The arrector pili muscle is responsible for causing 'goose-bumps' as it is attached to the hair follicle and pulls it into an upright position when the muscle is contracted.

Sebaceous glands

With the exception of the soles of the feet and the palms of the hands, these glands are found all over the body. There are more in areas such as the chest, face, back and the scalp, and less on the knees and elbows. They usually open out into a hair follicle, although some may be found on the skin's surface keeping the skin soft and supple by preventing moisture loss from the dermis. An invisible layer called the acid mantle is formed by sweat and sebum and protects the skin from harmful bacteria. Another function is to keep the skin waterproof and healthy. When the sebaceous glands increase activity, seborrhoea or oily skin occurs, which can lead to blocked pores and other skin conditions. The reverse will cause dry skin, flaking and dehydrated conditions.

Sweat glands

There are two types of sweat glands within the skin. Both types are deep in the dermis and consist of long narrow tubes or ducts that pass up through the epidermis to the surface, where the sweat is excreted through an opening in the skin called a pore. These glands are either:

- eccrine, or
- apocrine.

Eccrine glands are found all over the body and only secrete water and salts. Their only function is to regulate body temperature.

Apocrine glands are found in the armpits and genital areas and open into the hair follicles instead of the surface of the skin. These glands secrete water, urea and fats. It is the breakdown of this type of sweat that causes body odour.

To become a nail technician, you must learn about dermatology, the study of human skin, and this should cover skin disorders and skin diseases. The skin on the human body is thinnest on the eyelids and thickest on the palms of the hands and soles of the feet. It is part of our work as nail technicians to educate our clients on the processes they can use to maintain healthy skin on their hands and feet.

The functions of the skin

The skin has a number of jobs to perform to help keep the body in good working order. The following are six important functions in the skin's daily routine. To help you remember them, notice that their initials spell the word SHAPES.

- **S**ensation
- **H**eat regulation
- **A**bsorption
- **P**rotection
- **E**xcretion
- **S**ecretion

Sensation

Through its sensory nerve endings the skin responds to touch, pain, pressure and temperature.

Heat regulation

A healthy body maintains a constant internal temperature of 37°C or 98.6°F. In hot conditions, capillaries dilate dissipating heat, sweat is released onto the skin's surface and evaporation takes place, thus cooling the skin. In cold conditions, capillaries constrict, the arrector pili muscles contract causing the hairs to move to a vertical position, so trapping any escaping heat.

Absorption

This is limited, although certain substances, for example antibiotics, aromatherapy oils and certain chemicals, can be absorbed through the skin.

Protection

The skin protects the body from injury. The epidermis is covered with a thin layer of sebum. This is highly waterproof and antibacterial.

Excretion

Perspiration containing water, salts and chemicals is excreted via the sweat glands.

Secretion

Sebum is secreted from the sebaceous glands.

 Interesting Facts

One square centimetre of skin contains:

- 0.9 metres of blood vessels
- 3.6 metres of nerves
- 200 nerve endings
- 100 suderiferous glands
- 15 sebaceous glands
- approximately 10 hairs

The vascular system and its relationship to the lymphatic system

The vascular system is the chief transportation system of the body, carrying food, oxygen and other essentials to cell tissues, and taking away their waste products. The vascular system consists of three parts:

1   blood – a fluid in which materials are carried
2   heart – a pump which propels blood around the body
3   blood vessels – through which blood travels to and from the tissues

Blood is a red, sticky fluid. It consists of a clear yellow liquid called plasma, which carries dissolved substances such as glucose to the cells and waste products from the cells, and blood cells. There are two types of blood cells:

1   *Red* erythrocytes – these carry oxygen to the cells as oxyhaemoglobin
2   *White* lymphocytes – these help fight infection

Functions of the blood

- The transportation of food, glucose, fats, amino acids, vitamins, salts, water, hormones, white blood cells, removal of waste products and heat.
- Defence against disease or protection. The white blood cells fight invading foreign substances, for example bacteria.
- Clotting agents help to stop bleeding from wounds, close the wound and keep out bacteria.
- Heat/temperature regulator – exercising muscles and the working liver produce heat which is then distributed around the body.

The heart

The heart is a muscular organ about the size of a clenched fist. It is located in the chest and is an efficient pump keeping the blood moving within the body's circulatory system. Nerves from the autonomic nervous system regulate the heartbeat which in an adult is about 70–80 times per minute. The interior of the heart contains four chambers:

- the right and left atria which are the thin-walled upper chambers

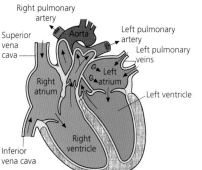

The heart

- the right and left ventricles which are the thick-walled lower chambers

The right and left sides of the heart are separated by the septum and valves allow blood to flow in one direction only between each of the four chambers.

With each contraction and relaxation of the heart, deoxygenated blood is pumped into the right atrium from the body and passes from there into the right ventricle. From the right ventricle the blood is pumped into the lungs to be oxygenated. The blood re-enters the heart by the left atrium and passes to the left ventricle from where it is pumped out to journey once again through the body.

Blood vessels

There are three types of blood vessels:

1 arteries
2 veins
3 capillaries

They all are tube-shaped and distribute the blood to and from the heart and to all the organs of the body.

Arteries are thick-walled muscular tubes that carry oxygenated blood from the heart to the capillaries at a very fast rate throughout the body.

Veins are thin-walled blood vessels that are less elastic than arteries and much nearer to the surface. They carry blood that lacks oxygen and nutrients back from the capillaries to the heart and lungs. Veins contain valves to prevent backflow of the blood; it is when these valves break down that you will see conditions such as varicose veins.

Capillaries are tiny, thin-walled blood vessels that connect the small arteries to the veins. They receive nourishment and eliminate waste products through their thin walls.

Blood supply to the arm and hand

The blood supply to the arm begins with the *subclavian artery* which branches off from the *aorta*. This becomes the *axillary artery* and then the *brachial artery* which runs down the inner part of the arm to about one centimetre below the elbow where it divides into the radial and ulnar arteries.

- The *radial artery* runs down the forearm next to the radius bone to the wrist. It can be felt as a radial pulse in the wrist where it is near the surface. It

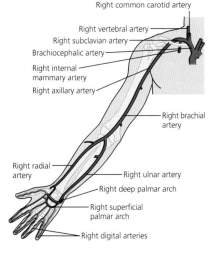

Right common carotid artery
Right vertebral artery
Right subclavian artery
Brachiocephalic artery
Right internal mammary artery
Right axillary artery
Right brachial artery
Right radial artery
Right ulnar artery
Right deep palmar arch
Right superficial palmar arch
Right digital arteries

Blood supply to the arm – arteries

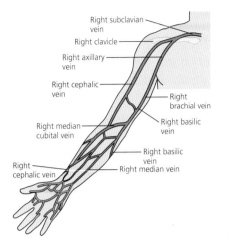

Right subclavian vein
Right clavicle
Right axillary vein
Right cephalic vein
Right brachial vein
Right median cubital vein
Right basilic vein
Right cephalic vein
Right basilic vein
Right median vein

Blood supply to the arm – veins

continues over the carpal bones to pass between the first and second metacarpal into the palm.

- The *ulnar artery* runs down the forearm next to the ulna bone, across the carpals and into the palm of the hand. Together they form two arches in the hand: the deep and superficial palmar arches. From these arteries branch others to supply blood to the structures of the upper arm and forearm, and also to the hand and fingers.

The venous return of blood from the hand begins with the palmar arch and the plexus, which is a network of capillaries present in the palm. Three veins carry the deoxygenated blood up the forearm:

1 radial vein
2 ulnar vein
3 median vein

The radial and ulnar veins run parallel to the radius and ulna bones and the median runs up the middle. Just above the elbow, the radial and ulnar veins join to become the brachial vein, and the median vein joins the basilic vein which originates from just below the elbow. As the veins carry on up the arm they link to form a network. Eventually the basilic vein joins the brachial vein and becomes the axillary vein.

Blood supply to the leg and foot

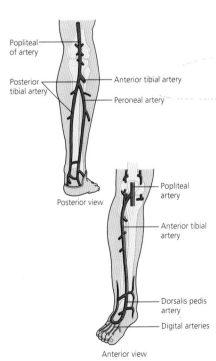

Popliteal of artery
Posterior tibial artery
Anterior tibial artery
Peroneal artery
Posterior view
Popliteal artery
Anterior tibial artery
Dorsalis pedis artery
Digital arteries
Anterior view

Blood supply to the leg – arteries

The *aorta* is a major artery which travels down the length of the trunk of the body to the lower abdomen where it divides into two main arteries which supply both legs. The artery in the thigh is called the *femoral artery* after the femur or thigh bone. At the knee the femoral artery becomes the *popliteal artery* and divides into two below the knee. One of these arteries runs down the front of the lower leg and is called the *anterior tibial artery*, while the other runs down the back and is known as the *posterior tibial artery*. This artery divides at the inside of the ankle and becomes the *medial plantar artery* on the inside of the foot and the *plantar arch* on the sole of the foot. The *anterior tibial artery* becomes the *dorsalis pedis* on top of the foot.

The network of veins in the foot become the *dorsal venous arch* on top of the foot. This travels up the inside of the foot to the ankle where it becomes a small *saphenous vein*. It runs up the back of the leg to the thigh where it is known as the *long saphenous vein*. There are two smaller veins called the *anterior tibial veins* which run up the front of the lower

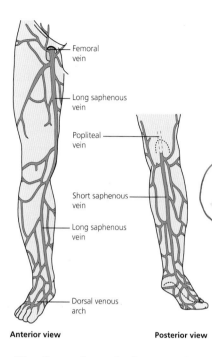

Femoral
vein

Long saphenous
vein

Popliteal
vein

Short saphenous
vein

Long saphenous
vein

Dorsal venous
arch

Anterior view   **Posterior view**

Blood supply to the legs – veins

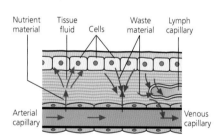

Nutrient   Tissue   Waste   Lymph
material   fluid   Cells material   capillary

Arterial   Venous
capillary   capillary

Lymphatic flow

leg while two other veins, the *posterior tibial veins*, run up the back. All four veins converge just below the knee to become the *popliteal vein* at the back of the knee and then eventually the *femoral vein* in the thigh. The *femoral and long saphenous veins* join at the groin and return to the heart.

The lymphatic system

The lymphatic system is a 'secondary' circulation system. It works closely with the body's blood circulation to rid the body of the waste the veins cannot carry.

The functions of the lymphatic system are:

1   To drain tissue fluid from all organs.
2   To prevent oedema. This is the excessive accumulation of fluid in the tissues leading to localised swelling. It is an example of fluid imbalance, and can be due to standing for long periods, or can be caused by an obstruction in the lymphatic drainage pathway, such as an infected lymph node.
3   The transportation of fats from the small intestine, or ileum, where they are absorbed by the liver.
4   To return to the blood protein molecules which are unable to pass back through the blood capillary walls because of their large size.
5   The production of lymphocytes which help to fight infection.

Lymph

The body consists of three types of fluid which are:

1   *Blood,* consisting of cells and platelets, plasma and various chemical substances dissolved within the plasma, which seeps through the capillary walls and circulates around the body tissues at which point it is called tissue fluid.
2   *Tissue fluid,* is the fluid drained from the tissues and collected by the lymphatic system, becoming known as **lymph.**
3   *Lymph,* is a clear, watery fluid resembling blood plasma. It contains all the components of blood plasma in similar concentrations except for the plasma proteins which occur in lower concentrations. Lymph contains fibrogen which helps with blood clotting, and leucocytes which help to fight any infection in the body.

The body needs the lymphatic system to be in good working order to stay healthy. The functions of lymph are:

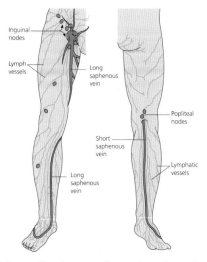

Lymphatic vessels and nodes of the leg

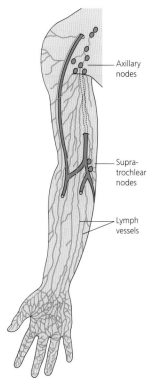

Lymphatic vessels and nodes of the arm

- to transport fat to the liver
- to prevent waterlogging of tissues
- the production of fibrogen
- the production of lymphocytes

Lymph nodes or glands

Lymph nodes occur in groups and are arranged in two sets: *deep* and *superficial*. They vary from the size of a pinhead to the size of a small fingernail. The nodes are made of tissue the function of which is to

- act as a filter to trap bacteria
- make lymphocytes
- produce antibodies and antitoxins

Lymphatic ducts

After being filtered into the nodes the lymph passes through more lymph vessels into the lymphatic ducts:

- thoracic duct
- right lymphatic duct

The *thoracic duct* is the main collecting duct of the lymphatic system. It receives lymph from the left side of the head, neck and thorax, from the left arm and the whole of the abdomen and both legs. It opens into the left subclavian vein.

The *right lymphatic duct* receives lymph from the right side of the head, neck and thorax, and the right arm. It is very short and opens into the right subclavian vein.

Circulation of lymph

Lymph is not pumped around the body in the same way as blood. The lymphatic circulation is maintained by suction and pressure. This is why massage within manicure and pedicure treatments can be so beneficial for your clients. The suction is caused by the negative pressure of the right atrium when the heart expands. Pressure is exerted by the contraction of the muscles and the action of the artery walls when the body inhales.

The skeletal system

For your own health and the welfare of your client you should have a thorough knowledge of the bones in the areas you will be working on, as you may come across conditions that contra indicate a particular treatment.

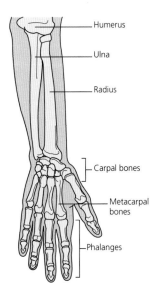

Bones of the arm

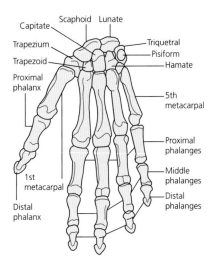

Bones of the hand

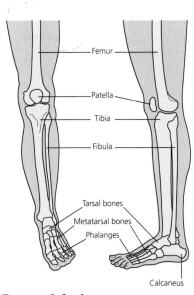

Bones of the leg

Bones of the arm and hand

The *humerus* is a long bone which extends from the shoulder joint down to the elbow. The shoulder bone is called the *scapula* and it joins the humerus at the shoulder joint. The other end of the humerus forms the hinged joint known as the elbow. The two bones in the forearm are called the *ulna* and the *radius*.

The ulna is slightly larger than the radius and runs down the arm on the side where the little finger is situated. It forms part of the elbow joint and its functions are to provide muscle attachment and also be weight bearing.

The radius runs down the arm on the side where the thumb is situated. It is a smaller bone than the ulna. The radius and ulna form a joint at the elbow that allows the lower arm to flex and extend. At the other end the radius and ulna form a series of joints that connect with the bones of the wrist, called *carpals*.

The carpals are a group of eight bones which form the wrist. The bones are arranged in two rows of four. The top row are the *scaphoid, lunate, triquetral* and *pisiform*. These four carpals all join with the ulna and radius. The lower row are the *trapezium, trapezoid, capitate* and *hamate*. These all form a joint with the bones of the palm. The bones slide or glide over each other to allow a variety of hand movements.

Metacarpals are the name given to the bones in the palm of the hand. There are five long bones in each hand, one relating to each digit. The *phalanges* are the small bones making up the fingers and thumbs. There are fourteen in each hand – three in each finger and two in the thumb.

Bones of the leg and foot

The long bone running down from the thigh is called the *femur*. It extends from the hip to the knee. Its functions are to be load bearing and provide muscle attachment. It forms a joint with the bones of the lower leg at the knee. The lower leg bones are called the *tibia* and *fibula*.

The tibia is a long strong bone situated towards the middle of the leg and its function is to support body weight, as well as being used for muscle attachments. It forms a joint with the *talus* at the *ankle*.

The fibula is a long slim bone situated towards the outer side of the leg. It is mainly used for muscle attachment. It forms a joint with the tibia near the knee and extends downwards to form joints with the ankle bones.

The *patella* is a flat bone situated at the knee joint, and is commonly known as the *knee cap*. It forms no joint with any

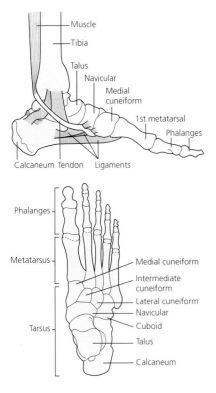

Bones of the foot

other bones because it is embedded in the strong tendon of the quadricep muscles at the front of the thigh.

The *tarsals* are seven bones that make up the ankle. They are larger than the carpals in the hand and are arranged differently to support our body weight and distribute it throughout the foot. The talus forms a joint with the tibia and fibula. The *calcaneum* performs an important function, attaching the muscles of the calf in the lower leg to the foot. This enables us to run, walk and move about effectively. Joints are formed by the *cuboid* and outer, middle and inner *cuneiforms* attaching to the bones of the foot. On the inside of the talus lies the *navicular* which is used for muscle attachment and movement.

The *metatarsals* are five long bones that make up the length of the foot. They form joints with the tarsals at one end and the bones of the foot at the other.

The *phalanges* are arranged in the same way as those in the hand and there are 14 in each foot with two in each toe. You may sometimes find that the phalanges in the little toes fuse together.

The muscular system

Movement of the body cannot happen without the contraction of muscles. Muscle tissue has four main characteristics:

1 it has the ability to shorten or contract
2 it can be stretched when it is relaxed, i.e. it is extensible
3 after contraction or extension it can return to its original shape, i.e. it has elasticity
4 muscle tissue responds to stimuli from a motor nerve provided by nerve impulses. When muscle tissue is contracted the following three things happen:
   – heat is produced
   – posture is maintained
   – movement is produced

Muscular movements aid the flow of blood and lymph through the veins and lymphatic systems

There are three types of muscle tissue:

1 skeletal – the movement of this is voluntary
2 smooth – the movement of this is involuntary
3 cardiac – the muscle that keeps the heart working

The muscles of the arms and legs with which you are concerned as a nail technician are skeletal muscles.

You will need to understand the following terminology which is used in the explanation of muscle movement before reading about the muscles and muscle groups.

Anterior – front

Posterior – back

Medial – middle or towards the mid-line

Dorsal – back

Lateral – side

Flexion – decreases the angle between two bones

Extension – increases the angle between two bones

Pronate – palm down

Supinate – palm up

Rotation – pivot about the joint

Abduction – away from the mid-line

Adduction – towards the mid-line

Dorsiflex – toes towards the knee

Plantar flex – toes pointed out

Invert – towards the mid-line

Evert – away from the mid-line

Muscles of the hand

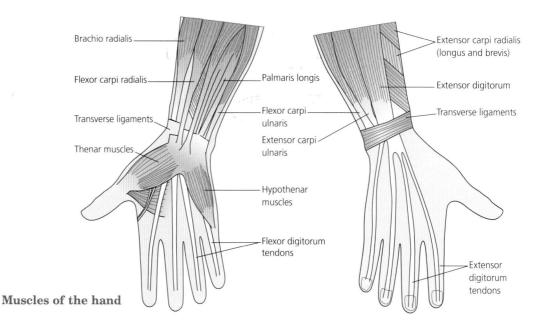

Brachio radialis

Flexor carpi radialis

Transverse ligaments

Thenar muscles

Palmaris longis

Flexor carpi ulnaris

Extensor carpi ulnaris

Hypothenar muscles

Flexor digitorum tendons

Extensor carpi radialis (longus and brevis)

Extensor digitorum

Transverse ligaments

Extensor digitorum tendons

Muscles of the hand

There are three main groups of muscles within the hand which provide the action required for gripping.

Hypothenar eminence – this muscle is positioned in the palm of the hand below the finger, and is attached to the carpals, metacarpals and the phalanges of the little finger. Its action abducts, adducts and flexes the little finger.

Thenar eminence – this muscle is also positioned in the palm of the hand, this time below the thumb. It is attached to the carpals, metacarpals and the phalanges of the thumb. Its action abducts, adducts and flexes the thumb and draws it towards the palm of the hand.

Mid-palm group – these muscles are in the centre of the palm below the middle three fingers. They are attached to the carpals, metacarpals and phalanges of the middle three fingers. Their action is to abduct, adduct and flex the middle three fingers.

Muscles of the arm

There are seven muscle groups in the arm.

Biceps – this muscle is found at the anterior aspect of the upper arm above the elbow. It is attached to the scapula at one end and the radius at the other. This muscle flexes the elbow and supinates the hand and forearm.

Brachialis – this muscle is found attached to the humerus and ulna across the elbow. Its action flexes the elbow.

Triceps – this muscle is found at the posterior aspect of the upper arm, it attaches to the scapula and humerus at one end and the ulna at the other. Its action extends the elbow.

Supinator – this muscle is found at the lateral aspect of the lower humerus and radius. Its action is to supinate the hand and forearm.

Flexors – these muscles are found at the medial aspect of the forearm, attached to the lower humerus, radius and ulna at one end and the metacarpals and phalanges of the fingers at the other. Their action flexes the wrist, fingers and thumbs.

Pronators – these muscles are found at the medial aspect of the lower humerus and radius. Their action pronates the hand and forearm.

Extensors – these muscles are found at the lateral aspect of the forearm, attached to the lower humerus, radius and ulna at one end and the metacarpals and phalanges at the other. Their action extends the wrist, fingers and thumbs.

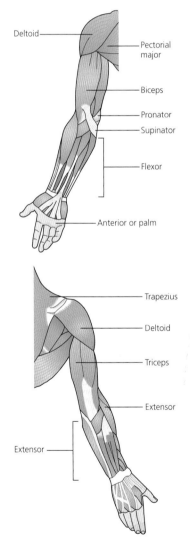

Deltoid
Pectorial major
Biceps
Pronator
Supinator
Flexor
Anterior or palm

Trapezius
Deltoid
Triceps
Extensor
Extensor

Muscles of the arm

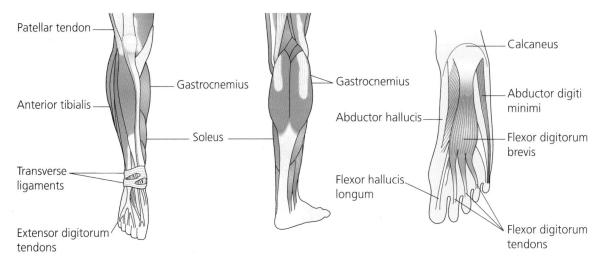

Patellar tendon

Gastrocnemius

Anterior tibialis

Soleus

Transverse ligaments

Extensor digitorum tendons

Gastrocnemius

Abductor hallucis

Flexor hallucis longum

Calcaneus

Abductor digiti minimi

Flexor digitorum brevis

Flexor digitorum tendons

Muscles of the leg and foot

Muscles of the lower leg and foot

The leg and foot also have seven muscle groups.

Gastrocnemius – this muscle is in the posterior aspect of the lower leg, and is the main muscle forming the calf. It is attached to the lower part of the femur across the back of the knee, and at the ankle to the calcaneum. Its action plantar flexes the ankle and the knee.

Soleus – this muscle is under the gastrocnemius in the calf, and is attached to the fibula and tibia at one end and across the ankle to the calcaneum at the other. The action plantar flexes the ankle.

Tibialis anterior – this muscle is situated along the skin at the anterior aspect of the lower leg, attached to the tibia at one end and the medial cuneiform and first metatarsal at the other. The action dorsiflexes the ankle and inverts the foot.

Tibialis posterior – this muscle is found at the posterior aspect, deep in the calf. It is attached to the tibia and fibula at one end and the navicular bone at the other. Its action inverts the foot.

Peroneus – this group of three muscles is found in the lateral and posterior aspect of the lower leg. They attach to the fibula and across the ankle to the underneath of the first and fifth metatarsals. Their action everts the foot.

Flexors of the toes – these muscles are deep in the posterior aspect of the lower leg and are attached to the tibia and fibula at one end and the phalanges of the toes at the other. Their action flexes toes and helps to plantar flex ankle.

Extensors of the toes – these muscles are found in the anterior and lateral aspects of the lower leg attached to the tibia and fibula and the phalanges of the toes. Their action extends the toes and dorsiflexes the ankle.

Anatomy of the natural nail

Anatomy of the natural nail

Learning objectives

In this section you will learn about:

- **the structure of the natural nail**

- **the growth pattern of the natural nail**

- **factors that can affect the growth and health of the natural nail**

Even in the early stages of a foetus growing in the womb, human nails begin to form. At fourteen weeks the foetus has developed the area where the nail plate will grow and the nail plate can be seen growing out from the proximal nail fold. The speed at which the nail will grow will depend on many factors, for example nutritional levels. Around the twenty-first week the nail plate will be completely formed and tiny fragile free edges can be seen. As always, throughout our lives, our toenails grow much slower than our fingernails.

Histology of the nail

The cells of the nail are flattened and filled with **keratin**. They have no nuclei and are thought to be similar to the cornified or uppermost layer found in the epidermis. They begin their life in the germinal **matrix** which extends to include the deep layers of the underside of the **proximal** nail fold. This area is where the cells divide and produce *keratinocytes*, capable of rapid terminal keratinisation. Keratin is a protein made in the body. It is a tough fibrous protein polymer made from amino acids. On average it is believed that the fingernail plate is approximately one hundred cells thick. As the cells leave the matrix most are already bonded. Inside the cells are long fibrous keratin tissues that bond into the next cell. Most cells have between three and six sides which interconnect and bond as the cells leave the matrix.

Unlike the cell structure of the skin there is very little lipid or fat between the keratinised cells of the nail plate. This may account for the fact that nails are ten times more permeable to water than skin. Usually the nail plate will have a low water content but under certain physical or medical conditions this can change. The base of the nail is developed from the germinal matrix and these cells have the furthest to travel, whilst at the same time the thin surface layer is formed by the deeper layers of the proximal nail fold

Interesting Facts

- Since nail extensions cannot affect the length of the matrix, clearly it is a myth that wearing nail extensions can make the nail plate grow thinner.

- Nail cells that have travelled the farthest are the oldest.

- The older we get the slower our nails will grow.

- Nails become more porous with age due to dehydration and are more susceptible to staining, chipping and peeling of nail plate layers.

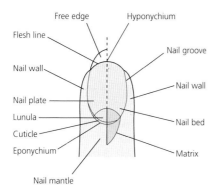

Cross section of the nail (front view)

Free edge · Hyponychium
Flesh line
Nail wall
Nail plate
Lunula
Cuticle
Eponychium
Nail mantle
Nail groove
Nail wall
Nail bed
Matrix

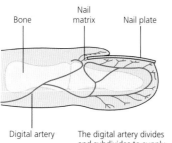

Blood supply to the nail and the nail bed

Bone · Nail matrix · Nail plate
Digital artery
The digital artery divides and subdivides to supply blood to the skin and nail bed

Technical Tip

The bed epithelium attaches firmly to the base of the nail plate and begins to pull away from the dermis. It forms tiny rails that fit into tiny grooves found at the base layer of the dermis. The rail and groove system allows the nail plate to slide across the nail bed as each nail cell grows towards the free edge.

and the proximal portion of the germinal matrix. If the matrix is short, the nail plate will be thinner, whereas a long matrix will produce a thicker nail plate. It is also a fact that the wider the matrix the wider the natural nail plate.

As nail technicians our work is mainly on the natural nail itself, but we do need to be aware of all the other structures that support the nail unit to be able to perform our job effectively. In this chapter we have looked briefly at the major systems of the body and in this section we will concentrate on the nail unit. This unit consists of:

- the nail bed
- the hyponychium
- the eponychium
- the perionychium
- the nail grooves
- the mantle or proximal nail fold
- the matrix
- the lunula
- the cuticle
- the nail plate
- the free edge

The nail bed

The **nail bed** is positioned directly under the **nail plate**. It starts at the front edge of the **matrix** (near the **lunula**) and continues through to the **hyponychium** just before the **free edge**. It is made up of two types of tissue:

1 dermis
2 epidermis

The epidermis is the upper layer of skin and is attached to the underside of the nail plate. Although it has the same name as that of the upper layers of skin on the fingers and hands its structure is slightly different and more closely resembles the skin on the inside of the mouth. This is more commonly referred to as the *bed epithelium*.

The dermis is the lower part of the skin and is attached to the bone underneath. It contains many thousands of tiny blood vessels that carry food, oxygen and nutrients to the nail unit whilst also taking away any waste and toxins.

The following elements are all seals that totally encompass the nail plate and the health of these structures is important to the health of the natural nail.

The hyponychium

The **hyponychium** is at the distal edge of the nail unit and is found directly under the free edge. It is composed of epidermal tissue and forms a watertight seal that prevents bacteria and viruses from attacking the nail bed. It is a thin strip of skin tissue that attaches the two lateral nail folds. If this seal is broken or damaged it could possibly lead to an infection.

The eponychium

The **eponychium** is the visible part of the skin fold that appears to end at the base of the nail plate. Sometimes this tissue is incorrectly referred to as cuticle. It has the same function as the hyponychium but is at the opposite end of the nail. When performing treatments on the nail the cuticle should never be pushed back further than the eponychium. This area should be treated with care and not pushed aggressively. If the matrix seal is broken infections can occur.

The perionychium

The sides of the body of the nail are bordered by a curved fold of skin known as the lateral nail folds or walls. The cornified layer of the lateral nail folds extends fractionally onto the nail plate, forming a seal against the environment. This seal is similar to the hyponychium and eponychium and is sometimes known as the **perionychium**. The grooves at the sides of the nail move along next to the lateral nail folds, and are known as the lateral nail grooves.

The nail grooves

The grooves at the lateral sidewall guide the nail plate down the finger.

The mantle or proximal nail fold

The **mantle** or **proximal** nail fold is a deep fold of skin at the base of the nail where the root is embedded. This area is usually worked on when performing a manicure treatment to keep the skin soft, supple and in good condition. If it is neglected and becomes dehydrated the skin may split or be torn and infection can occur.

The matrix

The **matrix** is a small area of living tissue directly under the proximal nail fold. All the nail cells grow in the matrix and if this is damaged in any way, the effects of the damage can be seen on the nail plate. In severe cases damage to the matrix can cause permanent deformities in nail growth. The developing nail within the matrix is very soft and care should always be taken when working on this area. As mentioned earlier, the length and width of the matrix determines the shape and thickness of the nail plate and this can only be changed by external factors such as physical or chemical damage. The matrix itself is white and it ends where the nail bed begins.

Natural nail and cuticle shapes

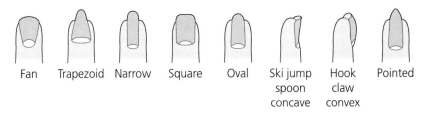

Fan   Trapezoid   Narrow   Square   Oval   Ski jump spoon concave   Hook claw convex   Pointed

The lunula

The **lunula** is the visible part of the matrix, often referred to as the 'half moon', and is white in colour and opaque. The cells in this area become transparent and are not yet fully keratinised. The lunula lies directly under the thinnest part of the nail plate and is not fully compressed, so it is much softer. This part of the matrix can be destroyed if damage occurs, for example from heavy filing or accidentally by shutting a finger in a door.

The cuticle

The **cuticle** lies just above the eponychium and acts as a watertight seal that prevents bacteria and other harmful pathogens from invading the soft tissue. The cuticle is the primary matrix seal and serves the same purpose as the hyponychium. It is essential to keep cuticles healthy to support the other structures of the nail such as the eponychium and if this seal is broken then infection can occur. The true cuticle on the underside of the proximal nail fold constantly sheds a layer of colourless skin. This shed skin attaches to the topside of the emerging nail plate and rides on the nail plate, seeming to grow from under the nail fold. It is one of the main areas of the nail unit where we perform treatments and on which we give our clients home care advice.

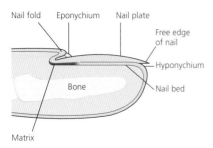

Nail fold   Eponychium   Nail plate

Free edge of nail

Hyponychium

Bone

Nail bed

Matrix

Cross section of the nail (side view)

The growth pattern of the natural nail

Keratin cells are born in the matrix and are initially white and round. As they are pushed forward on their path from the matrix they remain soft and translucent. They harden and become more compact as they move along the germinal matrix and onto the nail bed. They grow in a horizontal, lengthways direction. The dermis and the epidermis of the nail bed lock into channels, like train tracks, under the nail plate. As new cells are pushed from the proximal nail fold the nail plate is guided along these tracks. The plate is attached to the nail bed until it grows past the fingertip. The **distal** edge of the nail is the hyponychium found under the free edge. The nail plate becomes the free edge and old dead cells are pushed beyond this point and grow forward past the end of the finger.

Factors that can affect the growth and health of the natural nail

There are many factors that can affect the growth pattern and health of the natural nail. Some cannot be avoided and are due to *internal factors*, whilst others are caused by ourselves and our environment and are known as *external factors*.

Aspects of internal factors

- A doctor can sometimes tell from a patient's natural nails whether they are unwell and suffering from certain illnesses.

- Diet and nutrition play an important part in the health of nail growth. Malnutrition or poor diet can affect nail growth through lack of vitamins and nutrients. There are no foods that can make nails stronger than they already naturally are, this is a hereditary factor.

- Medication can affect nails by making them grow more quickly or by slowing down growth and affecting the health of the nail plate.

- Pregnancy can cause an increase in the growth rate of the natural nail between the fourth and eighth months and there can be up to 20 per cent increase during the months either side of the birth.

- Heat and climate can affect growth, as nails tend to grow more quickly in summer than in winter.

- Bad or poor circulation can affect the blood supply to the matrix and the nail bed and therefore affect nail growth. Disorders such as Raynaud's or diabetes will sometimes induce fingernail and toenail problems.

Aspects of external factors

- Trauma or impact can be either deliberate or accidental and, depending on its severity, can affect the nail in many ways. If the matrix of the nail is damaged it could cause permanent deformity or affect the growth pattern of the nail. Injury to the nail seals, eponychium, hyponychium and perionychium, can result in an infection around the soft tissue and can also affect nail growth.

- Chemical damage ranges from not protecting the nails when using hazardous chemicals to the overuse of substances such as nail hardeners with **formaldehyde** which can cause brittleness and, in the worst case, allergies. Water is also a chemical which can damage the natural nail if hands are constantly exposed to it without protection. There are some professionals who need to take care when working to use protective measures at all times from overexposure to water or chemicals.

- Good grooming is essential to keep the hands and feet in good health and working order. We use our hands and feet more than any other part of our body and they are subjected to quite a lot of wear and tear. There are straightforward ways to care for both:
  - keep hands clean and moisturised
  - keep fingernails and toenails at a sensible length
  - use gloves for housework and gardening
  - have regular manicures and pedicures
  - change shoes often, do not wear the same pair all day, every day
  - do not use nails as tools

The natural nail needs a constant balance of oil and moisture to protect its health and it is a daily battle for most people to maintain this balance. The nail plate will absorb water easily and can lose it quite rapidly, so care must be taken to avoid these extremes. Always ensure, as a professional, that you give your clientele good advice on home care and the retail items they will need to maintain the health of their hands, feet and nails. You should be a good example of your profession with beautiful, healthy, groomed hands and feet at all times!

Diseases of the skin and nails

Learning objectives

In this section you will learn about:

- **diseases and disorders of the nails**

- **diseases and disorders of the skin**

Checklist of nail diseases and disorders

A comprehensive list of nail diseases and disorders is given in the following table.

Checklist of nail diseases and disorders

ACAULOSIS UNGUIS	Infection of the nail with scopulariopsis brevicaulis
ANONYCHIA	Absence of the nail
BEAU'S LINES	Ridged nails, due to illness
DEFLUVIUM UNGUINUM	Brittle nails
DERMATITIS AND ECZEMA	Inflamed, irritated skin
EGG SHELL NAILS	Thin, white nails
HAPALONYCHIA	Soft nails
KOILONYCHIA	Spoon-shaped nails
LEUKONYCHIA	White, colourless nails or white spots
MACRONYCHIA	Large, but otherwise normal nails
MICRONYCHIA	Small, but otherwise normal nails
ONYCHALGIA NERVOSA	Intensely sensitive nails
ONYCHAUXIS	Thickened nails (old age, psoriasis, trauma, etc.)
ONYCHIA	Inflammation of the nail either post-traumatic or with paronychia
ONYCHODYSPLASIA	Abormal development of nail growth
ONYCHOGRYPHOSIS	Long, thick and curved nails
ONYCHOHETEROTROPHIA	Misplaced nails
ONYCHOLYSIS	Lifting away or separation of nail from bed
ONYCHOMADESIS	Splitting of nails into layers
ONYCHOMYCOSIS	Fungal infection, commonly known as ringworm
ONYCHOPHAGY	Nail biting
ONYCHORRHEXIS	Dry, brittle nails
ONYCHOTILLOMANIA	Picking at a nail from habit

PANARITIUM	Abscess at side of nail (whitlow)
PARONYCHIA	Inflammation of soft tissue
PLATONYCHIA	Increased curvature in long axis
POLYONYCHIA	Two or more separated nails on one digit
PSORIASIS	Abnormal thickening of the skin
PTERYGIUM	Excessive forward growth of the cuticle
TRACHYONYCHIA	Rough nails
USURE DES ONGLES	Wearing away of nails due to scratching
VERRUCA VULGARIS	Warts caused by viral infections

Bacterial infection

Bacterial infections usually take the form of **paronychias**. However there is another type of non-invasive bacterial infection which can be encountered in the nail services we provide. This can occur as a green to black discoloration on the surface of the natural nail plate, but underneath a lifted section of the product overlay. There is a general misconception that this discoloration is either a 'mould' or 'fungal' infection. The correct term is *pseudomonas bacteria* and, in fact, most dark discolorations are formed by bacteria and not fungi.

A bacterial infection can occur between the natural nail plate and the overlay. This can occur no matter what system is used, and for many reasons. The bacterial infection can be yellow or green in colour, the longer before it is detected the darker green the colour becomes. The green discoloration is a by-product of the bacteria and not the bacteria themselves. Therefore, the green discoloration is where the bacteria have already been. A point to remember is that bacteria will only thrive in a warm, moist environment with a good source of food.

Bacterial infection

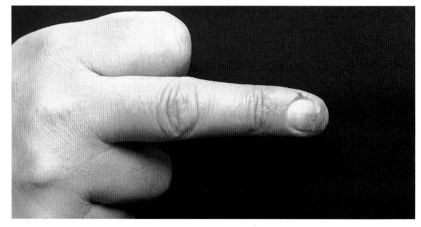

Technical Tip

If any product is touching the cuticle or side walls it will allow natural oils from the skin to find a route underneath the overlay. This provides a good source of food for the bacteria.

The *warmth* is supplied by heat from the rich blood supply to the nail bed directly under the natural nail plate, and the overlay will help to increase the temperature slightly. The *food source* can be moisture or non-living tissue that has not been correctly removed during preparation of the natural nail or application of the overlay.

Brittle nails

Brittle nails may be divided into four groups:

1 isolated splits at the free edge which can sometimes extend proximally
2 multiple splitting which resembles the battlements of a castle
3 lamellar splitting of the free edge of the nail into fine layers
4 transverse splitting and breaking of the lateral edge close to the distal margin

Bruised nails

Bruised nail

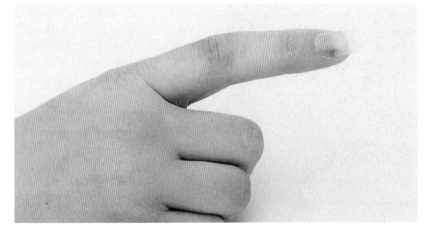

Bruised nails are due to a clot of blood which forms under the nail plate after impact or trauma. They vary in colour from red through to maroon and sometimes black. The client may lose the nail but a new nail will usually grow underneath. Sometimes the nail plate may need to be pierced to release the pressure, but this should be done by a qualified medical practitioner.

Beau's lines

Beau's lines are horizontal, traversing ridges which can be shallow or deep and often slightly elevated. This condition may affect the surface of all ten nails or just the thumbs –

and sometimes even just the big toes. Often the grooves are superficial or more marked in the middle of the nail. Grooves are often the result of an illness, appearing a few weeks after the onset of the illness.

Fragile or egg shell nails

Nails affected by this condition are normally thin and very curved on the free edge. They almost dip in the centre and have a white free edge. A client with this condition is not a good candidate for nail extensions, but will benefit from regular manicures.

Wet manicures should be avoided, as the nail plate will absorb the water and change shape by straightening when the fingers are soaked. After the polish is applied and the nail has dried, the shape will return to normal and the new polish will flake off. This is obviously disappointing for the client.

Furrows, ridges or corrugations

Furrows can run either horizontally, lengthways or vertically across the nail plate. Ridges that run lengthways are normal and can increase with age. Ridges that run across the nail plate could be caused by illness, trauma or poor circulation.

Courtesy of Blackwell Science Ltd

Furrows – ridges or corrugations

Hang nail or agnails

Hang nail is a very common problem caused by dry cuticles or resulting from the cuticles being cut. This procedure is not advised, as clipping excess cuticle on a regular basis just serves to perpetuate the condition. A client with this problem would benefit from the use of oils and regular manicures would also improve the condition.

Leukonychia or white spots

Leukonychia is simply bruising or trauma to the nail plate. This condition can be the result of the cuticles being pushed back too harshly. Remember that the newest cells are the softest, that is those at the cuticle, and they harden as they are pushed up towards the free edge. Sometimes the cause is accidental or can be the result of various types of manual work.

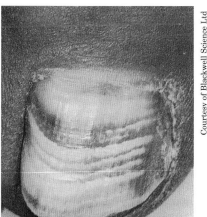

Courtesy of Blackwell Science Ltd

Trauma/eukonychia

Courtesy of Blackwell Science Ltd

True/eukonychia

Courtesy of Blackwell Science Ltd

Spotting by trauma

Courtesy of Blackwell Science Ltd

Habit tic

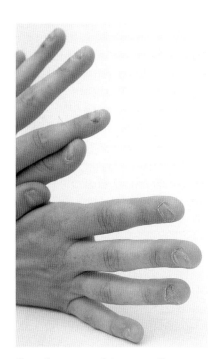

Onychopagy – bitten nails

Habit tic

A **habit tic** is caused by the client constantly picking or rubbing at the surface of the nail plate, usually at the proximal nail fold where the nail plate is softest. This is most often seen on the thumb. The condition is sometimes the result of a nervous habit – some clients are not even aware that they are doing the damage. After years of abuse, the damage can be permanent.

Onychophagy or bitten nails

Onychophagy or bitten nails is a condition that can sometimes be severe. Some nail biters just bite the free edge whilst others tear the nail below the hyponychium. Another sign of nail biting is broken and bitten skin around the cuticle or sidewalls. If the skin is broken or infected nail extensions should not be performed. Nail extensions can sometimes be the only form of help for a nail biter as they give instant beauty and length. It is very difficult for nail biters to grow their nails and most do not even realise they are doing it. Any little glitch or catch will send their nails straight back into their mouths. Nail extensions create instant order if they are maintained properly by the nail technician and cared for between appointments by the client. Sufferers should be able to grow their natural nails to a sensible length if they wear nail extensions for a few months.

Onychoclasis

Onychoclasis refers to a broken nail, normally occurring at the free edge. If the nail is broken below the free edge and has become infected do not treat the client. The cause is almost always due to mechanical trauma.

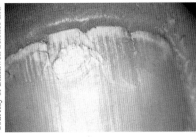

Onychorrhexis (longitudinal splitting/brittle nails)

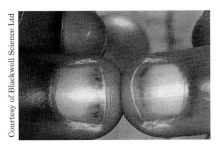

Splinter haemorrhage

Onychorrhexis

Onychorrhexis refers to split or brittle nails. A split can be lengthways and is normally caused by mechanical trauma, excessive filing or the overuse of cuticle solvents. All nail services can be performed, providing the split is not below the free edge.

Splinter haemorrhage

A **splinter haemorrhage** is the name given to a nail showing tiny streaks of blood that run lengthways up the nail plate and are sometimes mistaken for tiny hairs. They are caused by minor trauma.

Onychia

Onychia is an infection in or on the nail plate. This can be manifested as swollen tissue at the base. Redness, soreness or pus may also be present. Sometimes caused by insanitary tools or implements. Should be referred to a GP.

Onycholysis

Nail separation from the nail bed, or **onycholysis**, is seen as an increased white area from the free edge. Common causes are trauma to the free edge, sometimes due to length, **psoriasis** or an allergic reaction to nail products or drugs. Nail extensions should not be applied to client who has any separation, as extra length will only increase the problem. Nails should be kept short to avoid repeatedly catching them and to aid recovery. Onycholysis creates a subungual space that gathers dirt and keratin debris. The greyish-white colour is due to the presence of air under the nail, with the colour varying from yellow to brown.

Onycholysis

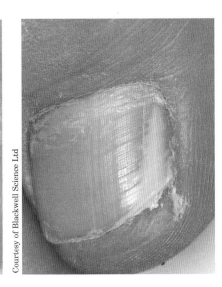

Technical Tip

If a nail technician is
applying nail extensions to
a client with severely
bitten nails he or she will
need to use some advanced
techniques for the client to
be able to keep the nails
on for the amount of time
needed to regrow the
natural nail. These
techniques are covered
fully in Chapter 6.

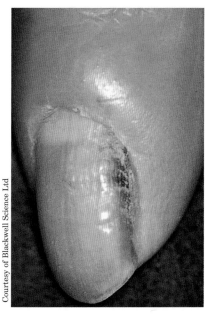

Paronychia

Onychomycosis or tinea unguium

Onychomycosis is an extremely contagious fungal
infection. The client should be referred to his or her GP and
not treated under any circumstances. The problem could be
the result of infection setting in after onycholysis or a break
in the tissue at the side or under the free edge. The
condition can be manifested as yellow or white patches or
even large areas of white that start at the free edge and
invade and grow towards the root. There can sometimes be
an unpleasant smell and the white areas look as if they could
be scraped off. In advanced stages, the disease could
penetrate the nail plate and cause superficial thinning,
sometimes peeling off and exposing a diseased nail bed.
Some occupations are more prone to this type of condition
such as those where the hands are constantly wet or are
exposed to detergents and cleaning chemicals.

Paronychia

Paronychia is an infectious inflammatory condition of the
tissue surrounding the nails. It is a common condition that
appears as a red and swollen area around the cuticle and
sidewall area of the nail. Pus formation may also be present
and the condition is usually quite painful. The cause could
be a cut or a break in the skin that has subsequently become
infected. Nail biters and pickers are prone to hang nails
which could lead to paronychia when the skin is bitten or
torn off. You may find that some older clients cut their
cuticles away which could be another route for infection.
Try and educate them into stopping this bad habit. The
condition is contagious and in some cases may need
treatment by a doctor. It is not wise to carry out any
treatments until the condition has cleared.

Psoriasis

Psoriasis is an inherited skin disorder characterised by
excessive cell proliferation. Histological changes in the nails
are similar to those seen in the skin. It can manifest itself in
several ways:

- discoloration of the nail
- pitting of the nail
- splinter haemorrhage
- extreme pitting of the nail plate

Discoloration of the natural nail can also involve onycholysis
and it is not advisable to work on a client with this condition.
You must always seek the client's doctor's approval before

attempting any treatment on a client with severe psoriasis, as there may be other conditions involved which you do not know of and cannot see. Psoriasis is not contagious and in around 36 per cent of cases is purely hereditary, although the condition can be brought on by stress. People who suffer from psoriasis of the nails should keep the length short and neat to prevent further damage. The nails will grow much more quickly on a person with this condition.

Psoriasis

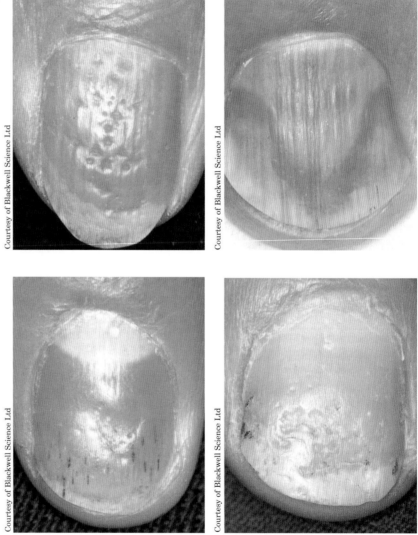

Courtesy of Blackwell Science Ltd

Pterygium

Forward growth of the cuticle is known as **pterygium**. This condition can and should be treated by the nail technician. If ignored, the skin can move up the nail plate towards the free edge.

Onychomadesis or nail shedding

Onychomadesis occurs most often after mechanical

trauma to the natural nail. The nail may loosen at the base and subsequently the new nail may push the old nail off.

Koilonychia or spoon-nails

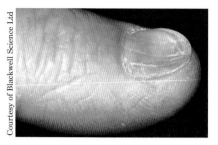

Koilonychia – spoon nails

A client with **koilonychia** has a nail plate which is flat or concave, giving the appearance of spoon-shaped nails. This nail shape can be hereditary and, if so, will never change. Other customers may develop koilonychia due to anaemia, which is more commonly known as iron deficiency. In such cases, the shape will return to normal after the condition has been treated. Koilonychia may also develop due to working conditions where the hands are constantly in oils or soaps. These soften the nail plate and cause it to turn upwards. The only way to cure the condition is to stop using the chemicals or detergents and allow the nail plate to return to normal. A new-born baby's nails are often spoon-shaped, but this will correct itself during the first year.

Hapalonychia or soft nails

A soft nail condition, known as **hapalonychia**, is usually due to the client's nails naturally retaining a lot of water, or it could just be the way their nails naturally grow. However, it could also be linked with conditions such as dermatitis or eczema due to an inflammation of the skin caused by an allergy or chronic irritation. It usually starts at the base of the nail next to the cuticle and works its way up the nail.

Onychogryphosis or claw nails

In clients with **onychogryphosis** the nail plate usually has a lot of grainy fibrous tissue coming from the hyponychium, which make the nail plate very thick and curved. If the nail is not kept short the curvature can make the nail look like a rams horn. Care must be taken when cutting the nail as it could cause bleeding. This condition is more common in toe nails than finger nails and can be caused by wearing bad fitting shoes. In the finger nails it could be caused by an injury. If the curvature is extreme or very thick then the client should be sent to his or her doctor or a chiropodist to be treated. This condition can be hereditary, or the result of psoriasis or trauma.

Onychocryptosis or ingrown nails

Also known as *unguis incarnatus*, **onychocryptosis** can be found on fingernails and toenails. It is more commonly found in toenails as people tend to cut them incorrectly. This condition can become infected and quite painful and should not be worked on if that stage has been reached.

Onychocryptosis – ingrowing nail

Onychocryptosis can be due to clients wearing socks or footwear is too tight or may be the result of a congenital defect from birth. An ingrown toenail occurs when the edges of the nails grow forward and are pushed into the lateral sidewalls causing inflammation, pain and in some cases a bacterial infection. In severe cases this condition may need surgery but, if caught early enough, can be treated by a chiropodist. When performing nail treatments on clients it is imperative that the nail technician takes care to remove any sharp edges on the natural nail and uses proper cutting and filing techniques.

Diseases of the skin

Contact dermatitis (eczema)

The skin is capable of withstanding a significant degree of chemical insult but if this is prolonged the body will react, particularly if the chemicals are harsh, and irritant **dermatitis** may develop. This condition appears as an inflamed or broken rash. Often the irritant will cause the initial rash and broken skin, and water will then deteriorate the skin further.

Impetigo

Impetigo is extremely contagious. The organism remains within the outer layers of the epidermis. It is found most often on the face and manifests itself as inflammation, blisters, pustules and yellow crusts. The client must be referred to a GP for antibiotic treatment, which is normally in the form of creams applied daily. This condition is contra indicated to all treatments.

Impetigo is more common in children and can be caused by a cut or wound becoming infected by scratching or the knocking off of scabs. Staphylococci bacteria can then invade the skin and cause infection.

Important Note

It is very important for nail technicians to understand how an allergy can take place and the safety measures they need to take to prevent this. This is covered in more depth in Chapters 2 and 5.

Allergic reaction

A swelling, rash, soreness or open sores may indicate an allergy to a particular product or chemical. The nail may also be white in colour or have white patches. The majority of products on the market today have a 48 hour cure time. After this time period it is considered by experts within the Nail Industry that more damage will be done to the skin and surrounding tissue by attempting to remove the product by soaking in Remover or Acetone. Medical advice should be sought by the client before any attempt at removal is made.

Herpes simplex

This is more commonly known as a cold sore. It is a skin infection caused by the Herpes virus and usually occurs periodically in sufferers. It is normally seen around the mouth area and, if you suffer with this condition, care must be taken when dealing with clients to avoid cross infection. Herpes simplex is a contagious viral infection.

Psoriasis

Psoriasis manifests itself as raised patches of red skin covered with very dry scales. This condition is not contagious, but the client should not be treated if the skin is broken in the treatment area. Stress, nerves, poor diet and also a genetic link can aggravate this condition. Psoriasis responds to sun beds, sunlight, steroids and sometimes coal tar treatments. Its implications for the nails in particular are discussed in the section on nail disorders above.

Scabies

Scabies appears as a raised itchy rash. It is caused by a mite and is highly contagious. It contra indicates all treatments. It is almost exclusively passed by direct contact, so care must be taken if you see any unusual marks on your client's skin. Always refer a client to a doctor if you are in any doubt.

Tinea pedis (ringworm on the feet)

Also known as athlete's foot, tinea pedis is usually found between the toes but can spread all over the foot. It can dry up and reappear later. This condition is caused by a fungal infection (mycelium). Ringworm is contra indicated to all treatments.

Tinea unguium (ringworm of the nails)

This condition is rare, but when it does occur it usually affects more than one nail. The infected area will turn a yellow or grey colour and the nails will become very brittle. In severe cases the nail plate may separate from the nail bed. If the ringworm has infected the hands the main symptoms can be recognised as red lesions occurring in patches or rings; itching can be slight or severe. Treatment is the same for both the hands and the feet and a doctor's help should always be sought. This condition is a highly contagious and contra indicates all treatments.

As a nail technician it is important to learn about and have a good understanding of the skin in order to be able to recognise when something is wrong – however do not ever attempt to diagnose. If we have a sound knowledge it will enable us to make informed judgements on when to treat clients and when they need medical attention. The *golden rule* is that if skin is inflamed, infected, sore or swollen *do not perform* the treatment but *refer the client* to a doctor for diagnosis and treatment. A letter giving permission for treatment to commence should be obtained and filed with the client's consultation card and a note made on the record card for insurance purposes.

Contra actions to nail treatments

Learning objectives

In this section you will learn about:

- **the recognition of contra actions caused by**
  - **manicure treatments**
  - **pedicure treatments**
  - **nail extension treatments**
  - **nail art treatments**

Every nail technician should be aware of all **contra actions** that could possibly occur during a treatment, or as a result of a treatment, and how to deal effectively with the condition. Some contra actions can occur with any treatments, for example an allergy to a product, whilst others occur as a result of a specific treatment being performed. The same contra action may have different causes in different treatments. In this section we cover all the main contra actions. Should you ever come across a condition you do not recognise or know about then refer your client to his or her doctor.

It is our duty as professionals to make our clients aware of any possible contra actions that could occur as a result of a treatment at the time of the consultation. If they have knowledge of these possibilities then they can contact you if something happens. Clients will respect your honesty when informing them of potential problems, such as lifting or premature loss, and will feel that they can talk to you. Further problems may result if they feel they cannot return to the salon for maintenance or correction.

Contra actions specific to manicure and pedicure

The following tables list the causes and solutions of the main contra actions you will come across in your work as a nail technician carrying out manicures and pedicures.

Discolouration of the nail plate

Cause	Solution
Not using a base coat under polish	Always use a good base coat even under clear polish.
Using products with formaldehyde	Always check with manufacturer or supplier for product ingredients.

Thinning of natural nail plate

Cause	Solution
Over-buffing of nail plate by technician or client	*Technician* – Use correct amount of strokes with natural nail buffer. *Client* – Should be educated on buffing techniques and how often this should be done. Buffing paste should be used in moderation.

Cutting of skin around cuticles

Cause	Solution
Improper use of cuticle knife	Follow correct procedure – Use cuticle knife with water or oil, at correct angle and from side to middle, turn over and side to middle again.
Pushing cuticles back too harshly	Use oil or cream to soften skin before pushing back.
Pulling at hang nails rather than cutting	Use nippers correctly. Place under hang nail and then cut and release, do not tear.
Using nippers to cut cuticle away rather than just nip excess	Never cut away excessive cuticle as this will cause scar tissue and the skin to thicken. Use creams or oils daily to remove excess.
Using new sharp abrasives near sidewalls or cuticle	Use the correct grit file for a natural nail – 240 or higher. Always use the file at a 45° angle and pull the skin at the sidewall away with your thumb and forefinger when filing. File from side to middle and then repeat on the other side to stop splitting or flaking of the free edge of the natural nail.

Excessive erythema of the skin

Cause	Solution
Too heavy pressure when performing massage	Be aware of different massage movements and where in the massage routine they should be performed.
Massaging on sensitive areas of the skin and body	Look at the areas to be massaged and determine movements and depth of routine for each area.
Skin reaction to the massage medium	Always carry out client consultation and find out if the client is allergic or sensitive to the ingredients of the products you are using. Always check that client has not had a sunbed or waxing treatment before a manicure or pedicure as this could over-stimulate the skin.

Ingrown toenails

Cause	Solution
Incorrect cutting of toenails	Toenails must be cut straight across and not too short and the corners must be rounded to prevent the sharp edge from growing into the skin.
Incorrect filing of toenails	Toenails should be filed across and edges filed smooth and rounded off.
Wearing of improper footwear	Advise clients to change shoes often, to not wear the same pair every day and to make sure they know their correct shoe size and width fitting.
Genetic deformity	Only surgery will correct any genetic deformities.

Contra actions specific to nail extensions

The following tables list the causes and solutions of the main contra actions associated with nail extensions.

Softening of the natural nail

Cause	Solution
Natural nail has been thinned by constant filing	Ensure you use correct grit files when prepping and use in direction of nail growth only. Use a light touch when blending in tips. Do not use a heavy hand when filing nails in the cuticle area during a maintenance.
Natural nail has been thinned by over-priming	Follow manufacturers' instructions for application of primer and always ensure nail plate is dry before applying product.
Natural nail not dehydrated before product application	Always carry out your prep steps before tip application and again before application of product to ensure all oil and moisture is removed.
Product has lifted and moisture is trapped between layers	Ensure product application has been carried out properly including proper preparation and tip application. Do not carry out a maintenance if there is any lifted area of product showing. If lifting is too severe then remove nail extension, cleanse and reapply.
Nail plate is wet before product applied	Do not carry out a water manicure just before applying nail extensions. Make sure that all preparation has left the nails totally dehydrated.

Over-blending of tips

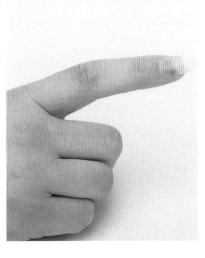

Splitting, thinning and flaking of the natural nail

Cause	Solution
Over-blending of tips	Light touch with correct abrasive.
Over-buffing of natural nail	Use pre-tailoring and pre-blending techniques for tip application (see Chapter 6).
Nail extensions too long, too thin or too thick	The length rules applies – the free edge should never be longer than the length of the natural nail bed. When applying product ensure that the stress area or apex is the thickest part of the nail and all other areas are thin and natural looking.
Client picking or biting extensions off	Educate your clients about correct removal techniques and timings of maintenance and the importance of keeping them. If you have a client who will not stop biting his or her nails off or who has them repeatedly too long, then refuse to do nails for this client.
Maintenance overdue and extensions unbalanced	A client needs to be educated on when to come back for maintenance and the consequences of not returning for appointments.

Thinning and splitting of the
natural nail

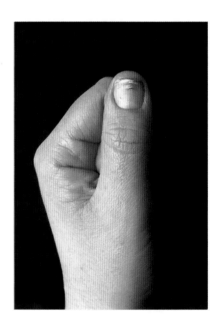

Premature loss of nail extensions

Cause	Solution
Improper preparation of natural nail	Ensure the correct preparation techniques have been carried out.
Nail extensions too long	Carry out an in-depth consultation into client's lifestyle and hobbies, looking at areas such as whether they have children, are they sporty, what type of career they have. Look at their natural nail shape and condition to evaluate what system, products and length they can take.
Changes in client's lifestyle	Look at a client's stress levels, diet and any medication that they are currently taking. Adjust treatments, products and length of nails to suit individual requirements.
Improper use of or inappropriate products	Always follow specific manufacturers' instructions for product use, as these may vary greatly. Never mix products from one company with those of another.

Lifting of product

Cause	Solution
Improper prep of the natural nail	Ensure correct preparation to remove all oil and moisture from the natural nail plate before application of products. This will ensure proper bonding and adhesion.
Medication and stress levels of clients	Carry out an in-depth client consultation.
Nail extensions too long	Carry out an in-depth client consultation.
Contamination of products, tools and equipment	Use your housekeeping rules and always work in a clean, safe environment.
Incorrect mix ratio	Make sure you have had good training in the application of your chosen system and follow your manufacturer's instructions for application of products.
Improper application of products	If products are not applied to manufacturers' instructions there could be adverse chemical reactions that will occur on your clients' nails, causing many problems. Never mix chemicals that are not compatible.
Clients not returning for maintenance on time	If clients are not informed of the importance of returning on a regular basis for maintenance treatments it will cause problems for you and take extra time you may not have allowed for. If the client does not return for maintenance they are putting the integrity of their natural nails at risk and they should be made aware of this, otherwise they will blame you.

Discolouration of the natural nail plate

Cause	*Solution*
Improper prep of the natural nail	Make sure thorough preparation is carried out on the natural nail ensuring nail is completely dry and dehydrated.
Lifting or cracks in the nail extension	Cracks or lifting will allow contamination to enter. Diagnose why nails have problems, for example: ● nails too long ● improper prep ● maintenance appointments not kept ● nail extension out of balance ● no homecare carried out
Overuse of primer	Ensure nails are clean and dry after application of primer and that manufacturer's instructions are followed.
Bacterial infection which may occur for any of the following reasons: ● improper prep ● maintenance appointment is not kept ● cracking of natural nail or nail extension ● client picking, biting, tearing or ripping off ● nail technician nipping off lifted product ● lifting of product at free edge, sidewall or cuticle allowing moisture to be trapped between layers	Remove nail and do not buff or reapply until condition has cleared.

Bacterial infection under nail extension

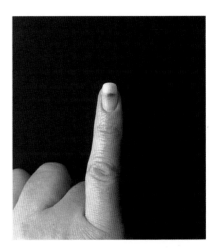

Technical Tip

Oxygen and UV light will help to inhibit the growth of bacteria. It is important to ensure that a nail extension is removed to allow the air to get to the natural nail plate. Do not apply a dark polish to cover the stain as this will block out the healing rays of natural UV light. Once the infection has started to clear, extensions can be reapplied but using cautionary measures such as proper prep. The stain will not disappear but will grow out with the natural nail. If the condition is severe and has turned black, the client should be sent to a doctor.

As the saying goes, prevention is better than cure. A nail technician cannot treat any nail infection and must never attempt to diagnose a condition. To do this could lay you open to a whole host of problems and could even lead to a client suing you. There are no products available to the general public or nail technicians that can cure nail infections, but good techniques and safe working practices can prevent them occurring and so protect you and your clientele. Always leave any medical diagnosis and treatment to the experts: the medical profession.

Chapter summary

Once you have worked your way through this chapter you will realise just how much information we need to have on the human body to be able to do our work effectively and safely, not just for the sake of our clients but also to be able to protect ourselves from stress, injuries and infections. The guidelines outlined here will protect you from possible contra actions occurring to your clients and ensure that you have the knowledge to work safely and within legal requirements. Every client has a different lifestyle, health level and treatment needs, and this chapter should help you to identify whether a treatment can take place and any measures you might need to take to make it as effective and safe as possible for all concerned.

Chemicals simplified

Chemicals are the substances of which all matter is composed so, effectively, everything around us is a chemical except for light, electricity and sound. In the strictest sense the water we drink, the tools we use and even ourselves are chemicals. This chapter aims to simplify this concept for you and covers the main chemicals that we use within the nail industry. Chemicals and their use within each nail system is covered as well as their relationship to each other. What chemicals are, how they work and how they are used is essential knowledge for every professional nail technician and without this information we cannot possibly understand how to perform our work properly and give sound advice to our clients. The chemicals involved in preparing the natural nail, applying nail extensions and their safe removal are all covered. There are other books available that will give you more detailed information on chemistry (see Bibliography). All of the information you need on the chemicals involved in each nail system is contained within this chapter. Every product supplier or manufacturer will have extra information on their products and you should make sure you ask for this whenever you attend a training course. Become familiar with the main chemicals and the processes involved in their use, for your own and your clients' safety. *Always follow manufacturers' instructions.*

In this chapter we will consider the following aspects:

- **introduction to chemicals**

- **chemicals in application**

- **a brief guide to the use of chemicals**

Introduction to chemicals

Learning objectives

In this section you will learn:

- **what chemicals are**

- **how to work safely with chemicals**

- **some chemical terminology**

Introduction to chemicals

It is necessary for nail technicians to have at least a basic understanding of chemistry, because almost every aspect of our work involves the use of chemicals. A good understanding of chemical reactions is an integral aspect of our safe working practices. Natural nail plates themselves are chemical substances, being made up of proteins called amino acids.

Everything in the world is either *matter* or *energy*. Matter is anything that takes up space or occupies an area. Matter can be in the form of solids, liquids or gases – for example ice, water or steam. Energy has no substance and is not made of matter. Energy can affect matter in many ways but it is not a chemical. Examples of energy are light waves, sound waves, microwaves or X-rays. Matter can be chemically changed, for example when water is heated it turns into steam or if it is frozen it turns into a solid.

Nail technicians use a range of products that physically change when used correctly and we have a responsibility to ourselves and to our clients to understand the chemical changes that take place when we work with these different products and chemicals.

What is a chemical?

The word chemical is often misused. When mentioned, it may strike alarm into some people and their immediate thoughts are 'dangerous', 'poisonous', 'toxic', or just an irrational feeling of fear, normally born out of a lack of knowledge. In fact, chemicals surround us at all times and include everything apart from light, electricity and sound. Electricity can be described as a flow of electrons (parts of an atom) between two charged poles. Light is the emission of photon energy from a source, for example the sun, a torch, light-emitting diodes, and so on. Sound is created by the vibration of air molecules. Light and electricity are energies that can have an affect on chemicals; sound can also affect chemicals, but not in any ways that concern nail technicians.

When the nail industry was in the early stages of its development, the products used were 'acrylics' and when compared to the products we use today they were greatly inferior. All new technology can take years to develop to its full potential. Consider mobile phones and the developments that have taken place and continue to take place in that market over a few short years. The nail industry is the same. Today's systems, products and techniques are far superior to those of yesteryear. Although nail extension products are still based on acrylics, they have advanced and are still developing every year.

As nail technicians, we should have a healthy respect for all the products we use, plus a good understanding of their specific use and the consequences of not following manufacturers' instructions. We must also consider the storage and protective measures that must be taken. Armed with this knowledge and the correct training, any remaining fears should disappear.

Working safely with chemicals

All the chemicals you are likely to come across in the nail industry can be used safely as long as certain rules are followed. Consider the checklist below:

- Store all flammable products away from ignition sources such as:
  – heat
  – sparks
  – flames
  – the boot of your car in extreme temperatures
- All product containers and lids should be firmly secured and kept away from children.
- Always aim to use or decant chemicals in well ventilated areas.
- Put chemicals or products away after use.
- Always use protective safety glasses to prevent eye damage.
- Take care with your hands, they should be clean and dry at all times and kept free of chemicals.
- Use metal waste bins, not plastic, preferably with a foot pedal operation.
- Keep COSHH or MSDS data sheets available on all products (see Chapter 2).

- Wear protective clothing – safety glasses and gloves – when decanting chemicals into smaller bottles or pots.

A–Z of chemical terminology

The nail industry cannot exist without the use of certain chemicals. When first learning how to become a nail technician this area can seem very daunting, with the complicated names and terminology of the chemicals we use. In what follows we will take a brief look at some of the most commonly used names and terms you will hear. Further explanation of the chemistry involved in nail technology is given in the subsequent four sections. For additional information we recommend *Nail Structure and Product Chemistry* by Douglas D. Schoon.

Acetone

Acetone has for a long time been labelled a 'bad chemical'. Many people believed it was responsible for all kinds of problems such as liver disease and cancer. However, nail technicians use such small amounts that it poses little, if any, threat. Acetone is an effective solvent that can be used safely in the salon environment to remove artificial nails. Some product companies also use pure acetone to dehydrate the natural nail plate. This is believed to improve adhesion, but will have a drying effect on the natural nail, albeit temporary.

Many nail technicians prefer to use a non-acetone polish remover to remove polish in the salon, because they believe acetone will cause lifting. This is not the case, as acetone will evaporate before any damage occurs to the nail extension. There is only a problem if lifting is already happening, in which case it is likely to be made worse. If a client has been wearing a red or dark-coloured polish, a non-acetone polish remover will not remove it so effectively. Non-acetone polish remover usually contains either acetate or methyl ethyl ketone as the solvent.

Acrylic

All of the three main systems in the nail industry contain **monomers** that are closely related. In fact all the systems are different forms of acrylic:

- **cyanoacrylates** – adhesive, wraps and no light gels
- **acrylates** – UV light gels
- **methacrylates** – UV light gels, monomer and polymer

Activator or accelerator

In the nail industry, an **activator** or accelerator is often associated with a wrap system (fibreglass or silk). It is used to accelerate or speed up the setting process of the resin after its application. The chemical that is used in the activator is called freon. If too much activator or accelerator is used or it is sprayed close to the natural nail plate, an undesirable heat reaction can take place.

Adhesive

An **adhesive** is a chemical that will allow two surfaces to bond together permanently. Many of the quality adhesives used in the salon are from the cyanoacrylate family, contain no animal by-products and are not water soluble. Good adhesion depends on a good technique and quality products.

Catalyst

A **catalyst** is a chemical that speeds up or slows down a chemical reaction. In the nail world we are looking at a speedy reaction – curing time can be measured in terms of seconds and minutes. Catalysts are usually weak alkaline substances which we brush or spray on and which cause an instantaneous reaction on our clients' nails.

Curing

Curing is the hardening or setting process of a liquid to a solid.

- A cure will take place when a gel system is placed under a UV lamp; this is when the gel hardens.
- Within the wrap system, curing takes place when activator or accelerator is brushed or sprayed onto resin.
- When using the liquid and powder system, the cure takes place during **polymerisation**.

Cyanoacrylate

Cyanoacrylate is an adhesive often used in the application of tips. This type of adhesive can be sensitive to moisture, and works well if slight pressure is applied during the tip application; this has the effect of squeezing out the air, which will aid the curing of the adhesive.

Formaldehyde

Some nail hardeners on the market contain as much as 3 per cent **formaldehyde**. A concentration of more than 1 per cent will cause the nail plate to stiffen. People using this type of product mistakenly believe they are strengthening the natural nail, but in fact the opposite is true, as the overuse of formaldehyde will dehydrate the natural nail and can be responsible for the nail plate becoming very brittle and then splitting and flaking. If using a nail hardener it is important to use it sparingly and to use a quality oil to rehydrate the cuticle and nail plate.

Safe and unsafe levels of formaldehyde

The concentration of formaldehyde in the majority of nail polishes is around 0.0015 per cent (fifteen ten-thousandths of 1 per cent). At this level there should be no problems, unless the client is allergic to formaldehyde. The continued use of nail strengtheners over a period of time may cause allergy problems.

Free radical

Free radicals are very excited molecules (i.e. molecules that move very quickly) that cause a chemical reaction. Our bodies use free radicals to perform thousands of vital functions each day – some of which can be considered good and some bad. For example, free radicals are involved in the ageing process and many skincare products contain chemicals that eliminate free radicals and so help to fight the ageing process. On the other hand, within our digestive systems, free radicals help to expel excessive amounts of substances such as cholesterol from our bodies.

Fumes

Fumes are not normally present in the salon environment. They are small particles of solids formed in smoke.

Glue

Glue, used as an adhesive, is normally a protein made from an animal by-product such as hide, hoof or bone. Glues are not water-resistant and some even dissolve in water. True glues are not always hypoallergenic and many clients overexpose themselves to them by using them to stick tips on for a prolonged period of time.

Initiator

An **initiator** is an ingredient within a product that will start a reaction, the speed of which will then be controlled by a catalyst.

- If you are using a gel system, the initiator is present in the gel but is activated by UV light. Daylight can therefore affect the gel so the pot must be covered as soon as the application has taken place.
- In a fibreglass system, the initiator is present in the

Technical Tip

Problems with the use formaldehyde can occur if there is prolonged use of formaldehyde-based products with a concentration of above 1 per cent.

activator or accelerator sprayed or brushed onto the resin, at which point a reaction will take place. The resin will dry without the activator or accelerator, but the reaction will be much slower.

- If you are using a liquid and powder system, the initiator will be present in the **polymer (powder)**. This is usually benzyl peroxide which when mixed with the monomer will cause a reaction to take place.

Methyl methacrylate

Methyl methacrylate (MMA) has been banned in the United States since the early 1970s. It is monomer and polymer that originated in the dental world. MMA is an extremely hard polymer that bonds well to the natural nail plate, but is very brittle and inflexible. If using MMA when an accident occurs the wearer may suffer severe damage: because of the rigidity of the product, the nail plate could be torn or ripped off the nail bed. Many nail technicians have suffered severe allergic skin reactions to dental products. Long-term use of MMA could cause respiratory problems. The majority of nail manufacturers switched from methyl methacrylate to ethyl methacrylate, a product which is far less likely to cause an allergic reaction.

Molecule

A **molecule** is a chemical in its simplest form. Water is a chemical made from two parts hydrogen and one part oxygen. The chemical shorthand for this combination is H_2O. One molecule of oxygen combined with two molecules of hydrogen makes one molecule of water. If the water molecule were broken down any further, it would not be water any more – it would go back to being molecules of two gases: hydrogen and oxygen. Molecules that cannot be broken down any further are called *elements*.

Monomer

Monomer is often referred to as the liquid part of liquid and powder system. **Mono** means one. A monomer is just one part or a single unit of a polymer. A line of monomers joined together would be called a **polymer**.

Oligomers

Oligomers are short single chains of molecules. They are either

- a polymer, meaning many molecules, or
- a monomer, meaning a single or one molecule.

Oligomers are present in UV gel systems.

Polymer

Polymers are very long chains of molecules linked together. Polymers can be liquids, but in the nail industry they are more usually solids in the form of a powder.

Polymerisation

Polymerisation is the setting that takes place when a monomer liquid and a polymer powder are mixed together. To achieve this process an initiator is needed to start the reaction (normally benzyl peroxide) and also a catalyst to control the reaction.

Primer

Primers are normally **methacrylic acid**-based and are corrosive. They must be used sparingly and with care. The acid in the primer will help to dissolve residue oils that are present in the nail plate and, if used correctly, primer will make the natural nail more compatible with certain nail coatings. The use of primer is much more effective if it is used in moderation and allowed to dry completely before any application of product. The use of primer can be advantageous if a client has an oily nail plate or suffers from perpetual lifting as it acts like a double-sided sticky tape with one side attached to the nail plate and the other side to the product. Primer can also help to prevent bacterial infections, but only if applied to the natural plate and kept well away from the tip or product when performing a maintenance treatment.

There is much new technology available today that does not require the use of primer, including gels and liquid and powder systems, but many nail technicians are reluctant to stop using primer because of its ability to prevent lifting and bacterial infections. However, with quality products, good preparation and application techniques this need is greatly reduced.

Solute

A **solute** is the substance that is being dissolved.

Solvent

A **solvent** is a substance that will dissolve another substance.

Toluene

Toluene has been used in the nail industry for many years to dissolve the ingredients in nail polish. Toluene will maintain the polish in a liquid form until it is ready to apply.

Technical Tip

Always wipe the primer brush on a clean paper towel before replacing it in the bottle. This will help prevent contamination. To check if the primer is in good condition hold the bottle up to the light, if you can see particles floating you should consider replacing it.

Volatile

Volatile is a term used to describe something which is not stable but is liable to change, for example products that will evaporate at room temperature.

Chemicals in application

Learning objectives

In this section you will learn about:

- **the chemicals used in nail extension application**
- **how they work and their chemical reactions**

A nail technician has to acquire many skills in a number of areas, but the most important skill is his or her technique in applying natural-looking, strong coatings over clients' natural nails, using a variety of techniques and products. To be able to do this effectively every technician needs a good, sound knowledge of how chemicals work and the processes involved in changing their state from one form to another, such as turning a liquid and powder into a solid.

Two types of coating are used in nail technology:

1 coatings that cure or polymerise
2 coatings that harden on evaporation

There are three types of nail systems but many different types of products used within them. All of these have one thing in common: every product creates nail **extensions** by a reaction called polymerisation. The three main ways of coating a nail with nail products are:

1 natural nail overlay – which covers the natural nail plate only
2 tip and overlay – which covers an artificial tip and the exposed natural nail plate
3 sculptured nail – which extends the coating past the free edge of the nail plate onto a form to create an extended tip

The products we use bond together to create a different form and we need to understand how some molecules bond naturally whilst others, owing to their positive and negative attraction, will require assistance in the form of heat, light or an initiator to speed up the setting process.

Acrylics

Nearly all the products used within the nail industry are from the same acrylic chemical family, including:

- light cure gels
- no light cure gels
- wraps
- liquid and powder

All of the systems require an initiator to start a reaction and a catalyst to control the speed of the action of turning the liquid into a solid, as explained in the previous section. All acrylics are man-made plastics and those that we use within the nail industry utilise the same chemical processes to form solids. This process is called polymerisation and it turns a liquid or semi-liquid into a solid.

Chemical molecules can be arranged and rearranged into almost unlimited combinations and the rearranging of molecules is known as a chemical reaction. Creating a nail extension is a classic example of a chemical reaction as billions of molecules must react or change to make one nail extension. Molecules can hook together in long chains containing millions of molecules. Longer chains are called polymers. The prefix 'poly' means many.

The prefix 'mono' means one, and a molecule by itself is called a monomer. A monomer is a molecule that makes polymers. It is important that you understand the meaning of monomers and polymers as these are two very important terms in a nail technician's vocabulary, whatever system is being used.

The liquid and powder system

The liquid in this system is the monomer and the marriage of monomers and polymers takes place when a monomer is mixed with a polymer containing an initiator (which in this case is usually benzyl peroxide). The initiator creates a heat reaction that splits the initiator in half. This reaction creates two free radicals. Each free radical energises a monomer. The energised monomer attaches itself to another monomer and this pattern is repeated in a domino effect until a polymer chain has been created.

The ratio of the liquid to powder units is very important when applying beads of product in the liquid and powder system. The correct ratio is vital to the performance and longevity of the product. Too dry a mix can make the nail extension too hard and brittle, whilst too wet a mix can result in a nail that is too flexible and is therefore weak and soft.

Consistency too wet

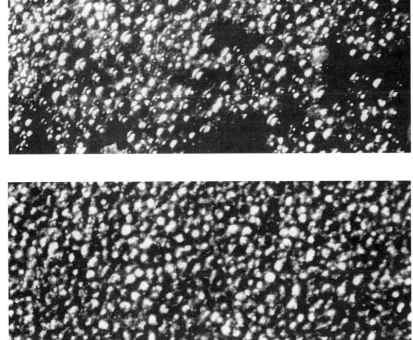

Correct consistency

Technical Tip

Most companies would recommend a medium wet bead, but you do need to check with your manufacturer what the correct mix ratio is for your product range.

Consistency control

There are a number of points to bear in mind when practising your mix ratio of monomer and polymer. These will be applicable to most of the products on the market.

Wet consistency	2 parts monomer, 1 part polymer
Medium wet consistency	1.5 parts monomer, 1 part polymer
Dry consistency	1 part monomer, 1 part polymer

- Too wet a consistency will give better adhesion but reduce strength.
- With a clean brush, make a bead in your normal way and lay the bead on top of a new tip at the **apex** in the centre; allow to settle for 15 seconds without touching bead with your brush – if a wet ring appears around the bead you know it is too wet.
- If the bead stays upright without gently dropping to half its size, then the mix is too dry.

The polymer powders used in liquid and powder systems

start out as monomers but may also be referred to as *homopolymers* – a polymer made from only ethyl or only methyl. The prefix 'homo' means the same, indicating that this polymer has been made entirely from the same monomer. Another term you may come across is *copolymer*. A copolymer is a mix of two or more different monomers. This will give a tougher, stronger and more flexible nail extension due to the choice of monomers in the blend. It also allows companies to design their own polymer blends.

Another point to consider when using the liquid and powder system is that the powders may come in various colours. It is useful to have a choice of colour as it can be employed to camouflage or enhance the natural nail. Powders are available in a range of clear, natural, pink and peach shades. There is no difference in the mix ratios of liquid to powder when using a coloured powder.

Other additives to the powder may include colour stabilisers and UV absorbers. These work to prevent yellowing and also to inhibit UV light, which can make the nail extensions discolour and become brittle.

The effects of oxygen

If there is too much oxygen around it is impossible for monomers to make polymers and this will affect the surface of the nail extension by allowing only a few monomers to join and resulting in a sticky top layer. The deeper molecules are shielded from oxygen by the monomers near the surface and are free to polymerise normally. This reaction can be seen on odourless systems as well as light cured products.

The gel system

Oligomers

These products are normally associated with gel systems. They are very similar to the monomer and polymer system. Gels are supplied pre-mixed, are placed on the nail and cured under a UV (ultra violet) light for approximately two minutes. The initiator in this system is the UV light.

Oligomers are also chains of molecules, but are shorter than polymer chains. They allow the UV light to penetrate the gel so that curing can take place.

Ultra violet light

The tubes in most nail lamps emit only UVA light to cure

Point to Remember

Generally, monomers are liquids as used in the liquid and powder system, whilst oligomers come in semi-liquid form as used in gel or resins.

nails. Tubes can vary between 5 and 9 watts and lamps usually have 1–6 tubes. There are many lamps available but most will only give out 38–45 watts of UV which is not harmful to the skin. The problems associated with light cured gels are that the light must completely penetrate the gel to polymerise all of the oligomers. This means that the product must be applied thinly and exposed to the correct amount of UV otherwise there is the risk of uncured product remaining on the natural nail bed. If the wattage in the lamp is too high it could cause heat reactions on the nail bed.

UV gel is more sensitive to oxygen than the liquid and powder system, as oxygen inhibits the polymerisation of the surface of the gel nail. UV gel will always have a sticky layer after curing which needs to be removed before buffing or polishing the nails.

The viscosity of gels varies greatly from one product to another. Viscosity relates to the thickness of a liquid. A lower viscosity gel is normally used to apply thin coats, whilst higher viscosity gels are used for building or sculpting.

Take the following points into consideration when learning your skills on the gel system:

- the thicker the gel that is applied the fewer the layers that will be needed
- some gels will not hold shape for long
- thicker gels are harder to master
- thinner gels are self-levelling
- gels are more resistant to solvents
- gels retain their surface shine longer
- thicker layers will shrink more than thinner layers

Wrap systems

Gel systems are, for the most part, a one component system; liquid and powder is a two-part system, and wrap systems are usually three-part systems. A wrap system consists of

- a fabric
- a resin
- a resin activator or accelerator.

The wrap system has been around for many years and was originally used by manicurists to repair natural nails or to wrap nails in silk to strengthen them.

Technical Tip

Always follow the manufacturers' instructions and use the UV lamp recommended for your system.

Fabric

A fabric mesh is used to give a cross-linked structure for strength and flexibility. Without the fabric, the resin would break down. Fabrics such as cotton, linen, tissue, silk and fibreglass can all be used within this system, but the strongest is a fibreglass mesh. Fibreglass mesh usually comes with a sticky back for easy application and some are supplied in a dispenser to keep the mesh from fraying and deteriorating before use.

Fibreglass

- Always choose a good quality fibreglass with a 50/50 weave as this will give you maximum strength.
- Fibreglass, as the name suggests, has a high glass content.
- Fibreglass should not overlap the nail.
- It is more difficult to make the mesh disappear than when working with silk.
- Fibreglass can come already pre-cut to shape, which saves time.

Silk

- The silk used in wrap systems is a very fine mesh of natural silk fibres.
- The silk disappears almost immediately when resin is applied.
- Silk is not as strong as fibreglass mesh.
- This is a good medium for coating a natural nail that has a shorter length.

Resin

The resin used by nail technicians belongs to the acrylic family and is a cyanoacrylate adhesive. There are two ways of applying resin:

1 with a nozzle on the applicator of the bottle
2 as a brush-on

Resin is used to wet the fabric and help it to disappear, giving the nails a natural appearance. It is also used to build up layers on a nail extension to give added strength and flexibility. As with any adhesive, there are various types and different qualities of resin. The type of resin most widely used and most suitable for nail extensions is ethyl cyanoacrylate. Viscosity also varies from one product company to another, but it is always advisable to use a high

Technical Tip

Too much moisture, i.e. water, will shock cure the product and cause a heat reaction on the natural nail. It can also lead to a breakdown in the product due to cracking.

grade for high quality and long-lasting results. Resin is sensitive to moisture and oxygen and will polymerise if exposed to either.

Resin activator or accelerator

Resin will cure with the natural moisture in the air, but this can take anything up to 20 minutes. If it is allowed to dry naturally it is also liable to peeling as it will have absorbed too much moisture. The safest option is to use an activator or accelerator to cure the resin quickly. This will also help to speed up treatments. Most activators are alcohol- or alkaline-based and, as we have mentioned before, can be sprayed onto or brushed over the nail.

Polymerisation happens in the same way as the liquid and powder and gel systems. However, the polymer chains that are formed lack strength, which is why they rely on the strength of the fibreglass. The polymerisation starts when the activator is sprayed or brushed onto the resin. The activator should be used sparingly, as excess heat reactions can occur if it is sprayed too close or too thickly. A fast cure will create a nasty heat reaction on the natural nail and lead to a weak structure.

You must ensure that your product company, distributor or manufacturer provides you not only with specific application instructions but also with product knowledge about the chemicals contained in the products you are using. Remember that it is a legal requirement to keep COSHH or MSDS sheets on all products you use. *Never* mix chemicals which have come from two different manufacturers as you could be exposing yourself and your clientele to chemical reactions you have no knowledge of.

Removers

The main solvent used in nail extension removal products is acetone. This is because acetone is very efficient and is the safest of the solvents we can use on our clients. There are other solvents that would do the job, but these can be damaging to the skin and dangerous to inhale.

Cross-linking makes it difficult to remove extensions. It is only those products that do not cross-link that are easy to remove, such as resin in the fibreglass system. The removal solvent swells the polymer network until it breaks into chunks and this can be achieved more quickly by warming the solvent when in use. As an analogy, consider immersing a roll of paper in water; the water will make the roll swell but will not dissolve it. The only way the roll can be broken up is to use a stick, just as we would use an orange stick to help remove the product from the natural nail plate.

A brief guide to the use of chemicals

Learning objectives

This section forms a checklist of the chemical components of products commonly used in nail extension application and manicure.

Chemicals in application

Product	*Chemical name*	*Uses*
Liquid	Monomer	Mixed with polymer (powder units) to form acrylic nails
Powder	Polymer	Mixed with monomer (liquid units) to form acrylic nails
Primer	Methacrylic acid	Anchors some products to the natural nail plate
Resin and adhesive	Cyanoacrylate family	Seals in fibreglass and bonds tips to natural nails
Fibreglass and silk	Threads and fabrics	Wraps for natural nails or tip and overlay
Activator or accelerator	Aromic amine and solvents such as freon, acetone, trichlorethane or ethyl ketone	Drying agents for slow curing adhesives
Nail polish remover	Acetone based	Removes polish
Non-acetone polish remover	Ethyl acetate, methyl ethyl ketone	Removes polish
Gel	Oligomer	Natural nail overlay or overlay over tip
Product remover	Solvents	Breaks down bonds in the product

Chemicals in manicure

Cosmetic	Main ingredients	Uses
Nail polish remover	Acetone occasionally used, sometimes mixed in oil. Mostly based on amyl, butyl or ethyl acetate	Dissolves nail enamel
Cuticle cream	Mixture of fats and waxes such as lanolin, cholesterol and sometimes white iodine, beeswax	Softens nail and surrounding tissue. Helps brittle condition when used in between treatments
Cuticle oil	Oils such as lanolin, petrolatum – with or without water	Softens nail and surrounding tissue
Cuticle remover	Oleic acid, glycerine, 2% solution sodium potassium hydroxide	Softens and removes dead cuticle
Nail white	White pigment such as zinc oxide (titanium dioxide) with wax or oil	Whitens free edge of nail
Paste polish	Powdered pumice, stannic oxide, talc or kaolin	Smooth irregular nail ridges or dry polish nails
Base coat	Butyl acetate. Toluene, nitrocellulose. Nylon and acrylics	Adhesive base for liquid nail polish. Smooth base
Nail enamel	Formaldehyde resin, butyl acetate, toluene nitrocellulose. Colouring dibutyl phalate additives	Polish and enhance nails
Top coat or sealer	Butyl acetate. Toluene dibutyl phalate as plasticiser	Protects enamel from chipping and scratching
Enamel dryer	Mineral oil. Oleic acid or silicone	Protects soft lacquer during hardening process
Hand lotion	Mineral, vegetable oils, lanolin, other fatty materials and plant extracts	Softens and protects skin
Nail enamel solvent	Ethyl acetate, butyl acetate, toluene	To thin enamel which has become to thick to use

Chapter summary

Once you have completed this chapter you will see how important it is not only to know how to apply your products safely, but also which chemicals they are made from, the chemical reactions that are taking place when products are applied and the specific instructions you may need to follow when using them. It is when problems occur that you will realise just how important it is to know your chemicals. *Prevention is better than cure.* Remember that technology changes at a fast pace and the chemicals involved in the professional nail industry are being enhanced all the time. Stay one step ahead and keep yourself informed of any new information on systems, chemical processes and application procedures.

The systems defined

The professional nail industry is changing constantly and every year manufacturers bring new products onto the market and the techniques involved in their use or application may change. This chapter looks at the procedures for manicure and pedicure and the massage routine involved in both. There are many specialist systems for both of these treatments on the market and you may find that your supplier or manufacturer recommends a procedure slightly different from the one outlined in this chapter. You may also find that, as time goes by and you gain more experience, your methods develop and you change your procedure slightly. It really does not matter which way round you proceed with this treatment as long as all the necessary areas of skin and nails are treated in an effective and safe manner.

This chapter also covers the preparation of the natural nail and all safety issues. The processes of applying tips and the three main nail systems are included but it must be remembered that manufacturers' instructions must be taken into account when performing treatments. Your teacher or trainer should show you how to do this and provide you with any specific step-by-step instructions. The advantages and disadvantages of each system are general and you must decide which best suits you and your working environment. Specific and generic aftercare are given but again you may need to add the information that your manufacturer recommends. We cover the technique of sculpting and the various sculpting forms you can choose to work on. This is a slightly more advanced technique and may require extra practice. The safe removal of all three systems is covered and how to give your clients advice on looking after their natural nails.

This chapter has a discussion of two specialist tools that are sometimes used by professional nail technicians. These are electric filing drills and the nail trainer. These tools are optional and may be used to enhance your skills. Their benefits and use are covered in detail. There is also a section on troubleshooting and this is to help the less experienced technician who may not have come across these problems before. Causes and solutions to each problem are given.

In this chapter we will consider the following aspects:

- **manicure and pedicure**
- **preparation of the natural nail**
- **tip application**
- **application, maintenance and sculpture**
- **removal techniques for nail extensions**
- **troubleshooting**

Manicure and pedicure

Learning objectives

In this section you will learn about:

- **why we carry out manicures and pedicures**
- **tools, equipment and products needed to carry out treatments**
- **manicure procedure**
- **pedicure procedure**
- **massage techniques and their benefits**
- **specialised treatments**

Why do we carry out manicures and pedicures?

Our hands and feet constitute an important part of our appearance and can influence our whole personality. People who have beautiful manicured hands usually have more confident body language and they will use their hands in a very different way from someone who is a nail biter. Alternatively, people with pretty pedicured feet are more likely to wear open-toed shoes or strappy sandals. Everyone's hands should be protected to prevent the skin from drying out and becoming rough or chapped. Nails should be protected from becoming broken, stained and flaky, with split and overgrown cuticles.

It is a lot easier for a manicurist to keep their clients' hands looking good with regular treatments rather than trying to cure problems on occasional visits. It is the same for feet, regular pedicures will prevent many foot conditions from happening or reoccurring. It is important to educate your clients on good home care so that they carry on your good work when they leave you. They will become more loyal because they know that you care about their hands and feet even when they are away from you. Make sure a home care package is part of your treatment – your clients need this, do not feel guilty about asking them to part with extra money.

Hands and feet

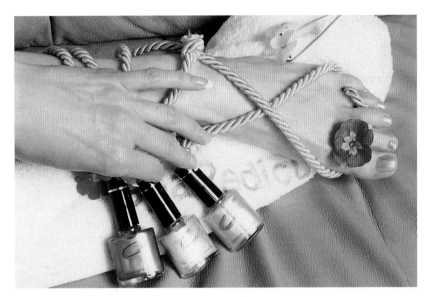

So what does a manicure or pedicure do?

Some of the benefits of a manicure or pedicure include:

- the cuticle and nail wall can be freed from the nail plate, avoiding hang nail formation
- infections are prevented
- prevention of minor nail damage, for example splits, tears or fragile free edges
- the outline of the nail is kept smooth to maintain an attractive cosmetic appearance
- the skin on the hands and feet is kept healthy and supple and free from infection

You must always work safely when carrying out any treatment and here are a few reminders of the important points to take into consideration when performing a manicure or pedicure treatment:

- always keep lids on bottles, never leave them loose or open
- always take creams out of pots with spatulas, never your fingers
- make sure all bottles are labelled correctly
- keep sharp implements stored safely and put them away after use
- change tissues and towels between clients
- make sure all equipment and tools are disinfected or sterilised correctly
- empty bins regularly
- do not have trailing flexes for people to trip over
- do not have water near any electrical appliances
- do not allow smoking in the salon environment

It is very important to make sure that all of your equipment, tools and products are to hand before you start a treatment. There is nothing worse than starting a treatment and finding out halfway through you have forgotten something. Your client will want a treatment that is flowing and not one that is constantly interrupted. There are many products on the market today and you may find a company that will sell you a 'system'. This creates a professional image as all the products and labelling will complement one another and give your treatment area a 'total' look. Here are a number of checklists for your manicure and pedicure station.

The manicure and pedicure area

The working area

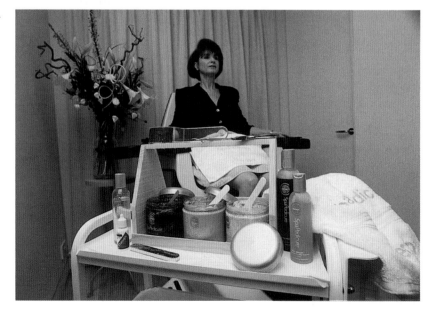

- a nail desk
- a pedicure chair for clients
- a comfortable chair for clients at the nail desk
- a manicure/pedicure stool with back support for you
- a metal bin with plastic liner
- an arm rest for manicure table (washable)
- sterilising solution and sterile container
- clean towels
- a dish for clients' jewellery
- a lamp for nail desk
- manicure bowl or pedicure bath

Tools and implements

A selection of manicure tools

- cuticle nippers
- cuticle pusher
- disposable or plastic spatula for creams
- nail clippers
- nail scissors
- natural nail buffer
- nail brush
- files and buffers
- pedifiles

Disposables

- disposable paper roll
- cotton wool
- lint-free pads
- orange sticks
- tissues

Manicure products

- hand sanitiser
- hand creams or lotions
- cuticle creams and oils
- base and top coats
- colour range of polishes
- polish remover
- nail soak
- buffing cream
- cuticle remover
- nail hardeners and strengtheners
- ridge fillers

The manicure procedure

It has been pointed out before there are many products on the market and you may find that some companies recommend their own way of performing a manicure. It would be a good idea to check with your supplier whether they recommend a certain routine using various products at different stages of the manicure. The following steps are for a basic manicure, including cuticle work and a massage. This procedure can be performed using any products you may choose. You can add to this basic routine a paraffin wax or hot oil procedure to make the treatment a more specialised one.

Manicure preparation

1. Prepare the treatment area and make sure you have good lighting.
2. Prepare your trolley; place products and instruments close to hand.
3. Check the appointment book to confirm client's name and find client record card.
4. Greet client, make sure he or she is comfortable, warm and supported.
5. Remove client's jewellery, put into a bowl on the trolley where the client can see it at all times.
6. Wash and sanitise your hands.

Sanitising a client's hand

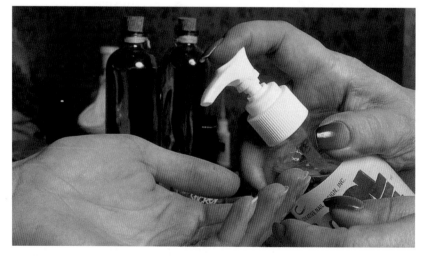

7. Inspect client's hands for contra indications or any adverse conditions and then wipe them over with an antiseptic solution or hand sanitiser, from the top of the wrist to the ends of the fingers.
8. Remove any old polish, starting with the left hand and repeating on the right. Make sure all polish is removed in

the cuticle area, along the sidewalls and under the free edge. Use an orange stick for difficult to reach areas.

9 Fill out the client record card and take a note of which polish colour your client requires, or if they have any special needs or wishes.

Manicure treatment

10 After consulting with your client on the length and shape they would like, file the natural nail with an emery board. Remember to keep the file at a 45° angle and never *saw* the nail back and forth.

11 If you are using a buffing paste at this stage, take a very small amount out of the pot with an orange stick and place a very small bead onto each fingernail. Swipe with your little finger down towards the free edge and not up to the cuticle. Use the buffer in one direction only from the base of the nail to the free edge.

12 Apply cuticle cream to the cuticle on each nail and massage in with the pad of your thumb in a firm rotary movement.

13 Place the left hand to soak in a manicure bowl, filled with warm water to soften the cuticles.

14 Whilst the left hand is soaking repeat steps 10–12 on the right hand.

15 Take client's left hand from the bowl and dry with tissue or soft towel. Place the right hand into the bowl to soak for two minutes.

16 Apply cuticle remover to the left hand to loosen tight cuticles and use a clean orange stick tipped with cotton wool to clean under the free edge. Then gently push the cuticles back with a pusher or orange stick tipped with cotton wool, using a circular motion.

17 Wet the cuticle tool and remove any non-living tissue or debris from the nail plate to give the appearance of neat and tidy cuticles.

Soaking a client's hands

Cleaning cuticles with tool

Safety Tip

Cuticles should *never* be cut across as this will cause the skin in that area to become thicker, exaggerating the problem and not curing it. Constant cutting or picking of the cuticle will cause scar tissue and give the surrounding skin the appearance of a thickened callous.

Massage with lotion

18 At this stage, but only if you need to, use nippers to remove any hang nails.

19 Repeat steps 15–18 on client's right hand.

20 Apply massage cream, lotion or oil to your hands and warm it up before applying to client's skin. Make sure client's arm is in a comfortable position before starting massage routine. Perform massage to both arms (see Massage routine, below).

21 If polish is to be applied then you will need to de-oil (squeak) the nail so that the polish will adhere properly. It is better to use a lint-free pad so as not to leave any fibres on the nail to catch in the newly applied polish. You may use polish remover or a nail dehydrator to 'squeak' the nail.

22 Polish the nails using one base coat, two coats of colour and a top coat, unless you are using a pearl polish, in which case you would use one base coat and three coats of colour.

Points to remember

The aim of cuticle work is to loosen the cuticle from the nail plate and not to force it back, thereby damaging the matrix.

1 Always push cuticles back gently, when you can feel the skin resisting you, stop.

2 Cuticle knives, or their equivalent, should always be used with water or oil for lubrication, *never* use them on a dry nail plate as this could scratch the surface of the natural nail plate or, even worse, cut soft tissue.

3 If using a cuticle remover, make sure it is removed from the skin and not left on for too long as it will have a dehydrating effect on the skin.

4 Care must be taken to ensure that only excess cuticle on the nail plate is removed and not any living tissue.

The massage routine

Massage treatments have been known of for centuries and were used by all of the ancient civilisations to heal and repair the mind and body. Think back to your own childhood and you may remember your mother massaging a hurt knee or a sore tummy. There are many forms of massage, some being more advanced than others, such as Shiatsu. Massage is the manipulation of soft tissue to help a person's total well-being. There are various massage movements but we will concentrate on the four most popularly used in a

Useful Tip

When performing a massage treatment you must be relaxed yourself otherwise your client will feel the tenseness in your muscles. You should enjoy the experience as much as your client.

Safety Tips

Remember to check that your clients do not have any medical conditions that contra indicate a massage treatment. Client's clothing must be protected from creams and oils.

manicure or pedicure routine. There are hundreds of different massage routines and we will go through a basic routine suitable for the vast majority of clients. You will find, over a period of time, that you will develop your own routine from favourite movements and others you may pick up by having treatments yourself or from watching colleagues. Find those that you are most comfortable with and practise until the movements flow, without you even thinking about what you are doing.

Massage should always be continuous movement and one of your hands should always be in contact with your client. If you interrupt the flow your client's enjoyment will be affected.

You must check that a client has no contra indications to a massage treatment. In general, anything you are not sure of must be referred to a doctor, such as a unknown skin condition. However, there are certain factors that would definitely need to be taken into account when deciding whether to incorporate a massage into a manicure or pedicure routine. For example:

- skin conditions that the creams and oils might affect, such as eczema or psoriasis
- varicose veins in the leg area - *massage lightly*
- chilblains - *knife like pain in the calf bone (shin splints) - light massage*
- diabetes - *light effleurage*
- Raynaud's disease - *no extreme temps hot or cold - effects extremeties - white fingers, + sensation*
- circulatory problems
- joint problems and arthritis
- any recent operations or scar tissue under 6 months old
- neuralgia
- bacterial infections
- loss of sensation of any part of the body
- particularly hairy parts of the body

Important note

Check that your client is not suffering from a more serious medical condition, such as a heart problem or cancer, although these may not necessarily contra indicate a treatment, a doctor's permission must be sought.

Massage movements – effects and benefits

Effleurage

Effleurage massage movement

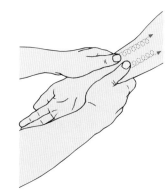

Effleurage is the first massage movement in any massage routine. It can be a very light, stroking movement or much deeper, according to the pressure applied. It is also the finishing movement to any massage routine. It is performed with the palm pads of the hands and pressure is exerted in one direction – always towards the heart to aid both venous and lymphatic flows. The hands and fingers of the masseuse are always returned to the starting point of the movement with no pressure but just light contact.

The beneficial effects of effleurage are:

- it aids venous circulation and indirectly arterial flow
- lymphatic circulation is improved, thus aiding the absorption of nutrients and the elimination of waste products from the body
- it aids desquamation, so cleansing the skin
- it aids relaxation

Petrissage

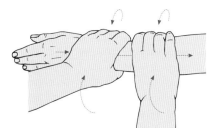

Petrissage massage movement

Petrissage is a compression movement that helps to tone muscles. It is a more vigorous movement than effleurage and it includes rolling, kneading, stretching and wringing the muscular tissue of the body. The movement may be performed with the whole hand, or individual fingers or a thumb. Petrissage must be performed slowly and rhythmically. During this movement the muscle is gently lifted away from the bone and alternately stretched, squeezed and then released. This improves blood flow which in turn helps muscle tone. The veins and lymphatic vessels are alternately emptied and filled. This movement will also help to soften any adhesions (where fibres within the muscles stick to each other due to mild inflammation), which may be present in the soft tissue.

The beneficial effects of petrissage are:

- desquamation or cleansing of the skin is improved
- muscle tone is improved because the blood supply is stimulated
- it brings fresh blood and important nutrients to the area of stimulation

Vibrations

Vibrations are fine tremulous movements, which are performed with the tips of the fingers or the whole hand. Both the arms and the hands of the manicurist must be relaxed and then contracted to produce the vibration movement which can be static or running.

The beneficial effects of vibration movements are:

- they are excellent for relieving tension in the muscles
- they are relaxing

Frictions

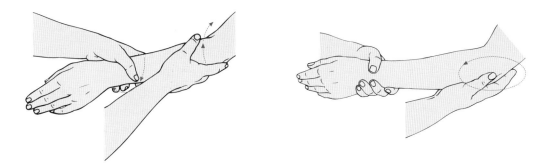

Friction massage movement

Friction movements are made up of small circular motions of the thumb or finger pads. These movements push the muscle against the bone, breaking up any nodules or adhesions present in the tissues. The movements are directed at the underlying tissues rather than the surface of the skin.

The beneficial effects of friction movements are that they

- are deep movements that produce a relaxing effect
- aid circulation
- have a tightening and toning effect
- break up fibrous tissue

Basic massage routine

1 Using the effleurage movement, stroke the hand up the front of your client's arm and gently come down the back. Pressure applied going up but not coming back down. Repeat three times with each of your hands.

2 Using your thumbs in a kneading circular movement, move up the front of your client's arm to the crease at the front of the elbow, slide hands back down and repeat movement three times. Be careful that you only apply enough pressure to make it comfortable for your client.

3 With the palm of your hand, pick up the muscle at the side of your client's arm and in a large, circular movement work towards the elbow. Repeat this three times either side of the arm with your right and left hands.

4 With your thumb, make circular friction movements around the elbow area and slide your hands down to the wrist. Repeat this movement six times on the wrist bone.

5 Lift the client's arm to an upright position and, supporting your client's wrist with one hand, gently flex and rotate their hand with your other hand. Repeat this six times. Be very careful with this movement, make sure it is performed slowly and check that it is comfortable for your client.

6 Lower your client's arm to the original position, with the palm turned upwards. Apply thumb effleurage to the metacarpal spaces, linking this with small thumb circles across the wrist three times.

7 Turn the hand back over and slide to the little finger. Circle the joints one by one and then gently rotate the finger and pull gently down the length of the finger to the end of the tip. Repeat on all fingers.

8 Effleurage up the entire hand and arm to the elbow six times. Each time apply slightly less pressure. Take both your hands and stroke either side of your client's hand to close the treatment.

The pedicure procedure

Pedicure products

You will need the following items:

- foot soak
- massage talc, oil or lotion
- hard skin exfoliator

Pedicure products

Technical Tip

When a client books a pedicure treatment, make sure they are advised to bring a pair of open-toed shoes or, if the weather does not permit this, that they allow sufficient time for drying.

- cuticle cream or oil
- polish remover
- polishes: base coat and top coat
- toe separators
- cuticle remover
- antiseptic solution

A pedicure treatment can be pure luxury as long as the client is warm and comfortable. Make sure your client is in a comfortable chair with a good back support, particularly important as you will be lifting their legs up and down. They will also need some privacy to change out of tights or trousers. A dressing gown and a modesty towel should be provided. Make sure you have inspected the feet thoroughly before proceeding with the first step of the treatment, sometimes you might not be able to see certain conditions until you have looked between the toes or underneath the sole of the foot. You should invest in some disposable surgical gloves which you can wear for this stage until you are happy to proceed knowing everything is healthy.

Pedicure preparation

1. Spray or wipe the feet with an antiseptic solution and inspect for any contra indications.
2. Remove polish and place both feet into soak for five minutes. At this stage you may wish to give your client a magazine to read.
3. Take one foot out of the pedicure bath and towel dry. The nails should be clipped back to the required length using

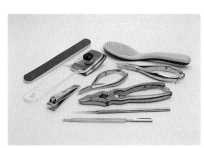

Pedicure tools

Clipping toenails

Cleaning cuticle area

toenail clippers. Do not try to cut across in one piece as this will split the nail. Then use an emery board to file across the top of the toenail. Any corners should be smoothed away to prevent ingrowing toenails. The toenail should then be bevelled and smoothed just like you would with a fingernail. Repeat on all five nails.

4 Apply cuticle cream and massage in with the pad of your thumb using a circular movement.

5 Push cuticles back with a hoof stick or cuticle pusher.

6 Using a cuticle knife, or equivalent, remove any non-living tissue around the cuticle and lateral nail folds on all five toenails.

7 Take a small amount of foot scrub in the palm of your hand and gently massage, in circular movements, over the ball and heel of the foot. Be very careful that your client is not sensitive in this area as it could ruin a wonderful treatment. Always use firm movements so that your client has confidence in you. You may want to rinse the scrub off in the foot bath and then gently use a pedifile if there is any hard skin left on the heel or ball of the foot. Do not use this tool on any soft areas of the sole.

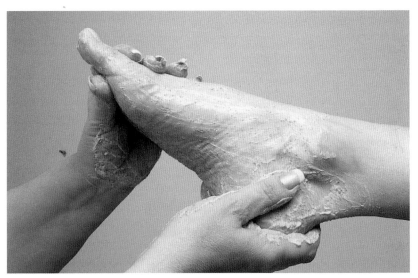

Foot scrub

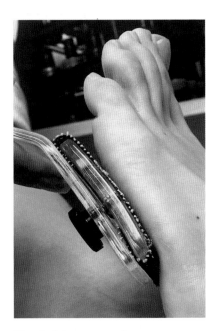

Hard skin removal

8 Repeat steps 3–7 on other foot. Keep the first foot wrapped in a towel whilst working on the second to keep the client warm.

9 Perform a massage routine on both feet and legs.

10 Squeak the nails if a polish is required.

11 Use toe separators or wind tissue in between the toes and apply a base coat, two coats of polish and a top coat.

The massage routine

1 Place cream, lotion or oil in the palms of your hands and warm. Apply to client's leg on either side and, working one hand after the other, perform effleurage movements towards the knee. Apply slight pressure on the way up and stroke lightly on the way back down. Repeat six times.

Application of oil on feet

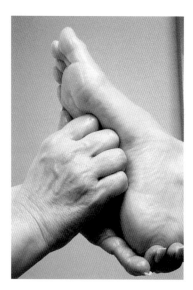

Massage routine on feet

2 With the palm of your hand, apply petrissage movements up the side of the leg in a circular movement. Once you have reached the knee, slide your hand down and repeat on other side of the leg. Repeat both sides six times.

3 Cup your hands and perform cupping movements on the back of the leg five or six times. If the sound is hollow you know you have got the movement right.

4 Slide your hands down to the ankles and circle around the ankle joint with your fingers six times.

thumbs down along back of calf circle around ankle

5 With the palms of your hands, rub from the top of the ankle to the heel in a friction movement. This is a very relaxing movement and produces a lot of warmth in the area.

6 Slide your hands underneath to the sole of the foot and, with your thumbs, work in a scissor movement across the bottom of the foot, working up and down the sole 2–3 times.

7 Take your thumb and forefinger and move up the achilles tendon with a slight pressure. Repeat six times.

8 Move your hands to the top of the front of the foot and, using small circle movements, move up between the metatarsals making sure that you do not apply too much pressure, making it uncomfortable for your client.

9 Rotate each toe twice and then gently pull and release.

10 Take the foot in a firm grip, with one hand supporting the heel and one hand on the ball of the foot, and rotate at the ankle joint three times in each direction.

11 Finish with three effleurage movements up to the knee and bring your hands down to stroke the foot at the top and on the sole, finally bringing your hands together.

A pedicure, for most clients, is a luxury treatment and is as much about their feet being groomed as it is about the psychological effect the whole treatment has. Always ensure that your client is seated comfortably and that the atmosphere is calm and relaxed. Feet are very often neglected, especially in the winter, and clients will need to be educated on how to look after their feet between treatments. Regular monthly pedicures will keep clients' feet looking healthy and in good condition.

Aftercare for manicure and pedicure treatments

It is important that before your clients leave the salon they have been given specific aftercare for the treatment that they have just received and that they receive the right retail items to help them do this. Remember, a new client will be so pleased with their smart nails or fancy feet that they will want to go out and buy items such as polishes. It is better that you encourage them to buy professional products from you rather than going down to their local chemist.

Here are a few points to take into consideration when giving aftercare to your clients:

- advice on further treatments and length of time in between
  - manicure treatments on average should be 2–4 weeks
  - pedicure treatments are usually once a month
- use non-acetone product remover
- always use base coat under a polish
- use a good quality top coat to prevent chipping of polish
- use hand cream or lotion every day
- use a cuticle cream or oil to moisturise soft tissue

- keep fingernails and toenails a sensible length
- use hand and foot exercises to keep joints supple
- wash feet daily and dry thoroughly, especially between the toes
- do not wear tight socks, tights or shoes
- use a pumice in between pedicures to keep hard skin under control

It is always a good idea to give clients an aftercare leaflet explaining to them the steps they can take to look after their hands and feet in between treatments. This will also prevent them from being able to say you did not tell them about the aftercare they should take. You can either make an aftercare leaflet yourself or some product manufacturers will be able to supply them to complement their products.

Clients will always appreciate you giving them sound advice and it might make a difference when they are considering whether to return to you or not.

Specialist treatments

There are many specialist manicure and pedicure systems on the market today and most major product companies will offer training to help you learn about these advanced techniques or products. The most commonly known additional treatments in manicure are hot oil and paraffin wax.

Hot oil manicures

A hot oil treatment is perfect for a client who has dry skin or cuticles and it can also help to moisturise dry, flaky and brittle nails. The heat involved in the treatment helps the oils to penetrate deeper into the nail plate, cuticle and surrounding skin. The oil can be used in a small bowl inside another bowl of hot water or alternatively it can be heated before you put it into the manicure dish. There are also heated mitts available that can be either microwaved or electrically heated.

A hot oil manicure can be as simple or as complicated as you wish it to be. Here is a simple step-by-step procedure for a basic hot oil manicure:

1 remove polish and file the free edges of the nails
2 soak nails in warm oil for 5 minutes
3 perform massage – using the oil already on the hand
4 carry out cuticle work
5 squeak and polish if required

If you would like to enhance this treatment even further for your client you can place their hands into plastic bags and place into heated mitts after taking them out of the oil. Leave their hands in the mitts for 5 minutes and then carry out the massage and the rest of the manicure routine. This will alleviate any dry skin conditions and is also an excellent treatment for those clients suffering from arthritis and rheumatism.

Always ensure that you use a good quality oil and not a cheap mineral oil, as this will not penetrate the skin as well.

Paraffin wax manicure or pedicure

Paraffin wax treatments can be used on both the hands and the feet. Most waxes are a blend of paraffin wax and beeswax and are extremely flammable. You will find that the paraffin wax used in manicure and pedicure treatments is always solid at room temperature and needs a special electric heater to melt it to a temperature of 50–55°C. It is not advisable to use any other heating method as it may not be safe. After the wax has been used it should be disposed of, especially if it has had other ingredients, such as aromatherapy oils, added or has been used in a pedicure treatment. Specialist wax baths are worth investing in as they will heat the wax to the correct temperature. They are then easy to use by dipping the hand or foot into the bath rather than having to paint the wax on.

Paraffin wax treatments have the following benefits:

- stimulate blood circulation
- improve the condition of the skin
- improve dry and chapped hands and feet
- relieve the pain of arthritis and rheumatism
- deep cleanse the skin

Paraffin wax treatment procedure

1 Check that the wax heater is on half an hour before your client arrives.
2 Check the temperature before using.
3 Protect the working area, yourself and your client from splashes.
4 Heat mitts before starting treatment.
5 Carry out client consultation, checking for any contra indications such as broken skin.
6 Cleanse and sanitise your own and your client's hands or client's feet.

7 Immerse client's whole hand or foot into wax bath, wait 5 seconds and repeat another 5–8 times.

8 Place client's hand or foot into a plastic protector and place into heated mitts or hot towels. Leave for 10 minutes, always checking that client is comfortable.

9 Unwrap hand or foot, peel off the wax and dispose of it. It is easier and less messy to do this as you pull the plastic protector off the limb.

10 Proceed with massage routine.

11 Carry out the rest of the manicure or pedicure treatment and polish.

There are many waxes on the market and some already have other ingredients added. Always check that your client is not sensitive to the ingredients in the wax.

It is a good idea to do some research before investing in a specialist manicure or pedicure system. Look at the cost effectiveness: How much can you charge for each treatment and how much longer will it take you than a basic manicure or pedicure? Always adjust your prices to reflect your extra time and investment.

Some specialist treatments incorporate the use of exfoliators and masks. These give added value to the treatments you perform.

Any extra products will mean the treatment takes longer to perform but usually, if used correctly, the client's skin will benefit for a longer period of time. Look carefully at the ingredients in your products and understand the features and benefits of each so that you can advise clients properly and so increase your retail sales.

Specialist pedicure mask

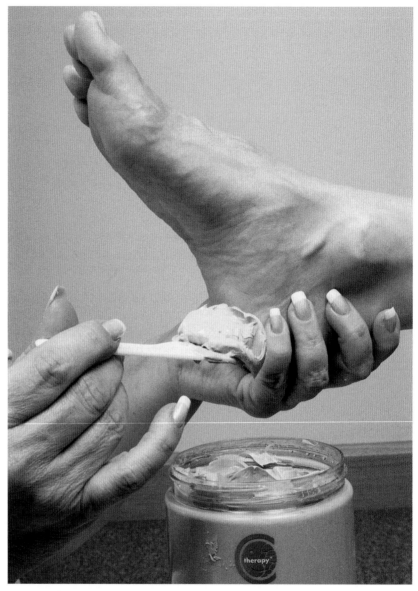

Specialist pedicure mask
applied to feet

Preparation of the natural nail

Learning objectives

In this section you will learn:

- **how to perform a mini manicure**

- **how to prepare the natural nail for nail extensions**

The proper preparation of your clients' hands is of the utmost importance before applying any nail enhancement products. If this is not done, it will not only put your clients' natural nail health at risk but also leaves you with only a weak foundation on which to build your product. Ultimately this could give you a bad reputation.

No matter what system you are using the natural nail should be prepared in the same way. You will find that most product companies will have their own names for products that actually do the same jobs. Check that they are what you need and do not use products that make false claims.

Technical Tip

If you choose to use an oil in preference to a cream, make sure that all oil deposits are thoroughly removed when dehydrating the natural nail and before any enhancement product application.

Safety Tip

One buff removes surface shine, twice or more removes nail plate layers. This is also true of using a heavy abrasive on the natural nail. You do not need to use low grit files to be effective, any file under 240 is totally unacceptable.

Performing a mini manicure

Before we apply nail enhancements we need to prepare the natural nail, making sure it is clean and free from any excess non-living tissue.

Technicians should wash their hands between client treatments and also make sure clients wash their hands. Apply a hand sanitiser to your hands and put some in the palm of the clients' hands, asking them to rub it in as well. If using a spray, spray your own hands first then the clients' hands.

At this stage you will carry out your consultation; make sure your client signs the client record card to say he or she agrees the treatment recommendations and that he or she has given you the correct information you need to be able to carry out a full treatment.

A small amount of good quality cuticle cream should be applied to each cuticle and gently massaged with the pads of your thumbs. This will lubricate and soften the skin in preparation for any cuticle work that you may need to perform. Gently push back the cuticle with a hoof stick, an orange stick tipped with cotton wool or a cuticle pusher. Make sure all metal tools are sterilised properly before being used on each client.

Pushing back cuticles

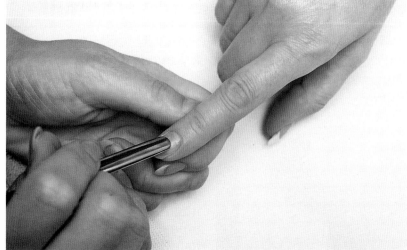

Removing non-living tissue

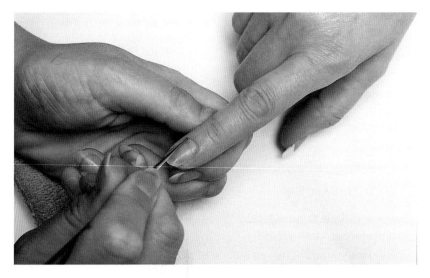

Filing natural nail

The nail plate needs to be free of any non-living tissue for the product to be able to adhere to it properly. If your client has excessive cuticles you may need to perform a water manicure a few days before commencing a nail enhancement treatment.

Any hang nails may be removed carefully with nippers. The cuticle should never be cut as this thickens the skin and can cause scarring. File the free edge of the natural nail to fit the shape of the deep stop point in the well of the tip. This will ensure the proper fit and maximum adhesion of the tip and will prevent moisture or dirt becoming trapped between the layers.

Remove shine

Remove any excess cream from the nail plate with a lint-free pad. Use a high grit buffer and gently remove the surface shine from the nail plate in the direction of nail growth only. This step ensures that all trapped surface oil and bacteria are removed.

By buffing in the direction of nail growth we can ensure that no damage is done to the soft tissue in the cuticle area. Remember the matrix is where all the new cells form and it is the softest part of the nail, so it needs very gentle handling.

Technical Tip

Removing the surface shine enables the nail dehydrator to work efficiently by breaking down the fat blocks in the surface of the nail. Test this effect by removing the surface shine from one nail and leave one unprepped, use the nail dehydrator on both and see the colour difference. One will be the same as it was originally and the other will look chalky and clean. It is difficult for any product to adhere properly to a nail plate with oils on its surface.

Removing surface shine

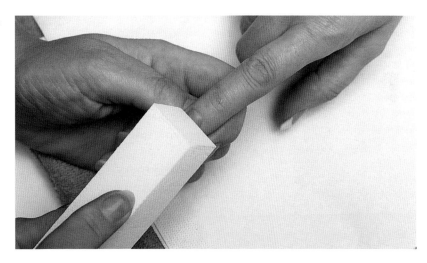

Technical Tip

We recommend that this step is performed on one hand only and then you apply tips or product. The reason for this is that if you leave it too long the natural nail oils will return – say within about 20 minutes. Also your client may touch their face or run their fingers through their hair in between you working on the first and second hands.

Cleanse and dehydrate the nail plate layers

It is very important to temporarily draw out all moisture from the surface of the nail. This gives the product the opportunity to bond fully, creating a good seal with the surface of the natural nail whilst also ensuring that no bacteria will be trapped between the natural nail and the enhancement. Take a lint-free pad or clean brush and apply nail cleanser and dehydrator to the surface of the natural nail. Pay particular attention to the lateral nail folds, cuticle and under the free edge.

Tip application

Learning objectives

In this section you will learn about:

- **the difference in tip materials**
- **the features of a good tip**
- **choosing the right tip**
- **pre-tailoring the tip before application**
- **blending techniques, manual or chemical**
- **application techniques**

Traditionally plastic tips were used to cover the whole of the natural nail. Technological advances have now developed strong, flexible, durable plastic tips that we can use with our nail systems to create beautiful, natural-looking nail extensions. These tips come in hundreds of shapes, colours and sizes. It would be impossible for us to list all of them in this one book but we have endeavoured to cover all the most important points a technician will need to know to be able to use tips effectively.

The difference in tip materials

There are two types of material used to make the tips we apply in nail technology today.

1 **ABS** (acrylonitrile-butadine-styrene) – all good quality tips will be made from this material. ABS is a plastic which goes through a great number of drying cycles before being moulded and therefore works better with cyanoacrylate adhesives. ABS tips tend to be more flexible and, added to their drier properties, this gives them better adhesion to the natural nail. An added benefit is that this helps eliminate the risk of air pockets when they are applied correctly. An ABS tip has a more opaque look and has a definitive colour that looks more natural than its acetate cousin. ABS is far easier to blend in and produces less heat when being blended to the natural nail.

2 Acetate – these tips have a higher oil content than ABS which means they are harder to blend and do not bond as well with adhesives. If a strong bond is not achieved the instant the tip touches the nail plate there is a tendency for the acetate tip to curl away from the natural nail. An

acetate tip does not have enough colour to look natural and is difficult to match to a client's natural nail colour. The extra filing required on an acetate tip will create heat, which when added to the heat produced from the setting of the adhesive and the use of some accelerators can give some clients an uncomfortable sensation of heat. Blending this type of tip is practically impossible without the use of a chemical tip blend. When trying to blend manually you will find that the plastic rolls or chips off, leaving an uneven seam.

All nail tips are plastic. They are made in injection-moulding machines, which force the melted plastic into moulds. The plastic cools quickly – approximately 10 seconds. The moulds, made of aluminium or steel, have different depressions for various sizes of tips. If the mould is of poor material quality the possibility exists for the sizes to change slightly as the mould is used over a period of time. High quality moulds which will not change shape are expensive to produce and you will find this is reflected in the price of the tips you buy. When the plastic comes out of the mould in the form of tips it looks like a tree. The tips are snapped off from either side and placed into tip boxes. Some manufacturers will recycle the waste by melting it down again. This process will help keep the manufacturing costs down, but is not beneficial to the quality of the tips. Plastic which has been recycled a number of times produces tips that are brittle and more yellow in colour in comparison to a 'virgin' ABS tip.

Always check with your supplier that the tips you are using are of a high quality plastic as these will last longer on your clients' nails, thus giving you a better reputation.

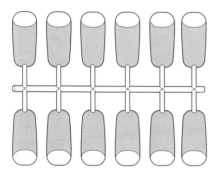

Tip tree

Features of a good tip

The tip acts as the cast to design a new look for the natural nail, creating a beautiful illusion for your client. When choosing a range of quality tips for your clientele take into account the fact that not every client has the same nail shape. A good nail technician will ensure they have a selection of tips to suit a range of nail shapes and sizes.

The essential features of a good tip are:

A selection of tip shapes

- virgin ABS plastic (as above)
- deep stop point
- thin contact area
- reinforced stress area
- good structural points

Deep stop point

This is the area in the well of the tip that butts into the free edge of the natural nail. This point of the tip should be deep rather than shallow to allow the natural nail to fit snugly into the groove of the tip. This will improve adhesion and also prevent any moisture from leaking between the tip and the natural nail plate. If the tip is fitted properly it will eliminate the risk of dirt sitting in the groove between the deep stop point and the natural nail's free edge. This is particularly important when fitting tips to irregular nail shapes such as a **ski jump** or on a nail biter. If the natural nail free edge is fitted properly into the deep stop point of the tip you will achieve a clean, natural-looking smile line after the tips have been blended. This will make the product application, if using white and pink powder or gel, much easier to achieve.

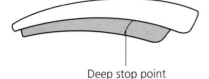

Deep stop point

Thin contact area

The contact area on various tips will differ. Some will cover more of the natural nail than others and some will sit on the free edge with the well already cut out. You may also find tips that have a 'V' cut into the well area to make blending easier and application on a wide flat nail more effective.

A good tip will have a thin contact area that will enable easier blending and achieve a clear, defined natural smile line to work on with your products.

Reinforced stress area

Another sign of a good tip will be the thickness of the stress area. The thickest part of a nail extension is the stress area or apex and the same should be said of a good tip. When the tip has been blended into the natural nail the stress area should remain the thickest part with the sidewalls and free edge being the thinnest. This will give added protection when a client is getting used to their longer length of nail.

Good structural points

There are various features of every tip that you will need to consider before deciding which ones to use. These are the features that will help you to select the right one for each client. There are four main structural points to look for:

1 sidewalls
2 'C' curve

3 lower arch

4 upper arch

Sidewalls

Sidewall

Look at your client's natural nail shape and choose a tip with either tapered or straight sidewalls to match. The sidewalls are one of the most important areas when fitting a tip to a natural nail as they provide reinforcement in a vulnerable area. When choosing a tip, look at the overall shape and whether or not it suits the natural nail shape. A tip should complement the natural nail and not exaggerate any irregularities. If the sidewalls of the tip do not fit perfectly into the natural nail grooves at the sidewall, this will create problems after the application of the overlay, has you will need to file through the newly applied product to redefine the shape, possibly weakening the structure.

'C' curve

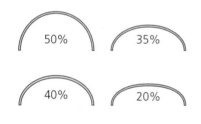

'C' curve

You will find that all natural nails will have different 'C' curves and this must be taken into account when choosing a tip to suit the shape of your client's natural nail. The tip needs to sit properly on the natural nail, otherwise your client will have problems keeping their nails on.

If you try to fit a flatter tip on a natural nail that has a deeper 'C' curve the edges will want to curl back up causing problems with sidewalls. Alternatively the opposite could happen if trying to fit a tip with a deeper 'C' curve onto a flat nail: it will want to spring back up and regain its natural shape. This might not happen until a few days later and could also cause your client some discomfort. If a tip does not match the 'C' curve of the natural nail, air pockets can develop between the product and the natural nail allowing bacterial infections.

Lower arch

Just like the natural nail, a tip should give the illusion of a continuation of the lower arch. This will be easier to achieve when the sidewalls are straight or slightly tapered, but is more difficult on a rounded nail shape. When pre-tailoring a tip for application make sure the lower arch is not digging into the flesh around the sidewall and the free edge of the natural nail. This is very important: when performing a treatment on a nail biter who has no lower arch, you need to create one.

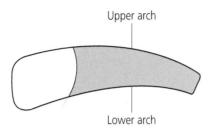

Lower and upper arch

Upper arch

Natural nails all have differing upper arches: some may be curved upwards, some flat and others may take a downward turn, for example claw nails. When choosing a tip to fit the upper arch of a natural nail you need to choose one that will complement the natural curvature or that will help to create an illusion of an upper arch that is not there naturally.

Choosing the right tip

When choosing the right tip to fit to your client's natural nails you will need to consider the following areas:

- sidewall to sidewall distance
- full contact area tip
- reduced contact area tip

Sidewall to sidewall

The tip should fit snugly into the nail grooves on either side of the natural nail plate. If a tip is too small then go for a bigger size and file to fit before application. *Never* fit a tip that does not fit perfectly from side to side as this could result in lifting, premature loss of the client's nails, splitting or cracks across the stress area and could also damage the client's natural nail. If a client has a flat nail or a fan nail, choose a tip one or two sizes larger and file down the sidewalls of the tip to the correct size, this will ensure that the tip will sit easier on the flat surface of the nail. Always make sure when sizing a tip that you pull back the sidewalls to expose the nail plate fully, ensuring complete contact with no gaps.

Most ranges of tips come in sizes 1–10, one being the largest and ten being the smallest. There are, however, some companies that manufacture slightly larger sizes such as 0.

Tip with full contact area

Most tips have a full contact area, but in a lot of cases you will be taking at least some of the contact area away before the application of tips to the natural nails. The contact area of any tip should never cover more than 30 per cent of the natural nail as the tip is only the platform for the product, it is the product that provides the strength in the nail extension unit. A full contact area is more susceptible to air pockets due to the larger surface area being bonded. This will not only show through the product but can also cause problems such as bacterial infections. A larger contact area

Technical Tip

When entering a competition or performing nails for a photo shoot you will need to look at the structure of the tips you are applying in much greater detail to make sure that they totally complement the natural nail you are working on. Judges and a camera will be harder on you than your clients.

Technical Tip

You may find that male clients and a small number of female clients have a nail plate that is just too wide for any size tip. You would then need to sculpt on a form. This is covered in the next section.

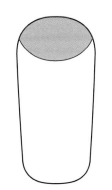

Tip with full contact area

will require more buffing and there could be a risk of damage to a client's natural nail. The finished nail will not look quite as clear and defined as a tip that has been applied with a smaller contact area.

Tips with reduced contact area

The newest type of tip on the market has a smaller contact area and is considered the fastest to apply. This is because the area to be blended is much smaller. However, this has its advantages:

- less filing is required on the natural nail
- less heat is created on the natural nail bed
- there is less chance of 'ghost' shadows being left across the blended area
- they are quick and easy to apply
- less adhesive is used
- there is a larger contact area for product, creating a stronger overlay
- there is less damage to the natural nail plate

Tip with reduced contact area

You will usually find that 'French' or 'white' tips all have a reduced contact area and are advertised as requiring no blending at all. However, the contact area will still need to be reduced further to match the natural free edge as this will differ from nail to nail. These tips are not suitable for clients who are nail biters or who have a really short nail plate as the percentage of white free edge to pink nail plate can make nails look top heavy and unbalanced. There is no real benefit to blending a 'French' tip into the natural nail, although it is quicker and more cost effective if your client wishes to have this type of look. By not blending a tip in fully you will sacrifice a little strength in the stress area. If your aim is to create a thin, flexible, strong enhancement then either blend or pre-blend before application of product.

Crystal clear tips

This type of tip is relatively new and is used mainly for artwork. If using clear tips on natural nails without any decoration you will need a nail plate that is pink, healthy and undamaged, otherwise they could look uninteresting and quite ugly.

These tips can be applied to the natural nail and blended or, by using the reduced contact area method, they can be left unblended. They can create a stunning look with jewels, rhinestones, bindis and other such decorations embedded into the overlay. You can also use coloured acrylics to design patterns such as flowers, zebra prints, pictures and much more. These tips are very versatile and can be used in many ways (see Chapter 7 for step-by-step instructions).

When they first start out in the nail industry most technicians feel they have spent a fortune finding the tips that they are happiest using. Always ask a supplier or manufacturer for a sample pack before buying so that you can test their tips to see if they have the properties you require. Always carry a few different types to suit all clients.

Pre-tailoring the tip before application

It is important to ensure that whenever you purchase your products you get full application instructions from the supplier. Techniques vary so much from one product to another that you could have serious problems if you do not check first that the way you are using them is the correct way.

Procedure for application of tips

1 Carry out a client consultation and choose the correct tip and adhesive to suit your client's needs.
2 Make sure all preparation steps are carried out fully.
3 Ensure your client's natural nail free edge matches the ridge in the well of the tip.
4 Size tips and pre-tailor to suit each client's natural nail shape.
5 Apply a small amount of adhesive to the tip of the client's natural nail.
6 Apply a small amount of adhesive to the well of the tip.
7 Press the tip onto the natural nail, holding the tip at a 45° angle – ensure there are no air bubbles.
8 The tip should be a perfect fit on the natural nail.
9 There should be no more than 30 per cent of the tip on the natural nail plate.
10 The well of the tip should be butted into the natural nail's free edge.
11 Do not allow any overlap on the sidewalls, or use a tip which is too small for the natural nail.
12 Ensure no excess adhesive is left under the free edge or on the surrounding tissue.

Technical Tip

If you try to use scissors you are likely to find the plastic will crack and form an ugly line across the nail. Use nail clippers and cut halfway across, then do the same from the other side and twist the excess tip off.

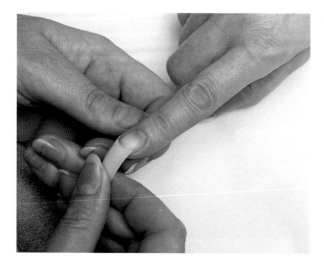

Tip at angle

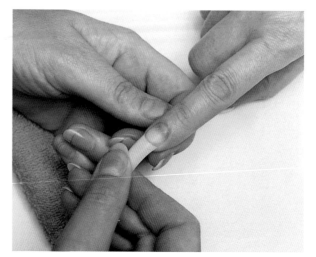

Holding tip and applying pressure

Cutting tip with tip cutters

Safety Tip

You might find holding your client's finger firmly with your thumb and middle finger will stop any uncomfortable rocking of the tip while you file the free edge.

13 Any excess should be cleaned off before the adhesive dries.

14 Cut tip to desired length with tip cutters or nail clippers.

15 Shape the free edge with a fine board, 240 grit or higher.

16 Define the sidewalls. Most of the pre-tailoring has been done before application, but you may need to slightly taper the sidewalls of the tip after application to blend into the sidewalls of the natural nail. Make sure that the lateral nail folds are held back when doing this to prevent catching the soft tissue.

17 To blend the tip to the natural nail start by using a 240 grit file or higher and, with a rounded motion, thin the entire tip evenly. Thin out **zone one** (the free edge) until it looks almost translucent, very carefully – you are working near the natural nail – refine **zone two** (the stress area) until there is no ghost shadow. Make sure the whole tip is thin and translucent.

Shaping free edge

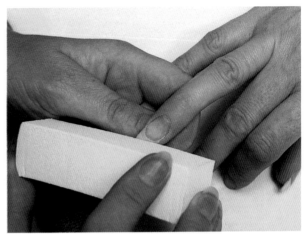

Blending tip with white block buffer

Safety Tip

There is a difference between placing the file in the lateral fold and pressing the file against the edge of the tip. If in doubt, tilt the file towards the centre of the nail before drawing the file down the sidewall.

18 Check the whole nail for any sharp edges or inconsistencies before going on to product application.

Safety tips

These tables cover some of the problems which can arise with tip application and their solutions.

Cracks

Cause	Solution
Poor tip fit	The 'C' curve of the tip should match the natural nail shape and fit snugly into the sidewalls otherwise excess pressure will cause cracking.
Poor cutting	Dull blades or cutting across with scissors.
Misuse of chemicals	Primer coming into contact with the tip will cause it to crack. The use of solvents as tip blends will also weaken the surface of the tip and can build in weaknesses.

Bubbles

Cause	Solution
Too little adhesive	Make sure that adhesive is placed on both surfaces. You will need to gauge how much is needed depending on the size of the tip and natural nail.
Not enough pressure when applying tips	Most adhesives are pressure set and will bond better with more pressure. Do not be afraid of hurting your client, just have a firm grip and hold for the right amount of time for that product.
Poor fit	If a tip is too small it will have excessive stress placed upon it and will want to come off. Alternatively, if the tip is too large, gaps will appear in the corner and cause weaknesses where the tip has not adhered to any surface.

The three systems: their application, maintenance and sculpture

Learning objectives

In this section you will learn about:

- **the general points of each system**

- **advantages of each system**

- **the application, maintenance and aftercare of each system**

- **toenail application**

- **the advantages and process of sculpting**

- **becoming a proficient nail technician**

- **using drills**

There are different 'ways' in which you can apply artificial nails according to the products used and how they are applied. Each method is known as a 'system' and there are three main systems. When first starting out on your career as a nail technician we recommend that you master one system first, as it is practically impossible to be a master of all three initially. Trying to learn all three effectively can be confusing. Most experienced technicians can use more than one system, but will usually have a favourite. Consider the following factors before deciding which system you want to work with:

- cost

- availability of courses in your area

- availability of further training

- provision of support by manufacturers

- what system is most popular in your area

Do not get drawn into the trap of spending large amounts of money on equipment and products for all three systems at the start of your course of career: you may find you never use some of them. Ask for a demonstration and see which one appeals to you the most. Invest in one system with a second as a back up. Eventually as your career path widens, you will find yourself favouring one particular system but perhaps using all three on your clients.

We will look at each system in turn, considering its advantages and disadvantages, the tools and equipment required and any safety issues specific to each system. We will also discuss the application, maintenance and aftercare advice required.

The liquid and powder system

The acrylic, or liquid and powder system as it is often called, is considered to be the strongest system used in the nail industry. Some manufactures use the latest cross-linked polymer technology. Safer products such as ethyl methacrylate are used now. In the past, acrylic systems used dental products that had an adverse effect on the skin. Being a nail technician today and using a liquid and powder system can be very satisfying since there are many coloured

Finished acrylic nail

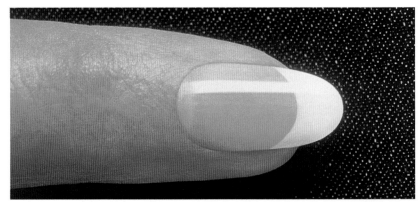

powders available to create a range of interesting effects and designs.

The two components of this system are:

- monomer liquid
- polymer powder

When liquid monomer is mixed with polymer powder it changes from a liquid to a solid. This process is called polymerisation (see Chapter 5).

Advantages of this system

- nail extensions can be flexible, thin and natural-looking
- sculpting is successful
- a permanent French manicure can be achieved
- it is the strongest system for heavy-handed clients
- maintenance is quick and easy once proficient
- it can correct irregular natural nail shapes
- some products can be heat sensitive

Disadvantages of this system

- it takes time to remove
- it is time consuming when learning
- dust could be a problem until proficient
- it is the most difficult to master
- odours can be a problem in some environments
- some systems need a primer

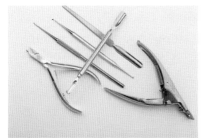

A selection of tools

Tools and equipment required

- sanitiser
- hard surface disinfectant
- sterilised tools
- towels
- disposables
- cuticle oil
- tips
- adhesive
- files and buffers
- nail preparation products

- primer if required
- liquid and powder system
- dappen dish
- base coat, top coat and chosen polish
- a proper extraction ventilation system
- sable brush

Brush care

A sculpting brush to a nail technician should be the same as good quality scissors are to a hairdresser. Some of the top hairdressers can pay hundreds of pounds for the right scissors and a nail technician should always use the best quality brushes to create beautiful nails. The right brush will not only last longer but will perform better when being used. Your brush should be personal to you and never shared. You will personalise the shape of your brush to suit the techniques you prefer working with and if another technician borrows your brush they can undo all of your good work in moments.

When purchasing a new system take these factors into account:

- For liquid and powder use sable brushes.
- For gel you may use a nylon brush.
- Some brushes are tapered, some pointed and some flat – choose which is best for you, everyone works differently.
- Consider the brush size and how much liquid it will hold; this can alter your bead size.

When you first purchase a new brush you will need to carry out basic maintenance, including:

- training your new brush
- cleaning your new brush
- storing your brush

Safety Tip

Never touch the hairs of your brush with your fingers as this could lead to overexposure for you and contaminate the brush with the oils from your fingers.

Training

Like a new hair-cut, your sable brush must be trained to your touch. Before using, dip the hairs into the monomer to saturate them, then glide it through a towel or tissue to taper it. Guide any flared hair back into the taper by continuing to dip the brush into the monomer and guide it back through the towel until trained. Any single hairs that will not reshape should be cut at the base and not plucked.

Technical Tip

If using a nylon brush, follow the same steps for storage, but you may clean the brush with a solvent as this will not damage nylon fibres. A nylon brush should only be wiped with solvent and never soaked as this may destroy the structure of the brush.

Once trained, be careful to protect, store and properly care for your brush to ensure a longer life.

Cleaning

Only ever clean your sable brush in monomer. Never wash in soapy water, acetone or brush cleaner. These substances will dry out the hairs of the brush and make it difficult to use. If the brush clogs, soak it in monomer until the product has softened and then guide the brush through a paper towel using an orange stick for any stubborn particles. Re-shape the brush in monomer, wipe and store correctly.

Storing

Storing your brush safely is very important. If the brush is not stored horizontally or flat the 'old' liquid could contaminate the next set of nails. The barrel of the brush may hold excess liquid if it is not stored and cleaned properly and if you experience any 'yellowing' of the product this is usually the reason why. Your brush should always be in its own container or wrapped in tissue after use. If it is left on a nail desk, or in a drawer with files, it could collect debris that will contaminate your clients' nails.

Safety rules

- Do not touch the cuticle or soft tissue with the brush or product.
- Never use monomer without the polymer.
- Always follow the manufacturer's instructions for application.

Application

This procedure for liquid and powder application is generic and in no way takes the place of specific manufacturer's instructions.

Prepared nail

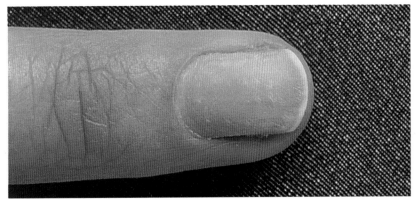

1   Perform steps to prepare the natural nail for nail application.

2   Apply tips, shape and blend.

Shaped and blended tip

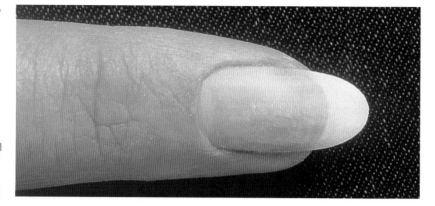

3   Cleanse and dehydrate nails again, on one hand only.

4   Use primer sparingly, if required.

5   Dip the clean brush into liquid and pull up the side of the dappen dish, ensuring the amount of liquid is not excessive.

6   Draw the very tip of the brush through the surface of the powder, drawing a fine line across the surface. The amount of line you draw will determine the size of bead you pick up. You need to decide the size of bead in relation to the surface area you are working on. You may need to alter the amount of liquid in your brush to alter your bead size. Check with your manufacturer what the right consistency or mix ratio is for your chosen product.

Application of white powder in zone 1

7   Make sure all the powder is absorbed into the bead on the tip of the brush before placing it on the nail. If there is excess powder left then it usually means your consistency is too dry.

8   If using white powder place the bead in the centre point of the free edge, halfway between each sidewall and halfway between the flesh line and free edge line. Push

Technical Tip

Remember that the liquid in your brush is activating your bead and if you work your product all the way out to one side first you are likely to get a bump in the other side, or one side will be thicker than the other.

the bead down in the middle, keeping the brush at such an angle that the highest point of the bead stays near the smile line. Press the bead to the left and at the same time nudge the edge of the white into a slight curve (this will start to give you your smile).

9 Take your brush to the left side again and finally push it into the corner, making sure the edge is crisp. Repeat this on the right side. Then bring the brush over the nail at an angle to press the product into a smooth surface. By angling the brush downward it ensures a thin free edge whilst the bulk of the product stays in the apex.

10 Ensure your brush is clean and free from white powder before placing it back into your dappen dish, otherwise your liquid will become cloudy.

11 Repeat steps 5–7, but this time with clear, natural, peach or pink powder. Apply in the centre of the nail just above the smile line but not touching it. Allow it to settle, count to 3, press the brush into the centre and then press the product out to either side. Do not press the product all the way to the sidewall because when you smooth it over it will go onto the skin. Press out to about 4 mm from the sidewall and then draw the brush down over the nail. This will ensure that the product sits nicely on the edge of the nail in the lateral folds, without touching the soft tissue. Draw the brush lightly over the whole surface to give a good contact. Make sure the brush is at a slight angle to give a thinner application nearer the cuticle whilst keeping the bulk of product in the apex area.

Application of white powder in zone 2

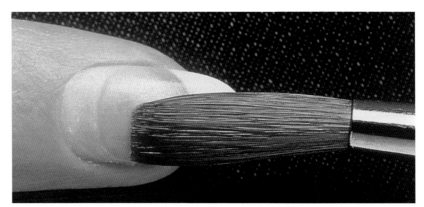

12 Repeat steps 5–7 but with a much smaller bead. Place in the centre of what is left of the exposed natural nail and press the bead in the centre. When pressing the bead nudge it slightly towards the cuticle and then draw the brush back over the product. This will ensure that there is no ridge at the cuticle and will save any heavy filing in a delicate area. Press the bead to either side and smooth over to give even coverage.

Application of white powder in zone 3

13 Finish the surface of the nail first using 240 grit, if needed. Then graduate to white block, or equivalent, and then use a three-way buffer to finish to a high gloss shine.

Finished nail

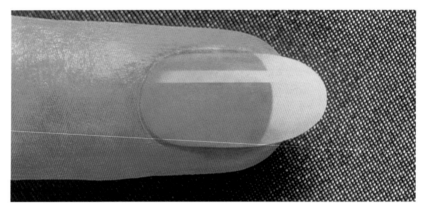

Technical Tip

Check with the manufacturer's instructions as to the curing time of the product before filing and buffing can take place. If you are not sure, tap your brush on the finished nail and if you get a sharp click then it is dry and ready to buff. Check the sidewalls and free edge first for any rough edges.

Aftercare advice for liquid and powder

Every client without exception should be given good sound advice on how to look after and maintain their 'new nails'. The advice is basically the same for all systems and here are all the points you need to take into account when designing a client leaflet for aftercare advice:

- leave only 2–3 weeks between appointments
- ring the salon if any problems occur
- always use non-acetone polish remover
- always use a base coat under a coloured polish
- always use a top coat to keep polish neat and chip free
- book appointments before leaving the salon to avoid disappointment
- contact the salon if any nails are cracked or broken to enable the technician to allow extra time
- wear cotton-lined rubber gloves if using bleach or detergents

- use a cuticle cream or oil daily to keep skin soft and supple
- use a hand lotion daily to keep hands looking good
- treat nails as jewels not tools, do not use them to 'pick'

Remember if you physically give each and every client an aftercare leaflet – be it your own or one you have purchased from a product supplier – you cannot be blamed for not informing them of any of the points above. If clients do have problems at least you know the advice you have given is written in black and white.

Maintenance

The timeframe for a client returning for maintenance on liquid and power is the same as for any other system, so do not believe claims that 'one system lasts longer than any other'. It is always the growth rate of the natural nail that will determine the frequency of maintenance appointments for any nail system. It is important to have your client's record card ready when they arrive so that you can assess the growth, how they have coped with their new nails and any damage that may have occurred. Assess the nails, fill out the details on their card and then proceed with the treatment.

The products and equipment needed will be the same as for a new set of nail extensions.

1   Carry out client consultation.
2   Sanitise your own and your client's hands.
3   Carry out any cuticle work.
4   If there are any nails missing, apply tips at this stage.
5   Look at the shape and length first and carry out any correction needed.
6   The length should be taken down, back to the original recommendation you made at the consultation on the client's first visit. If the length is not shortened, when the client returns for the next maintenance treatment they will have four weeks growth, and by then all your recommendations for treatment will have changed. The client may request the length be left, if this is the case you must note this on the client record card. If the client makes this request on a few visits he or she may experience problems. The client will probably only remember they have problems with lifting, cracking or loss now and they will not remember that it is they who changed the client agreement you made at the original consultation.
7   Take a 240 grit file and gently file down the side walls to straighten.

Safety Tip

Never use nippers to take away lifted product, as this will lift product that is bonded to the natural nail and only take the lift further back down the nail.

Technical Tip

Always file into good product that is adhered to the natural nail plate just above the lifted area, then the lifted area will flake away. If you file on top of the lifting you will only increase the lifting up the nail plate.

8 Thin down the free edge with a 240 grit file at a 45° angle. Remember, if you are replacing a white French manicure overlay you will need to remove most of the last application of product in this area. If not, just thin the area slightly. Thin down or remove the bulk of the product, remembering that the stress area has moved up the nail towards the free edge. Redefine this as **zone two** – the new stress area.

9 Working very carefully, buff the product in **zone three**, the cuticle area, so that you cannot see the seam where the natural nail has grown. If there is any lifting you will need to correct this before applying any new product and careful buffing should be performed without damaging the health of the natural nail.

10 Make sure the nail is free from dust and use a nail dehydrator to cleanse the new growth area.

11 If you are not performing a backfill go to step 13. If you are performing a backfill (redefining the French manicure look) apply a small bead of product to zone one and create your new smile line, being sure to push product into the corners of the sidewalls.

12 Place a second bead of product into the centre of zone two, pushing the product to the sidewalls and then over zone three towards the cuticle. Depending on your product control, this can be achieved in one or two beads.

13 If not backfilling place a small bead into the centre of zone two and press to the sidewalls, pulling a thin coating of product to the free edge. Place a second bead of product into the centre just below zone two and then pushing over zone three towards the cuticle. Make sure to press the product down at the cuticle, this will help prevent lifting.

14 File and oil buff all ten nails to a shine.

15 Ask client to wash his or her hands to remove excess oil and dust.

16 Polish if required.

17 Remind your client about aftercare advice.

18 Book next appointment.

The fibreglass (silk) system

All nail systems have their roots in the family of acrylics and the fibreglass system is no exception. Unlike natural fabrics such as silk, cotton and linen, which soak up resin, fibreglass retains its integrity and adds flexibility and strength to the resin. Fibreglass systems use a wrap and a resin:

- Fibreglass mesh is the 'fabric' or wrap used in this system and provides flexibility and strength.
- Ethyl cyanoacrylate is the 'resin', or liquid adhesive, used in all wrap systems. The liquid encases the fabric and has little strength without it.

Wraps and resins vary greatly from one supplier to another and you will need to test a number of products before investing in any wrap system. As before, ask product suppliers for a demonstration or a trial sample.

Fibreglass fabric can be clear, white or pink and can be purchased in strips or a dispenser box. A dispenser is a good idea: it keeps the fabric free of dusty filings and also reduces handling by oily fingers. Contamination by oily fingers will create a barrier to the resin and it will be difficult to make the fibre disappear. Fabrics are available in different densities, those that are more loosely woven provide less strength. Some fabrics have an adhesive backing which make them easier to apply, but if the adhesive on the back is too sticky it will make it difficult for the technician to handle and it will be harder to make the fabric 'disappear' when the resin is applied.

The quality of resins will vary from supplier to supplier. Resins are cured or dried by an activator which speeds up the drying time. Resins will also vary in viscosity (thickness) and there are some that will yellow very quickly as they age – you will also find that these resins will become brittle and be liable to break easily. Try to use a resin that is of a medium viscosity and is non-yellowing.

Advantages of this system

- nail extensions are flexible, thin and natural-looking
- it is a versatile system for repairs or overlay of the natural nail
- it is easy and quick to remove with little or no damage to the natural nail

Disadvantages of this system

- it is difficult to correct irregular natural nail shapes
- the product ages more quickly than other systems
- a spray activator can cause respiratory problems, so masks may have to be worn
- spray activators can also cause problems for clients with sensitive skin
- cyanoacrylate resin vapours can cause eye problems
- it is time consuming when learning

Tools and equipment required

- sanitiser
- hard surface disinfectant
- sterilised tools
- towels
- disposables
- cuticle oil
- tips
- adhesive
- files and buffers
- nail preparation products
- fibreglass or silk
- sharp, small scissors
- resin (brush-on or nozzle and applicator)
- activator or accelerator (spray or brush-on)
- base coat, top coat and chosen polish

Safety rules

- Do not touch fabric with your fingertips, otherwise it will not 'disappear' when the resin is applied.
- Make sure the fabric or resin does not touch the skin.
- Spray the activator from at least 40–45 cm away from the hand, otherwise your client may have a severe heat reaction.
- When spraying activator always spray down towards the hand and not near the face.
- Use a proper extraction ventilation system.
- Always follow the manufacturer's instructions for application.

Application as an overlay on tips

This system is easy to master but may seem fiddly for a beginner. A spray or brush-on activator may be used depending on your own preference; they are equally effective. This system contains three main components:

- the resin
- the fabric – fibreglass
- the activator or accelerator – spray or brush-on

The same general advice applies: always check with your supplier and follow the manufacturer's instructions for specific application procedures. The procedure described here for fibreglass application is generic and in no way takes the place of specific manufacturer's instructions.

1 Carry out an in-depth client consultation.
2 Sanitise your own and your client's hands.
3 Carry out the following preparation steps on the natural nail:

  – clean cuticle area

  – remove any surface shine from the natural nail

  – use a dehydrator to cleanse and remove any moisture

4 Holding each finger in turn and at a slightly downward angle, apply a thin layer of resin over the entire surface of the nail plate. Remember always to leave a tiny free margin around the cuticle and sidewalls.

  – always hold the resin bottle horizontally so that the flow of resin can be controlled

  – always spread the resin over the nail with the side of the nozzle

Basing the nail with resin

5 Activate the resin by spraying activator over all ten nails:

  – position client's hands so that the fingers are inverted and over the palms of the hands, nearly clenched

  – spray at least 40–45 cm away from hands

Tip application

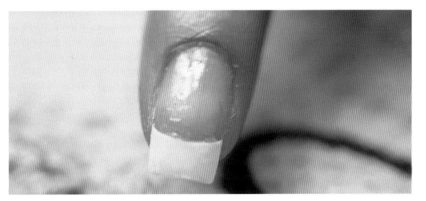

6 Apply shape and blend tips to all ten nails.

7 Cut fibreglass to match cuticle and sidewalls and press onto all ten nails:

- do not touch fabric with fingers, use paper and scissors to place in position
- press the fabric firmly into position with paper or a lint-free pad
- leave a small free margin around the cuticle and sidewalls

Application of fibreglass

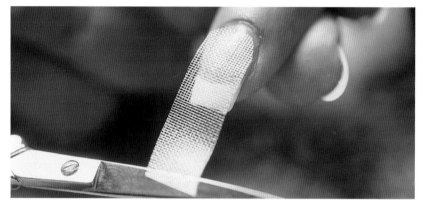

Fibreglass cut to shape

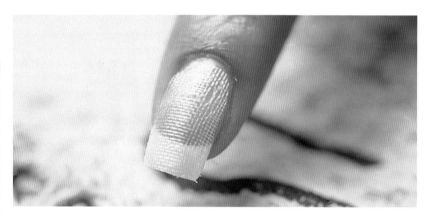

Technical Tip

If a client wants a longer length or is particularly hard wearing on his or her nails, place a 'stress' strip across the stress line. This will add a little more strength.

Application of stress strip

Stress strip cut to shape

8 Gently apply a coat of resin, being careful not to drag the fabric away from the nail. Place the resin, using the nozzle, in a line down the centre of the nail and then glide from side to side, ensuring all the fabric is sealed and has disappeared.

Application of resin

9 Mist the activator over each inverted hand.
10 Apply another thin coat of resin to all ten nails.
11 Mist the activator over each inverted hand.
12 If the nails need buffing at all do it at this stage and clean off any dust.

Buffing nails

13 Apply another thin coat of resin to all ten nails.

Application of final coat of resin

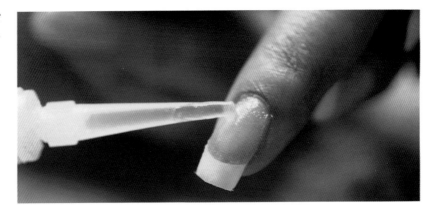

14 Mist activator over both hands.

15 Finish off nails by buffing to shape and then to a high shine.

Finished nail

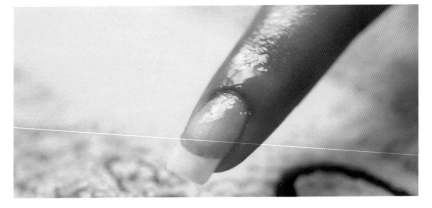

16 Ask your client to wash his or her hands to remove excess oil and dust.

17 Polish if client wishes.

Technical Tip

If using a brush-on resin you should activate after the application of all the layers of resin, or you will risk activating the whole bottle of resin when replacing the brush. Clean the brush before returning it to the bottle of resin and this should reduce the possibility of contaminating the resin.

Maintenance

Fibreglass nails should be maintained roughly every 2–4 weeks, but this will obviously depend on the growth rate of your client's nails and how he or she looks after them during that time. Although initially it seems quite time consuming to apply fibreglass extensions, once you have had a lot of practice you will find it as easy as any other system. The maintenance is basically the same as for the other systems and should take around the same amount of time. Obviously if there are problems, such as lifting, then it will take slightly longer.

1 Carry out a client consultation and look to see if there have been any problems since you last saw your client. If there have analyse why and use corrective methods.

2 Sanitise your own and your client's hands.

3 Carry out any cuticle work that needs doing.

4 If there are any nails missing apply tips at this stage.

5 Look at the shape and length and carry out any correction needed.

6 Take a 240 grit file and gently buff the surface shine from the surface of the entire nail extension. Then, working very carefully, buff the product in zone three, the cuticle area, so that you cannot see the seam where the natural nail has grown. If there is any lifting you will need to correct this before applying new product and careful buffing should be performed without damaging the health of the natural nail.

7 Cleanse and dehydrate the new growth area.

8 Apply a thin coat of resin to all ten nails and mist with activator.

9 Apply a thin strip of fabric in the new growth area on all 10 nails.

10 Apply a thin coat of resin to the new growth area making sure the nozzle does not drag the fabric away from the nail.

11 Mist activator over all 10 nails.

12 Apply another thin coat of resin over all 10 nails.

13 Mist activator over all 10 nails.

14 Buff nails and finish to a high gloss.

15 Ask your client to wash his or her hands to remove excess oil and dust.

16 Polish if required.

Aftercare advice for fibreglass

Remember that aftercare advice is vitally important so that your clients can look after their new nails between appointments. This means there will be less work for you to perform on rebalance treatments.

- Leave only 2–3 weeks between maintenance appointments.
- Ring the salon if any problems occur.
- Always use non-acetone polish remover.

- Always use a base and top coat.
- Always use a cuticle cream or oil.
- Keep rebalance appointments.
- Contact the salon if extra time is likely to be needed for maintenance appointment.
- Use hand creams or lotions daily.
- Take extra care with fibreglass nails as they are not quite as resistant to knocking and banging.
- Treat nails as jewels not tools!

The UV gel system

The UV gel system is a pre-mixed product that comes ready to use by the nail technician. It is only one material rather than a mixture and usually has to be cured with a UV light machine. The differences in the various gels on the market are:

- their viscosity (the thickness)
- whether they are clear or coloured

All gels are from the acrylic family and are based on both the methacrylate and acrylate families. They share the same properties as the liquid and powder system. All gels are made from oligomers which are short, pre-joined chains of molecules that are neither monomers nor polymers. Nail extension products that are liquid are called monomers and the powders or solids are called polymers. Gels do not fall into either category, which is why they are called oligomers. Gels have a thick consistency and the higher the thickness or viscosity of a gel the lower the evaporation and odour levels.

UV light must penetrate completely through the gel for it to polymerise or cure all of the oligomers properly. Unless the UV light is very powerful, care must be taken not to apply too thick a coat of gel. If there is any residue of uncured product left on the nail it could lead to an allergic reaction.

It is always a good idea before investing in a gel system to try out the products first. This will allow you to see how they look and how long they last. A good product will not only look good on application but will still look as good when a client returns for a rebalance. You will also need to take into account the fact that some gels can produce tremendous heat while there are some that are classed as 'cool' gels. Being familiar with your chosen system and the products that you are working with can save time and help to prevent problems

Advantages

- it is very easy to apply
- gels are very low odour, which some clients may prefer
- gels can be slightly more flexible than other systems, but not necessarily
- there is always a permanent high gloss shine on finishing
- they can look very natural if applied properly.

Disadvantages

- good ventilation must still be used – remember that low odour products are no safer to use than those having a high odour
- gels are not as strong as liquid and powder
- they are not as easy to remove and repair if they crack or break as other systems
- a complete cure is necessary or overexposure can occur
- gels carry a higher risk of allergic reaction due to their sticky heavy consistency; never allow product to touch the skin
- some gels can create a 'heat' sensation on curing under UV light

Tools and equipment required

- sanitiser
- hard surface disinfectant
- sterilised tools
- towels
- disposables
- cuticle oil
- tips
- adhesive
- files and buffers
- nail preparation products
- primer, if required
- UV gel
- gel brush
- UV lamp
- base coat, top coat and chosen polish

All three systems, including gel, are safe to use as long as all the manufacturers' instructions are used and safety rules deployed. If a nail technician is suffering from an allergy or any other health problem which they believe to be work-related, it is probable that they have developed bad habits and need to look at the way they are working – before they cannot work at all!

Safety rules

- always keep UV lamps in good condition
- change UV bulbs every 6–12 months – check this time limit with the manufacturer
- always use your supplier's recommended curing time for the gel
- use thin rather than thick coats of gel
- keep products where they belong, on the nail plate only
- practise good housekeeping and careful sanitation and sterilisation
- keep dust and vapours to a minimum by good application techniques
- always use extraction ventilation to clean dust and vapours from the working area
- always follow manufacturer's instructions strictly for product application

Application

There are many gel systems that you can use and we cannot possibly give you instructions on how to apply all of them in this chapter. You *must* follow the manufacturer's instructions for application and you will find these will differ from company to company. Some product companies will have just one gel, whilst others might have produced a three-phase system including a base, a builder and a top coat gel. There are others that claim they sell gels that are not acrylic – but remember all gels are acrylic. Ask for a demonstration or a trial kit before investing large sums of money in a whole system.

This procedure for the application of gel is generic and in no way takes the place of specific manufacturer's instructions.

1 Carry out an in-depth client consultation.
2 Sanitise your own and your client's hands.
3 Carry out the following preparation steps on the natural nail
   – clean cuticle area
   – remove any surface shine from the natural nail

– use a dehydrator to cleanse and remove any moisture

4 Apply tips to all ten nails.

5 Take up a small bead of gel on the tip of a sculpting brush and apply it to the centre of the nail. Work the bead over the nail surface in small circular movements covering the whole nail but maintaining a small margin around the cuticle and sidewalls. Complete on the four fingers of one hand, cure and then repeat on the four fingers of other hand. Once the fingers have been done, repeat the process on the two thumbs and cure under a lamp.

6 If a white tip is required for a 'French' nail, then use a white sculpting gel and apply to the free edge of the tip, working into a smile line along the natural nail smile line. Follow the same process as in item 5.

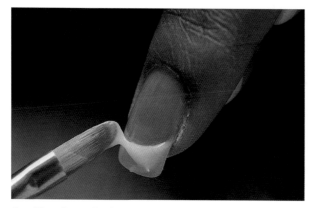

Application of white gel in zone 1

Application of white gel in zones 2 and 3

7 Using a sculpting brush, take up a slightly larger bead and place it in the middle of the stress area. Gently draw the bead down to cover the tip first, leaving the bulk of the gel in the centre of the nail. Then gently draw the bead back up to the cuticle and work over the top part of the nail, leaving the bulk of gel in the centre, or stress area, for strength. Do four fingers and cure, then repeat the process on the four fingers of the other hand and finally repeat on the thumbs.

8 You may need to wipe residue from the surface of the nail with an appropriate cleanser at this stage before buffing.

9 Shape nails with a high grit file and buff with a white block.

10 Use cleanser to remove any dust caused by filing.

11 Apply a small bead of finishing gel to the centre of the nail and float over the entire surface. Cure for 1–2 minutes. Use the same process as above: four fingers, the other four fingers, then the two thumbs.

Safety Tips

- Make sure you cure for at least 2 minutes.
- Leave a small margin around product and do not allow it to touch the skin.

Finishing nails in lamp

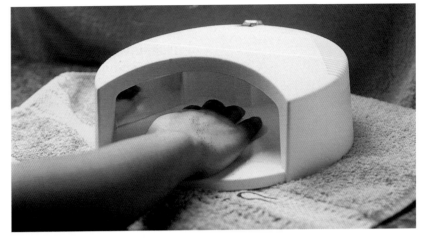

Maintenance

The timeframe for a client returning for maintenance on gel nails is the same as any other system, so do not believe claims that 'one system lasts longer than any other'. It is always the growth rate of the natural nail that will determine the frequency of maintenance appointments for any nail system. It is important to have your client's record card ready when they arrive so that you can assess the growth, how they have coped with their new nails and any damage that may have occurred. Assess the nails, fill out the details on their card and then proceed with the treatment.

The products and equipment needed will be the same as for a new set of nail extensions.

1   Carry out an in-depth client consultation.

2   Sanitise your own and your client's hands.

3   Carry out any cuticle work that needs doing.

4   If there are any nails missing apply tips at this stage.

5   Look at the shape and length first and carry out any correction needed. A client may need the length taken down or decide that they do not like the square look and want the corners softened.

6   Take a 240 grit file and gently buff the surface shine from the surface of the nail extension. Then working very carefully buff the product in zone three, the cuticle area, so that you cannot see the seam where the natural nail has grown. If there is any lifting you will need to correct this before applying new product and careful buffing should be performed without damaging the health of the natural nail.

7   Make sure the nail is free from dust and use a nail dehydrator to cleanse new growth area.

Safety Tip

Never use nippers to take away lifted product as this will lift product that is bonded to the natural nail and only take the lift further back down the nail.

8 Apply a small bead of product to the centre of the new growth area and push up to the cuticle. Then draw down over the exposed natural nail to meet the existing product. Be careful to leave a small margin and do not allow product to touch the skin. Apply to four nails and cure, repeat on the other four fingernails, repeat on thumbs.

9 Apply a small bead of builder gel and repeat item 8.

10 Clean off residue and buff if necessary.

11 Apply a final bead of product and draw down over the whole nail to ensure a final shine. Cure and wipe off residue.

12 Polish if required.

Aftercare advice for gel

Every client should be given good sound advice on how to look after their 'new nails'. The advice is basically the same for all systems and here are all the points you need to take into account when designing a client leaflet for aftercare advice:

- leave only 2–3 weeks between maintenance appointments
- ring the salon if any problems occur
- always use non-acetone polish remover
- always use a base coat under a coloured polish
- always use a top coat to keep polish neat and chip free
- make an appointment before leaving the salon to avoid disappointment
- ring the salon if any nails are cracked or broken to enable the nail technician to allow extra time
- wear cotton-lined rubber gloves if using bleach or detergents
- use a cuticle cream or oil daily to keep skin soft and supple
- use a hand lotion daily to keep hands looking good
- treat nails as jewels not tools, do not use them to 'pick'

Remember if you physically give each and every client an aftercare leaflet – be it your own or one you have purchased from a product supplier – you cannot be blamed for not informing them of any of the points above. If clients do have problems at least you know the advice you have given is written in black and white.

Toenail application step by step

Many clients now request toenail extensions and it is not unusual for just the large toenails to be extended or covered after an operation for in-grown toenails. This should only proceed after healing has taken place and new growth is established. Toenails may be extended or overlaid for any of the following reasons:

- deep ridges in the toenails
- permanent damage to toenails
- misshapen toenails
- thin or weak toenails
- toenail picking or accidental damage

Tools and equipment required for all toenail extensions

- sanitiser
- hard surface disinfectant
- sterilised tools
- disposable towels
- towels
- cuticle oil
- files and buffers
- nail preparation products
- primer, if required
- liquid and powder system
- dappen dish
- base coat, top coat and chosen polish
- a proper extraction ventilation system
- sable brush
- UV lamp if using a UV gel system

Application

1. Prepare area for treatment.
2. Perform client consultation.
3. Prepare treatment plan and obtain client's signature.
4. Sanitise technician and client.
5. Check client for contra indications (skin and nail disorders).
6. Remove polish.

Technical Tip

Tip application on toenails is not always successful, especially on the large toe because of its size. Sculpting is much more successful but requires more skill. You should consider carefully which system to use.

- A fibreglass system would probably not be suitable as the large toe usually requires sculpting techniques.
- A UV gel system is suitable for toenail application. Use a good sculpting gel or builder gel for the best results. If purchasing a UV lamp for this purpose consider its height, size and shape as you may need to raise the foot with a towel so the client is not balancing their foot in the lamp.
- Liquid and powder systems are suitable for toenail extensions.

Technical Tip

If applying extensions and performing a pedicure ensure the toenail is completely dehydrated before application of product.

Technical Tip

If applying a sculpting form to the large toe, you may need to cut two paper forms and join them together:

- cut the first form by reducing the left-hand side

- cut the second form by reducing the right-hand side

- peel off the backing and join them together, making the join in the centre smooth and even with a pair of scissors

- fit in the usual way

7 Apply cuticle cream to all ten nails.

8 File and shape all ten nails.

9 Perform preparation on nails to be extended:
  – push back cuticles
  – remove surface shine
  – apply natural nail cleanser

10 Apply primer if necessary.

11 Fit sculpting form to the toe and secure. Fit only one form at a time as this will prevent the form moving accidentally. Then proceed with product application and repeat the process on the next toe.

12 Apply product to the sculpting form and the free edge of the nail in zone one. Remember not to extend too far or too thickly as this will cause the client pain when wearing shoes.

13 Apply product to zone two, press to the sidewalls and push up to the beginning of zone three, pressing as thinly as possible.

14 If necessary apply to zone three, remembering that this area should match the natural nail completely.

15 Remove sculpting form, file, buff and finish as per manufacturer's instructions.

Maintenance

If the overlay is very thin, regular pedicures by the technician to shorten and thin the toenail will make it possible to grow the nail extension off. However, if the client's toenail is damaged and the overlay is there to camouflage or disguise a shape or disorder, the client will need to have regular maintenance appointments.

Aftercare

Aftercare is the same as for regular fingernail extensions.

Sculpting techniques

It is very difficult for a complete beginner to grasp the technical skills needed to perform sculpting whilst they are leaning how to apply product. The skill is not only in the product application but also the proper placement of the sculpting form and knowing how to create the correct shape. When using a tip the outline of the nail is easily created, but when sculpting on a form you need to be more creative.

In this section we will look at:

- the advantages of sculpting
- the various types of forms

- the structural points of a good sculpted nail extension
- the nail systems and sculpting
- step-by-step sculpting
- points to look out for when maintaining sculptured nails

To be able to complete Unit 19 of the Level III Beauty **NVQ** you will have to prove to an assessor that you can perform a competent sculpting treatment.

Sculpting can be a big time-saver in the salon and there are many advantages:

- it saves time as there is no tip blending
- it is easy and quick to replace one nail and match the natural nail shape during a manicure
- sculpting techniques are the only way to successfully extend claw nails
- if a corner is missing when performing a maintenance treatment it is possible to thin down and sculpt, instead of soaking the nail tip off
- if the free edge of a nail tip has broken it can be sculpted back on instead of having to remove and then replace the whole extension
- sculpting saves shortening the client's natural nail length when they wish to grow their own nails
- sculpting is a more cost effective treatment as tips can be expensive.

Sculpting forms

There are various sculpting forms that can make it easy to create beautiful nail extensions. The material used for various forms can be:

- metal
- teflon-coated
- plastic
- paper

Metal forms

Metal forms are cost effective because they can be sanitised and re-used again and again. They need to be carefully shaped before fitting to the natural nail as it is difficult to achieve a good shape once they are placed on the finger. Metal conducts heat so these forms are not suitable if sculpting with UV gel. Heat can also be caused if the mix ratio of liquid and powder is too wet.

Forms

Teflon-coated forms

Teflon-coated forms are more expensive but can still be cost effective as they are also re-usable. Another advantage is that they grip the side of the finger and keep the form in place. However, they have metal sides which will conduct heat.

Plastic forms

Plastic forms can also be re-used and sanitised. Some are available in various sizes and shapes to match different fingernail shapes. This is advantageous, but it can be time consuming to fit each individual form until you become used to the various sizes.

Paper forms

Paper forms are probably the most widely used and versatile form that a technician can use. They can only be used once,

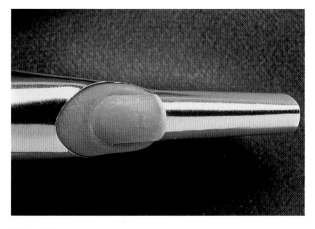

Metal forms

Plastic forms

Paper forms

Customising paper forms

but come in various shapes that can be cut to fit and suit all nail shapes. Some have tabs that can be joined together to keep the form in place whilst working. Two forms can be cut and joined together for extra large nails. Paper forms are the easiest to use on toenails.

The structural points of a good sculpted nail extension

You should not be able to tell the difference between a sculpted nail and one that has a tip and overlay. They should both have the same characteristics. There are clients who can wear sculpted nails successfully and those whom you would never attempt to sculpt on.

Suitable clients

You can apply sculpted techniques to clients

- with a low level lifestyle who do not perform any heavy work
- who have a long natural nail bed that is in good condition
- who suffer from a hook, or claw, nail shape, as sculpting can correct the hook
- who want to match one odd broken nail to their others
- who have a chipped or broken nail, which is easy to correct with a form

Unsuitable clients

You would not attempt to sculpt on clients with

- a flat nail shape, as it is difficult to create an arch or apex without making the nail too thick

- a ski jump nail shape, as it is practically impossible to correct this with a sculpting form
- bitten nails, as the bulbous skin at the end of the nail plate will push the sculpting form into an unnatural position
- a crooked nail plate or where the sidewall of the natural nail plate is missing – this would be hard to correct with a form and tips are much more suitable for this
- thin or natural nail plates which are in bad condition; nail extensions are like houses – they need a good foundation to build on

The nail systems and sculpting

Sculpting techniques can be achieved using all systems, with varying degrees of success.

Points to consider when using fibreglass

Fibreglass can be used as a sculpting material but a number of factors must be taken into consideration, such as the curve and the strength of the natural nail. A weak, flat nail will give the nail technician all kinds of problems with shape and strength. This client would not be a good candidate for sculpting in this medium.

Fibreglass could not be extended much further than the natural nail for the following reasons:

- it is very unlikely that all ten nails will remain the same shape after they have been activated
- it would be very difficult to maintain the original structure after several maintenance appointments, because resin is prone to dry out and become brittle with age
- it is difficult to build a strong structure with this medium without the help of a tip so they will not last well

Points to consider when using UV gel

Gels can successfully be used to sculpt nail extensions, but care must be taken when placing into the lamp to avoid the forms being dislodged. The following points should be considered:

- A builder gel is essential to give the strength and support that the tip would normally give to the nail structure.
- If a builder gel is not available you could use fibreglass to reinforce the structure.

- After curing the form needs to be removed and the nails cured again from the underside.
- Ensure that the finished nail has all the correct structural points to maintain strength and durability.

Points to consider when using liquid and powder

This is the most popular and effective system to use as a sculpting medium. If properly applied it offers strength and wearability for your clients.

- It is the easiest system to use for sculpting.
- It is easier to build in the shape and structure.
- It is easy to correct chips or breaks when maintaining the nail extensions.
- Working on a form will give more time to create nail shape than when working on a tip as the form will not give out as much heat, so the setting time is slightly slower. This allows more time to create a beautiful smile line.

Step-by-step sculpting

When creating sculpted nails on a client the following stages are the same for all systems:

- client consultation
- preparation of the natural nail
- fitting of the form

The client consultation and the preparation of the natural nail have been discussed in detail elsewhere in this book, but it is worth looking at the fitting of the form a little more closely.

Fitting the form

Whichever form you choose to use – and you will need to try a number before choosing the one you are happiest with – it has to fit perfectly under the small free edge of the natural nail. An experienced technician will keep a selection of different shapes or types of sculpting form in stock.

Fitting a form can appear to be a daunting task for those who have never tried it before. Practise with cheaper paper forms on a hand trainer and you will find that you soon feel comfortable. Bear in mind the following points when fitting the form:

- With the exception of a metal form, you will need to create a 'C' curve. To do this, hold the form between the thumb and forefingers and bend to shape whilst placing it under the free edge.

- Take the form in at a slight angle and push it up under the natural nail free edge to match the natural nail's 'C' curve. This will ensure there is no seepage of the product on the underside of the nail. A leak could create a uncomfortable shelf on the underside of the sculpted nail.

- If the form has sticky tabs, make sure they are attached under the finger to keep the form in place.

- Only fit one form at a time and perform the sculpting before moving onto the next finger. If you try to fit all five forms at once one of them could be dislodged, creating a misshapen nail.

- If a metal form is to be used, you can shape with a wooden dowel or pencil to create the 'C' curve. Be aware that the 'C' curve is not the same, even on the thumb and fingers of one hand, so you may need different sizes of dowels.

- A metal form needs to be placed under the free edge and pinched into the sides to hold it secure. Sculpting should be performed immediately after fitting whilst holding the form in place.

The steps below describe a basic procedure for performing a sculpted nail and in no way replace any specific manufacturer's instructions for application. The system we have chosen for this sculpting demonstration is liquid and powder.

1 Carry out an in-depth client consultation.
2 Sanitise your own and your client's hands.
3 Prepare the nail plate.
4 Fit a sculpting form to one finger at a time.
5 Apply a white bead of product to zone one (free edge), in the centre.

Technical Tip

To create a perfect smile line, make three large presses to evenly distribute the product out to the sidewalls and then make tiny presses along the smile line to create a clean sharp edge.

Application of white bead in zone 1

6 Press the bead into the centre or apex, and then press out to the side and nudge up to the sidewall; repeat on other side. Use the side of the brush to create the lower arch and repeat on the other side.

7 Apply a second bead of natural colour product to zone two (apex). Press in the centre and then to either side, ensuring no product touches the skin. Then smooth over to meet zone one.

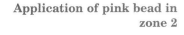

Application of pink bead in zone 2

Application of pink bead in zone 3

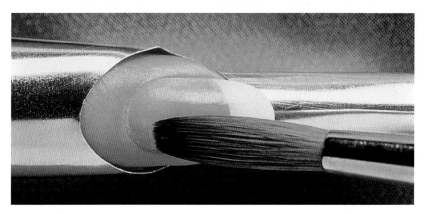

8 Apply a final bead of product to zone three (cuticle area).

9 Repeat on all ten nails.

10 Pinch the form to release the product and pull away gently, ensuring there is no discomfort for the client.

11 File and buff the surface of the nail to a high shine.

12 Ask your client to wash his or her hands and polish if required.

When using a new product your supplier should always offer training in sculpting techniques so that you will be able to use their products to their maximum potential.

The procedure for sculpted nail extensions is the same maintenance as for the system used.

Finished nails

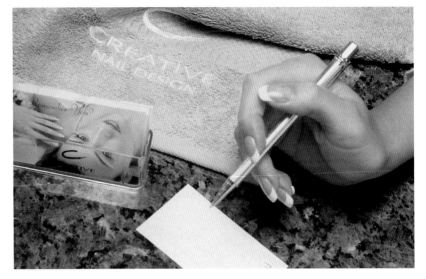

Removal techniques for nail extensions

Learning objectives

In this section you will learn about:

- **the chemicals involved in the removal of nail extensions**

- **safety tips**

- **removal procedures**

The removal of nail extensions should only be performed if a client no longer wishes to keep the nail extensions. A client who has their nail extensions correctly maintained can keep them on for a few years without needing to change or renew the product. If a client is constantly having new sets of nail extensions applied it will damage the health of their natural nail and could lead to a number of other problems. We work in an industry that is totally chemical-based and we need to be aware that those chemicals can affect the natural nail adversely.

The chemicals used in the removal process

Nail extensions can only be soaked off using a **solvent**. Most nail technicians will use a solvent that contains **acetone** as this is the quickest and cheapest way of soaking nail extensions from the natural nail. A solvent will break the bonds between the **polymer** chains and not dissolve the overlay. The stronger these bonds are, the harder it is to soak off the nail extensions.

The easiest system to remove is fibreglass, as this has no cross-linking structures. Cyanoacrylate resin in the fibreglass system has the weakest bonds which makes it much quicker and safer to use than the other two systems. The liquid and powder system is the next easiest to remove, but will take longer and need slightly more buffing. The hardest to remove is UV gel, as the bonds that link the structure are the strongest of all three systems.

Acetone is widely used within the nail industry but it should be used with great care as it has drying properties that could affect your client's natural nail plate and surrounding skin. If a client's nails are continually soaked in acetone they may have an adverse reaction such as splitting, flaking or excessive dehydration of the nail plate. As long as all the safety procedures are taken into account and nails are not soaked too often, then using acetone should have no long-term effect. If a client is suffering from any skin or nail condition this should be taken into consideration before soaking the nails in a solvent.

Safety rules

- Always make sure there is only enough solvent to cover the fingertips in the soak-off bowl.
- Only allow your client to soak for the correct amount of time.
- Never leave a client alone when performing a removal.
- Make sure that the client's clothes are protected.
- Make sure there are no cuts or abrasions in your client's soft tissue before immersing fingertips in solvents.
- If a client is not having nail extensions put back on, make sure the skin, cuticles and natural nails are rehydrated.

You will need to determine at the initial client consultation how long your client wishes to keep their nail extensions on. Take this into account when giving aftercare advice. If a client wants to keep the nails on for a specific event, for example a wedding, then you need to make sure they have sound advice on when to return for the removal. If he or she does not want to return for maintenance your client will need to be made aware of the dangers of not returning to have the nails removed correctly. Make sure you charge accordingly for this service.

Removal procedures

There are two main ways to remove nail extensions safely. Both involve the use of solvents.

This is the main removal procedure used by most technicians.

Technical Tip

The heat will accelerate the removal process by breaking down the bonds. Keep the hot water topped up during the removal and it will save you time.

1 Place two china or glass dishes filled to a depth of approximately 2–3 cm of product remover into two larger dishes of hot water.
2 Before immersing your client's fingers into the product remover, cut back any length and take off any polish.
3 Submerge fingertips into the bowls and cover the hands with a towel to keep the heat in. This will also stop your clients from taking their hands out to look at them.
4 Leave the nails to soak for approximately 20 minutes.
5 Take off the towel, lift one hand out and wipe off excess fluid. Gently remove the product with an orange stick.
6 Repeat on the other hand.
7 Ask the client to wash his or her hands.
8 Check the cuticles and reshape the free edge with a thin file.
9 Reapply nail extensions *or* apply hand cream and polish if required.
10 Advise your client to return for manicures if they are not having nail extensions reapplied.

Technical Tip

If the polish is not taken off before removal you may find a dark colour will stain the natural nail and be difficult to remove. This usually happens if the natural nails are very dry and brittle.

The second method of removal is slightly more time consuming but just as effective. Try both before deciding which one you prefer.

1 Cut back the length of your client's nails and remove any polish.
2 Soak ten balls of cotton wool in product remover and apply to each fingertip, making sure the cotton wool is placed across the whole nail, then wrap in tin foil.
3 The client's hands may then, if you prefer, be put into plastic bags and placed in heated mitts for 20 minutes.
4 Remove one hand at a time and gently remove product with an orange stick.

Technical Tip

When the nails are placed in solvent they become soft and when the nails are taken out of the product remover they will harden. The nails should remain in the solution until all the product has softened otherwise the removal will take much longer.

Then follow steps 7–10 above.

When a client has their nail extensions removed for the first time they will always think that their natural nails seem thinner. Most of the time this is an illusion and is due to the fact they have become used to strong, flexible nail extensions, making their own seem weak by comparison. Gently point this out to your clients if they remark that their nails have been damaged.

Remember, if you have followed your manufacturer's guidelines and all the safety techniques, your clients will have beautiful, strong natural nails even when their nail extensions have been removed.

The Nail Trainer

The only way to become a proficient nail technician is to practise. For many years nail students have been compelled to do all their practice on live models. Although this real-life approach is possibly the best, there are, in fact, several disadvantages to having students begin their learning on a live model, the most obvious being the problems of getting enough practice in the early days. However, there is now a real alternative with the Nail Trainer.

The Nail Trainer

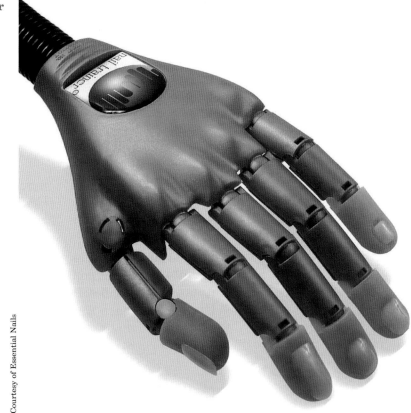

Courtesy of Essential Nails

The Nail Trainer is a lifelike hand that feels like a real person. It has different sizes and shapes of nail plates which match the range of shapes that are required within Unit 19, Level III Beauty NVQ, a rotating wrist joint, a flexible arm to clamp to the work table and fully articulating fingers.

Your work can be removed and kept as a record of achievement and the hand is suitable for all three nail systems in addition to nail art and air brushing.

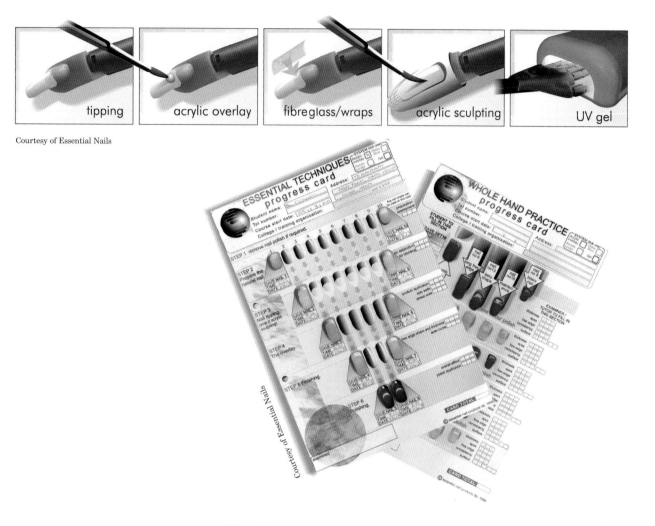

Courtesy of Essential Nails

This doesn't entirely remove the need for human practice. You won't be able to prepare the natural nail plate on the Nail Trainer, as there is no cuticle. In addition, removal techniques, client consultation and aftercare advice also require a living person. However, since it was launched, the level of student drop-out has fallen dramatically while the percentage of trainees finding work easily because their skills have progressed quickly is much higher.

Using drills and electric filing machines

A number of questions surround the use of electric filing machines, for example:

- Do electric filing machines damage nails?

- What type of machines are available?
- What you should look for in a machine?
- How and when can you use the machine?

To drill or not to drill, that is the question! The question of whether it is safe to use a drill when performing nail treatments is probably one of the biggest debates in the industry and most technicians are still very divided over the use of drills. As in every other area of the nail industry, the key is education.

A drill cannot damage a client's nails on its own – it will need an operator to use it to perform any work on a client's hands or feet. If that operator is not trained properly in its use, then a great deal of damage can be done to a client's fingernails or toenails. But then could we not say that of normal hand files and buffers, nippers and nail chemicals? Could all of these, if improperly used, damage our clients' health? Yes they could, so if you are considering using a drill, then make sure that you have proper training in its correct use.

Drills can be used to

- buff down product that has been applied incorrectly
- correct the shape of a nail extension
- cut out a new smile line when performing a backfill
- save time

When considering whether to invest in a drill, ask yourself whether you really need one if your product application is as good as it should be? Perhaps you do not need to perform your treatment any faster? Consider whether your clients are likely to mind you using an electric drill.

Electric drills are mostly used with the liquid and powder system. It is unlikely that a fibreglass user will need to use a drill, partly because it could do a lot of damage to the structure of fibreglass.

There are a number of different types of machine on the market:

- Micro motors – the handpiece contains the motor and the bit holder, whilst the controls are in a separate box.
- Hand-held micro motors – everything is mounted in the handpiece.
- Cable driven – these are meant to be used as craft and hobby tools and are not suitable for the nail industry.
- Belt driven – these are the most old fashioned and

Author Note

We have included this section in the book as many technicians do choose to use a drill and we believe everyone should be given the opportunity to work with the tools of their choice.

tend to be used more in dentistry; they can be off-putting for clients.

If you are thinking of purchasing an electric drill then ask for a demonstration on yourself so you can see the drill being operated by someone who knows how to work it. This is usually a good indication of whether the company selling it to you will give you good training. Consider how it feels and how easy it is to use. Drills can vary in price – do not choose a cheaper model to save money, you must take into account all the safety aspects as well.

When buying a machine you should consider:

- Size – if you are mobile you will need to carry lots of equipment or sometimes work in a restricted space.
- Variable speed – you should be able to adjust the speed to your preference rather than having three settings: low, medium and high.
- Reverse function – this is extremely helpful for left-handed technicians.
- Changing bits – this procedure should be quick and easy and not need extra tools.
- Foot pedals – you may prefer to work this way.
- Running true – this refers to the vibration level and should be tested with the bits fitted.
- Bits – how many come with the drill and how easy is it to replace them.
- Warranty period – are loan machines available while yours is repaired, what maintenance is required and how long repairs take.
- Price – look at your budget and why you feel you need a drill.

Before purchasing a drill look at the bits that come with it and their use. Make sure that you have good instructions or have attended a training course on the way to use the drill effectively and safely.

The following paragraphs describe a few of the areas of the nail that can be worked on with a drill.

Shaping

When shaping a nail extension, make sure the drill is held at the correct angle of 20° to the top of the nail. Work the bit from left to right making sure to lift it off the nail plate at regular intervals. Do not use too coarse a grit as this will only put grooves into the nail surface that you will have to file out again. The edge of the nail should be finished with a nail file and not with the drill, to save your client any discomfort.

Cuticle area

Be extremely careful when working in the cuticle area not to allow the drill to touch any exposed natural nail or the soft tissue along the cuticle or sidewalls. Work the bit from side to side so it the product graduates smoothly into the natural nail.

Filing the sides

Begin by shaping the sides and tip from the top view with a hand-held file. Hold the nail so that you can see it in profile and file with the bit held horizontally to the side of the extended nail until the shape you desire is achieved.

Defining the 'C' curve

To refine the concave and convex curves of the tip, hold the nail looking straight down the barrel and place the bit right up against the underside edge so that the bit touches every part of the edge, thus defining the 'C' curve.

Buffing

Use a chamois buffing bit to finish off the nails to a high shine but make sure that the client's hands have been washed and are free of oil and dust.

Finishing

Be sure to go over the entire nail before switching to a finer bit and then repeat the same steps. Remember that the coarser bits are always used first, graduating to a medium or finer bit to shape and finish.

Backfill

The shorter backfill bits are designed to cut out the area where the white tip has grown out. Using the bit at a 45° angle, cut a new smile line just above the old one. It is important to remember that acrylics that have been on the nail for some time may have aged slightly and discoloured. At least 60–70 per cent of the white should be taken off before applying new product.

To work safely, consider the following points when using a drill.

Heat reaction

Friction is the main cause of heat and pressure is the main cause of friction. Sanding bands will heat up most quickly and you must remember to constantly lift the bit as you work. This will allow the air to cool the nail between each period of contact.

Red rings on the natural nail

These indentations on the natural nail can be caused not only by a drill but also by heavy hand-filing. They are usually only seen on a nail that has been maintained by a heavy-handed technician. When using a drill, it can be caused by the bit being held at the wrong angle and digging into the cuticle area.

Cleaning and sanitising

It is important to remember when using a drill that it is like all your other equipment and needs care, attention and cleaning. The bits should cleaned between each client treatment. The dust should be removed first and then the bits should be soaked in an appropriate cleaning solution and the machinery wiped down. Once the bits have been disinfected they should be stored in a clean, dry container until required.

Speed – RPM

The average speed of nail drills is between 7,000 and 15,000 revolutions per minute (RPM). Never use a drill that has a higher revolution than 15,000 RPM.

If a client has received an injury or experienced discomfort at another salon you will have a hard job persuading them that the drill is safe in your hands. Always let them make the final choice – you may risk losing clients by insisting on using a drill. Drills will not suit all clients, but if your nail skills are excellent you may not need to use it all the time.

Troubleshooting

Learning objective

In this section you will learn about:

- **the correction methods for irregular nail shapes**

No two clients will have the same natural nail shape and some shapes will be more challenging than others. The range of nail shapes that you will need to cover to complete Unit 19, Level III Beauty Therapy NVQ are:

- fan
- claw
- spoon
- severe nail biter

Average   Ski jump   Hook   Bitten   Square   Fan   Oval

Natural nail shapes

The table below will help you to determine which techniques to use when correcting these nail shapes. You may need to see a demonstration of how to perform treatments on these shapes, so ask your trainer or use a video to help you. If you perform the same treatment with the same products and techniques on all of your clients they will return for maintenance treatments with a number of problems. *Remember that prevention is better than cure.*

Corrective methods for problem nail shapes

Nail shape	Solution	Products used
Fan	Trim back natural nail to the free edge line. Match width of free edge of natural nail to deep stop point of tip. File sides of tip to fit snugly into side walls.	Flatten tips with gel adhesive. Overlay with any nail system.
Ski jump or spoon	Trim back natural nail to the free edge line. Cut out the contact area of tip to minimum. Attach at a downward angle checking side view to make sure that the tip curves downwards.	Gentle arched tip with gel adhesive. Overlay with any nail system.
Hook or claw nail	Trim free edge leaving small portion exposed. Apply sculpting form and correct angle of upper arch with product. Using a tip could accentuate the downward curve of the natural nail.	Use sculpting forms, liquid and powder or gel systems.
Nail biter	Use tip with reinforced stress area and sidewalls. Create or cut a saddle in the sidewalls so tip sits flat over skin instead of being forced upwards. Cut out contact area so tip sits on the edge of the natural nail leaving as much nail as possible exposed for the product to give maximum strength. Use a gel adhesive to give greater flexibility and shock absorbency.	Gentle arched tip with gel adhesive. Overlay with any nail system.

Chapter summary

This is a large chapter which has given you a lot of information to absorb. You may find you do not need all this information at once, but over the course of a few years within the industry it will provide useful reference information. For instance, you may initially learn how to perform only one system, but after a few months or years you may learn a second or third. The basics will always be the same, but with technology changing you should always check with your manufacturer for any changes to procedures.

The art of decorating

This chapter covers all types of nail art from basic painting techniques to embedding jewels into acrylic nails. It covers simple hand painting to more advanced pictures that will take a lot more practice. Polishing techniques and buffing nails are an important part of a technician's work and the processes, tools and equipment, and products are all listed in this chapter. Nail art equipment is also covered and step-by-step descriptions of a range of simple designs are included. For those who are more adventurous there are advanced techniques such as airbrushing and 3D work. This chapter will take you through using the equipment, how to keep it clean and the colour theory needed to be able to mix colours and create beautiful designs. There are many airbrushes on today's market and you will need to research which one suits you and your budget before investing your hard-earned cash; there is a guide on the main points to look for in an airbrush system. Working with other materials, such as rhinestones and coloured powders is a relatively new area within the nail industry but we have included a few designs for you to try. You can also go on to experiment with other materials such as lace and colour powders to create new stunning designs. Try to find a company that provides advanced training.

You may not wish to incorporate nail art into the list of treatments you offer to your clientele initially, but you may discover after a short period of time that there is a demand for this treatment and, therefore, want to add it. Use this chapter as a reference point for starting out on your career as an artiste.

In this chapter we will consider the following aspects:

- **finishing techniques**
- **nail art products, tools and equipment**
- **basic nail art**
- **the art of airbrushing**
- **taking nail art to the next dimension**

Finishing techniques

Wedding nails

Learning objectives

In this section you will learn about:

- **using finishing tools to achieve maximum results**
- **buffing the natural nail to a high gloss and shine**
- **achieving that 'no scratch' shine on nail enhancements**
- **achieving a perfect one colour polish, including shading and shaping techniques**
- **achieving a perfect French polish**

Every manicurist or nail technician should be able to finish a treatment using techniques that leave their clients' nails looking as good as possible. The art of finishing is like decorating – do a quick, slapdash finish and cut corners and the result will look bad, will not last, giving you a bad reputation. It is every client's right to have his or her nails finished properly, whether natural or polished.

Finishing tools

The following tools are used in the finishing process:

- files/abrasives
- buffers
- oil
- cotton wool
- orange stick
- enamel remover
- base coat
- enamels and polishes – various colours
- top coat
- quick dry

Safety rules

- Using new files for each client is a good hygienic and safe working practice and will help to cut down the risk of cross-infection.
- Purchase washable files that can be scrubbed and sprayed with a disinfectant between appointments.
- Store in a clean, dry and safe place. You could use an envelope with the client's details on it and clip the client card to the envelope.
- A dusty file will increase your finishing time and create additional work.
- If you accidentally cut your client (usually with a new file) dispose of the file immediately in a sealed bin liner.

Files and abrasives

Never use any file with less than 180 grit as these will be too heavy for a nail enhancement and cause scratches in the surface that will be hard to buff back out. If working on a natural nail you should use nothing less than 240 grit on the nail plate surface unless performing corrective work.

A selection of files

Buffers

There are various buffers that can be used on natural nails and nail enhancements. They fall into two main categories:

● chamois (pronounced *sham-ee*)
● graduated buffer files

There are thousands of different files on today's market. Most product companies recommend their own files as these have been made to complement the products they manufacture. When learning your skills it is usually best to be guided by these recommendations until you have gained more experience and feel able to experiment with others.

Chamois buffers

Due to the rapid advancement of nail technology, there are many good buffers available. If using a chamois buffer, which is the old-fashioned way, you would normally use it with a paste polish. The only drawback with this method is that only a small amount of paste should be used so that the paste polish is not pushed into the cuticle area.

The abrasive qualities of paste polish along with the buffing action smooth the nail surface into a shine and help bind the nail plate layers together at the free edge. This method would not help any serious problems such as psoriasis as the action is too gentle. This buffer is mainly used on natural nails and can be made from a soft suede-like leather or even a soft plastic. It is used not only to buff the natural nail to a high shine but to help smooth out any ridges or corrugations on the surface of the nail. Some manicurists use a pumice paste to help with deeper ridges.

Chamois buffers come in two types. The first has a closed top handle and should be used resting your thumb along the edge of the buffer for support. You may also place the middle and ring fingers through the handle.

Buffing natural nails

If you are buffing a client's natural nail you would only use a buffer and never a low grit file. These are only for use with nail enhancement products. To finish a natural nail to a high shine:

● Clean under free edge with an orange stick to get rid of any dust or creams.
● Wipe the natural nail with a lint-free pad using either polish remover or natural nail cleaner. *Note* – this is called 'squeaking' as it removes oil.
● Position buffer down the nail and not across. Use light movements and buff in one direction from the

A white plastic buffer can be washed and wiped with disinfectant, whereas chamois buffers cannot. This means they are more hygienic and safer to use. Chamois is good for clients to use at home.

Safety Tip

Always make sure when using any files or buffers that a light touch is used. This prevents any stress occurring to the natural nail and the surrounding soft tissue and also helps to prevent RSI.

Point to Remember

Buffing also increases blood flow to the surface area of the natural nail so it aids circulation, bringing important nutrients to the natural nail.

Technical Tip

- Graduated buffers can also be used to gently buff any scratches from stick-on gold nails.

- Spray nails with water before buffing, this can reduce the heat sensation caused by buffing.

- Lift buffer away from the nail to prevent friction.

top of the nail to the bottom and then diagonally in an 'X' motion to ensure the whole nail plate is shiny. Repeat approximately ten to twelve times maximum for each nail.

'X' filing

Graduated buffer files

There are many graduated buffers. Some are two-sided and others will have three sides. One side has fine-grade emery paper and the other an even finer surface to achieve a high gloss shine. Each are on either side of a strong foam which is either in the shape of a block or of a natural nail file. Some manufacturers use fabric instead of emery paper. The choice is up to you, they all do the same job.

As with most tools, the more you pay, the better quality the tools will be, in most cases. You may find more expensive files last longer. Keep a note, if using new files, how long they lasted compared to your existing ones. If buffing a natural nail you may find, if there are no problems, that you will not need to use the emery side of the buffer. The coarser side should only be used to:

- gently buff down the ridge between nail product and the natural nail
- gently buff any ridges in the natural nail
- smooth a nail plate pitted with psoriasis or dermatitis
- smooth flaky edges of a natural nail
- remove any yellowing or surface-staining of natural nails
- remove any excess adhesive or nail product without damaging the natural nail

Graduated buffers are more popular now than old-fashioned chamois buffers because they are usually cheaper and can be disposed of more often. Also there is no need to use messy paste polishes.

Buffing techniques for nail enhancements

The nail system you are using will depend on what files and abrasives you may use. A good nail technician should be able to create a beautiful nail with the minimum of filing. Not only does this cut down on time but it is safer and creates stronger nail enhancements. One of the hardest processes to learn when first starting out as a nail technician is not only how to use a file but how to hold it comfortably.

Here are a few tips on how to hold your file, if you do not find these comfortable don't worry. There is no right or wrong way. Do what is most comfortable for you. Watch other, more experienced technicians to see how they work with their files.

- Always hold the end third of your file which allows you a larger surface area to work longer, smoother and firmer strokes.
- Hold the client's hand from underneath so you can see where you are filing. This also allows a firmer grip so your client's finger is not moving from side to side.
- Use the base of your thumb as a guide of where to file. This will keep the file steady.
- Use your thumb against the client's nail plate whilst filing to reduce stress to the client's nail.
- Always keep files moving and never file in just one spot.
- Do not touch your client's skin with your abrasives. Hold the lateral nail walls away as you are buffing and protect the cuticle area with your thumb when working around that area.
- Use a thinner board for refining product around cuticles and sidewalls.
- Avoid over-filing as this can cause friction burns or even onycholysis (nail plate separation).

You will need to look at your nail enhancement from its top view, side view and down the barrel (or 'C' curve) to decide how much filing needs to be done.

Analyse where you need to file any bulk away first as this area will need more buffing than others. Always use a rounded motion to give gentle curves in the correct places.

- Don't be afraid to turn your client's fingers into your line of vision rather than turn your body.
- Use a good lamp so that you can see the highlight on the nail and determine any flat spots or scratches.

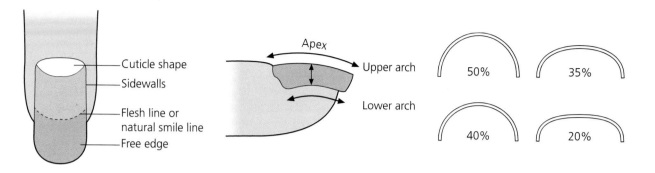

Nail – top view, side view, barrel view

- 'X' file to be sure finishing is even from side to side.
- Check each nail from every angle.
- Check length is even from nail to nail.

Once you have refined the shape so that the nail is thin in zones one and three (cuticle and free edge) but thickest in zone two (apex or where the flesh line is visible) you can then go on to do the surface refinement. Using a high grit file or buffer – a white block is most popular – buff the surface of the entire nail so it looks even in colour with no scratches. Use a shiny buffer to bring the surface of the nail to a high shine.

Now you are ready to decorate your client's nails, if that is their choice, onto the most beautiful, well balanced, enhancement. Check the highlight under your lamp. It should be a continuous straight line all the way down the nail.

Oils

There are many oils on the market and most reputable nail companies market oils as a retail item. If you are using oil on your client within the treatment it gives you the opportunity to talk about home care and the retail products every client needs. Oils can be used to help dry, split cuticles and also help to dry polish.

Put a thin layer of oil over the entire nail surface once the nails are 'touch dry'. Leave your client for 5 minutes by which time the nails should be dry and all the oil absorbed into the surrounding soft tissue. A good example to give a client on why they should use oil is to ask: 'How many times do you wash your hands in one day? Would you wash your hair or face as many times and not use conditioners or moisturisers?'

Make sure you use a good grade of oil that will absorb into the nail enhancement and soft tissue and not a cheap

Technical Note

Make sure you use 'X' filing to ensure the sidewalls and cuticle area are not dull, but are as shiny as the rest of the nail. Ask your client to wash his or her hands to eliminate dust and apply oil if polish is not required. Massage the oil into the nail, cuticle and under the free edge to take any dryness away from the soft tissue.

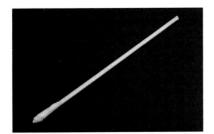

Cotton wool tipped orange stick

mineral oil that will just sit on the surface and do nothing. Check with the manufacturer what the key ingredients are in all products you are using, including oils. Oils can be referred to as fats and may have been extracted from animal or plant sources. Like all organic products, that is those derived from living matter (e.g. apples and an apple tree), they can degrade with time and 'go off' or become smelly! They need to be kept in a dark, cool cupboard to ensure a longer shelf life.

Cotton wool and orange stick

If you wind a very small amount of cotton wool around the end of an orange stick, it can be used to clean any dust from underneath the nail. If the polish has 'bled' into the cuticle or sidewall, use a small amount of polish remover on the end of an orange stick tipped in cotton wool to remove it.

Enamel removers

Removers are used to dissolve and remove nail enamels from the nail. They can also be used to 'squeak' or de-oil the nail before applying polish on the natural nail, as the natural nail will hold oils on its surface.

The main ingredient in most removers is acetone and some organic solvents. However, the majority of nail companies use non-acetone removers, as acetone is believed to weaken tips, various wraps (i.e. fibreglass) and acrylics. Most removers now use solvents that are less drying and some may have added moisturising agents, such as aloe vera. Other ingredients include colourings to distinguish removers from other liquids, perfumes or fragrances, water and alcohol.

Base coat

Always use a good quality base coat specific to that purpose, that is not one which can serve as a base and top coat. Base coat and top coat have different qualities and polish will last longer if these are used properly. Base coat is the first step in any polish procedure and a good base coat will stay sticky even when dry. This allows the polish to adhere really well and helps it to last longer.

Base coat usually contains more resin than coloured polish, which gives it its tacky consistency and enables it to adhere to the nail. Most base coats are clear, although some may have a colour additive purely to distinguish them from other clear polishes such as top coats and nail strengtheners or hardeners. Some of the main ingredients are:

- resins and solvents
- nitrocellulose
- ethyl acetate and butyl acetate
- isopropyl alcohol

You may wish to use a nail strengthener or hardener as a base on a natural nail. Make sure you follow the manufacturer's instructions for application and consequently advise clients about continued use.

A ridge filler could also be used to help the appearance of the final polish look smoother. Ridge fillers are usually thicker than base coats and help to camouflage any irregularities or deep ridges in the nail. They take slightly longer to dry than normal base coats. Base coats usually have a lower viscosity and are lower in non-volatile ingredients which allows them to dry more quickly and be applied more thinly.

To apply the base coat

- Make sure the nail is free from dust and oil.
- Pull the brush out of the bottle, pressing against one side to get the correct measure of base coat needed.
- Press the bead into the middle of the nail about 3 mm away from the cuticle, towards the cuticle and then pull it down in a vertical line to the free edge leaving 1–2 mm margin at the cuticle area.
- Turn finger slightly to the left and repeat, leaving 1–2 mm free margin.
- Turn finger to the other side and cover the right side of the nail.
- Three thin strokes should be plenty to cover the entire nail.
- Allow a few minutes to dry, although the surface should stay slightly tacky.
- Nails are now ready to be polished.

Enamels and polishes

Coloured polishes, enamels or lacquers (pronounced *lack-er*) – the names all refer to the same item – are used to add colour or high gloss to the natural nail. Every week companies around the world design new colours and the choice we have as professionals is astounding and very beautiful. Nail polishes have been available since the early 1900s and were first made in the USA but various races have been decorating their hands and nails for centuries.

Some of these include the ancient Indians, Egyptians and Chinese. They used natural products such as henna and other plant extracts.

Polished nails

The polishes we use today are made up of a mixture of various chemicals that allow us to produce beautiful, many coloured and long lasting nail designs. A brief description of some of the most used chemical ingredients in polishes follows.

- *Nitrocellulose* is a film-forming substance which is the bulk product of most polishes. It needs the addition of other chemicals to help with drying, to counteract shrinking and to stop discoloration with ageing.
- *Resins* are used to help reduce shrinkage when a polish dries, as well as improve adhesion and flexibility. Resins provide the finish gloss on the polish surface but unfortunately they reduce the hardness of the polish.
- *Solvents* are used to alter the consistency of a polish. The consistency must be right to allow even coverage with the brush. Butyl and ethyl acetate are the main solvents used to 'wet' the nitrocellulose. It is normally mixed with toluene to stabilise ingredients and regulate evaporation.
- *Plasticisers* are used to regulate evaporation and reduce shrinkage. Plasticisers can improve a polish's flexibility but can also prevent it from adhering to the natural nail.
- *Colorants*. There are two types of polish:
  – cream
  – pearlised
  Cream polish contains insoluble colours mixed with

iron oxide and titanium dioxide. Pearl polishes get their effect from reflective transparent crystals of guanine. These can be obtained from the scales of fish or from synthetic products such as mica flakes that are coated with titanium dioxide. A cheaper alternative is to use bismuth-coated mica flakes.

Colour theory

When your clients choose a polish colour, they normally pick colours they are attracted to rather than those that complement their skin tone. It is really important to have some knowledge of colour theory when working in the nail industry, as we are decorators as well as manicurists and nail technicians. Every good decorator should be able to use their knowledge to get maximum results.

Ask the client whether he or she is going somewhere special and wants to match a certain look. Take into consideration the condition of the nails and surrounding soft tissue. All your clients will have experienced trying clothes and immediately knowing they are not right for them, whether it is the cut or – more often – the colour that does not flatter them. The wrong colour against some skin tones can make people look sallow, ruddy or even ill. Other

Colour pops

Technical Tip

Polishes vary greatly in colour consistency; some might need only one coat and some as many as three or four to give a good depth of colour.

Colour wheel

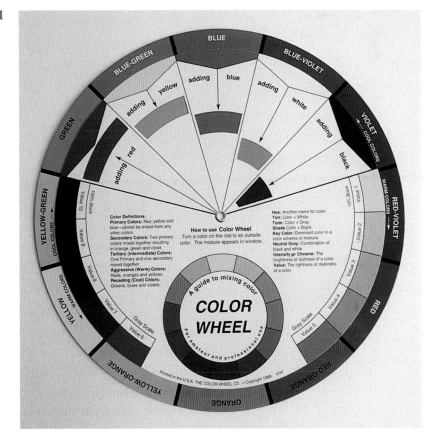

Technical Tip

Look at the following when helping a client to choose a polish or nail art design:

● colour of client's clothes and accessories

● client's make-up, hair colour and skin tone – look at the inside of their wrist for best idea

colours can make the skin radiate with health and camouflage any skin imperfections. The same applies to colour on the nails. If your client's natural nails are short, or even bitten, then applying a bright red polish will make them look cheap and gaudy and draw attention to the short length. You might want to suggest a paler colour that will give the illusion of length or even try a French polish which, with a deep smile line, can make the nails look longer than they really are.

Some clients may have already visited a colour specialist and been colour coded. This is the process whereby the specialist, with the help of many colour swatches, matches colours to the client's skin tone, and then puts them into what is known as a colour season. These seasons are:

● winter
● summer
● autumn
● spring

Autumn skin tones

These people will be able to wear warm colours, being usually freckly and having a pinkish tone to their skins.

Winter

These clients will have more of a blue cast to their skin and will be able to wear both cooler and more vibrant colours.

Spring and summer

People in this category are usually best in brighter and lighter versions of winter and autumn colours.

There will always be clients who fall between each category; if this happens look at what polish colour suits them best. Here are a few tips from each season:

Winter

Winter tones can be extremely varied and either have a yellow or blue cast to the skin. If the client is yellow-based then using polishes with the same colour base will give the skin a sallow effect. If blue tones are used this will soften the yellow.

Winter skin tones can vary from very pale to black skin tones. Blue-based and strong colours like the primary colours are called for and not browns, golds and orangey reds.

Summer

In the same way as for winter colouring, the skin has blue tones but usually with a slight pink or pinky beige hue. It is inadvisable to use yellow-based colours as these will appear to make the skin look unclean and emphasise any fine veins and capillaries. Choose softer colours than for winter, but with the same base blue tone. Again, avoid oranges and golds.

Spring

Clients who fall under the category of spring usually have fair complexions, most of the time with gold undertones and perhaps some freckles. These types of skin can vary greatly from creamy or peachy to very pale beige. Use yellow-based colours to add warmth and make the skin look healthy. Avoid colours that will clash with the yellow base, for example colours such as deep reds with blue tones.

Autumn

This type of skin will usually be seen on a redhead or a blonde with red tones. A yellow-based colour will even out this skin tone. Use strong colours, such as yellow or gold-based browns, terracotta, peach and bronzes. Try to avoid colours such as blue-based pinks, reds and purples.

- The three *primary colours* are red, blue and yellow. All other colour combinations come from these three.
- The *secondary colours* are orange, which is a mixture of yellow and red, green, which is a mixture of blue and yellow, and purple, a mixture of red and blue.

There is further information on colour in Chapter 7.

Although it is traditional to use cotton wool to remove polish or to squeak the nail before the application of polish, you will sometimes find it leaves tiny fibres on the nail, no matter how careful you are. Lint-free pads are now available and are excellent for absorbing the right amount of liquid and leaving the nail free of fibres. This means that fewer pads and less polish remover are used. One pad will remove the bulk of the polish from all ten nails and a second will remove excess polish. A further advantage is that you are not constantly soaking your client's skin and drying it out with large amounts of polish remover. Try to purchase pads with a tab for you to hold, as this will prevent your fingers being overexposed to chemicals and the polish and nail design that you are wearing from being damaged.

It is always wise to test polishes before you buy, especially if

Technical Tip

When choosing colours look at your client's hand condition and age. Some colours will help disguise lines and wrinkles and others will accentuate them.

Technical Tip

Polishes contain a solution of nitrocellulose in a volatile solvent such as acetate. This evaporates quickly each time the liquid is exposed to the air, which is why our most well used colours become tacky quickly.

Technical Tip

Nitrocellulose-based nail polishes are 'thixotropic', which means they get thinner when agitated. Keep tightly sealed between use, store in a cool place and agitate between the hands before using. Never shake a polish bottle as this causes air bubbles and will not give a smooth surface.

Technical Tip

Never use polish remover to thin down your polish. Remover may contain oils and water which would prevent the polish from hardening properly.

you are buying in a whole range from one supplier. Either ask for a sample bottle or try a test on your own nails for a few hours or even a few days. See how the polishes stand up to the test of time and how easy they are to apply.

Here are a few qualities to look for in a good polish:

- even colour consistency
- good colour after two coats
- smooth flow with no streaks when applied
- dries to a high gloss finish
- colour pigment does not stain natural nail
- has a quick drying time
- no colour separation in bottle
- should dry to a hard, scratch-resistant coating

Nail polishes can be thinned with a solvent or a mixture of solvents that form the same base as the polish. You must use the thinner compatible with your range of polishes or one that your manufacturer recommends for your particular range.

Application of enamel or polish

The application of base coat, polish and top coat are all basically the same. You will need to consider the size and shape of the nail when deciding on the amount of polish for each application and possibly how many strokes for each nail. Obviously a short, round nail will require a different amount of polish from a very long, square nail.

Here is the easiest way to hold the polish bottle:

- If you are right handed, hold the polish in your left hand and vice versa.
- Hold the bottle in the palm of your hand.
- Support the bottle with your ring and little finger against the pad of muscle at the base of your thumb.
- Tilt the bottle slightly – the less polish there is in the bottle the further down the palm you will have to tilt the bottle to reach the polish at the bottom.
- Hold client's finger in between your index and middle finger and your thumb.
- Rotate client's finger and hold back lateral sidewalls when polishing to get an even coverage without touching any soft tissue.

Technical Tip

The manicurist's or nail technician's arm should be leaning on the desk for stability when polishing. It is much more difficult to achieve an even coverage if your client's hand is waving in the air.

There are various ways of applying polish but the easiest is the three-step method. The first coat should be a thin layer, leaving a 1–2 mm margin free in the cuticle area and along the sidewalls.

1 Apply the first stroke as for the base coat, place the brush three-quarters of the way down the nail in the centre of the nail, pushing the colour slightly up to the cuticle without leaking into the soft tissue.

2 Slightly turn the finger to one side and cover the left side of the nail, making sure the brush is pulled all the way down to the free edge.

3 Proceed in the same way for the right side of the nail.

Polish application

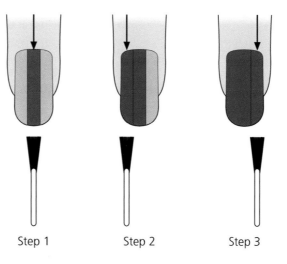

Step 1   Step 2   Step 3

You would apply a second coat the same manner, but use very slightly more polish for good coverage. Make sure all the edges are covered and the surface is smooth. You may need to add another coat, if the consistency of the polish is thin, to deepen the colour.

Here are a few more tips to help your polish application techniques:

● By placing the brush in the middle of the nail plate the majority of the polish will be in such a position that it can be worked evenly over the entire nail.

● Do not keep stroking the brush over the surface of the nail as the solvent is evaporating and the polish will become tacky and streaky.

● If mistakes like streaking or a missed area do occur, the second coat will usually rectify this.

Point to Remember

Ask your clients for payment, to get out their car keys, make their next appointment and help them put on their coats before polish application. This will avoid 'digs' and 'smudges' in the fresh polish.

Technical Tip

Practise your smiles on tips or practice cards to achieve deeper curves. The French polish is so versatile you can incorporate it with other artistic designs such as flowers, pearls, rhinestones, lace and many other techniques. For further discussion of these embellishments, see the section on Nail Art.

Useful Tip

Have some tips on a display board to show your clients. Remember not everyone will know what a French polish is.

- If a larger mistake occurs, the nail should be cleaned off and started again.

- Make no more than 4 strokes on a small nail and 6 on a larger nail.

- If a client has a wide nail, leave a free margin along the sidewalls to give the illusion of a slimmer and longer nail.

- If you have a client who constantly 'chips' their polish along the free edge, take a small nail art brush and remove 1–2 mm of the polish along the free edge.

- If a client smudges a nail before you have finished you can take a small amount of polish on the brush and work over the smudge to soften it and then brush over the entire nail to make it smooth.

- Sell a bottle of the same colour polish to the client for touching up or for matching their toes to their fingers.

- Suggest colours that complement skin tone as well as make-up and clothes.

Make sure your client does not bang his or her hands down on a dusty tissue or towel as this will cause the dust to rise up and land on the wet polish. There is no way to rectify this other than to start again.

The perfect French polish

The French polish has got to be the most requested treatment within manicures and nail enhancement treatments. As a nail technician, you will either love it or hate it. A significant number of manicurists and nail technicians do not offer it simply because they find it difficult to perform. You will need to consider these points before attempting the French look:

- the nails have some free edge, but not too much

- your enamels or polishes are not thick and sticky

- you have a steady hand

Performing a French manicure can make a short nail look longer and slimmer if done properly. Whether you are using

French polish – chevron

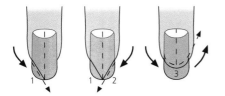

French polish – rounded

polishes or nail enhancement products, look at how a smile line makes the nail look as if it is smiling or how a line can look like a grimace or even make it look sad.

The easiest way to perform a French finish is by airbrushing, but this can be expensive to set up. A French finish can be done in three ways:

- chevron
- rounded – starting with chevron
- rounded

You will see that the white starts off as a chevron and then you turn it into a smile.

Chevron and rounded-chevron

- Apply your base coat as before.
- Apply white polish to the free edge of the nail starting on the left and sweeping the brush across and down to the bottom right hand corner.
- Repeat on the other side, working from right to left.
- If the smile effect is required, swipe the brush across the nail, but not in a straight line, dipping it slightly to achieve a curve.
- Apply clear, sheer pink, peach or natural polish over the entire nail using the 3-stroke method as before. Be careful to use the correct shade for your client's skin tone.
- Apply a top coat over the entire nail.

Rounded

- Pull the brush out of the side of the bottle and lose about half the polish.
- Take the side of the brush with enamel on and swipe across from one side to the other, dipping slightly in the middle to create a smile line.
- Take the brush and work the bulk of the polish down the nail to the free edge in 3 strokes (less if it is a small nail). Work down the middle and then either side.

Technical Tip

Using a top coat on top of a colour will prevent chipping and peeling of the enamel.

Technical Tip

- Remember polish is drying so don't overwork it, as you will get streaking. Place the polish where you want it and let it find its own level.

- You can always neaten a smile line with a small art brush and some polish remover or nail dehydrator.

- Always allow a little longer for a French polish to dry.

Technical Tip

- Try not to let clients blow on their nails, as inevitably they will smudge one while their hands are wafting around.

- Do not use polish driers between polish layers as this will cause the polish to peel or bubble.

- Use the chosen colour on the rest of the nail, as above.

- Apply top coat, as above.

Top coats

Top coats are used to seal polish in and provide a hard gloss protective cover for natural nails or coloured enamels. A top coat should be applied as a thin, even colour over the whole nail. However, remember to leave that tiny free margin around the cuticle and sidewall.

Some top coats might also act as quick dries, but it is always best to use products that are made specifically for that purpose. Don't forget, if a product makes a spectacular claim, always test it before buying.

Apply top coat in the same way as base and polish. One thin coat only is required.

Quick dries

A nail quick dry is optional and doesn't need to be used for any other reason than that the client needs to be drier quicker. Quick dries can come in the form of:

- polishes/top coats
- sprays
- electric or battery blow-dryers
- oils

Nail art products, tools and equipment

Nail art designs

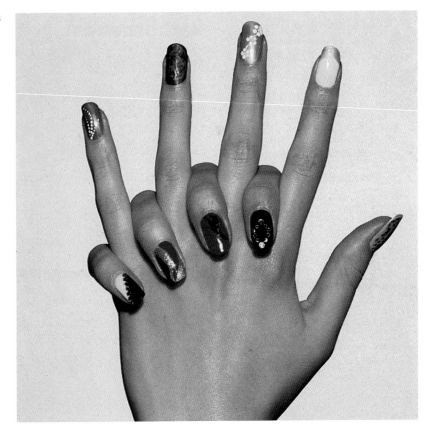

Learning objectives

In this section you will learn about:

- **the products needed to perform nail art**

- **the tools needed to create the designs**

- **equipment for the nail artist**

Not every client wants outrageous designs on their nails, but nail art is not just about crazy nails. It can be very subtle and beautiful. You will need to collect some basic tools and equipment to be able to offer this service. We have listed the most popular items on the market, but it is a good idea to visit trade shows and talk to distributors of nail art products, to see if any new products or techniques are being developed.

Nail paints

Nail paints are normally non-toxic, water-based acrylic paints that come in a variety of colours. These paints can be diluted for specialist paint effects or mixed together to create

Nail paints and polishes

Flexi-brushes

A selection of brushes

a spectrum of colours. Your brushes can be easily cleaned in liquid soap and water.

Nail brushes

Fine detail brush

Normally a small, fine-tipped brush. These are excellent for precise detailing.

Liner brush, medium

These are ideal for producing thick lines and colour on nails.

Liner brush, long

This is a very thin, narrow-bristled brush which is terrific for creating long straight lines.

Fan brush

The bristles of this brush imitate the look of a fan. You can use this brush to create sweep effects across the nail.

Shading brush

A broad square of bristles. You can shade and float colour as well as use a mixture of colours on either side of the bristles to create swirl effects.

Glitter dust brush

It is best to use a sable brush for this technique, as nylon can deteriorate very quickly. The effect is created with glitter dust and mixer. Your brush will have to be cleaned with nail varnish remover.

Other nail art tools and equipment

Marbling tool

This tool has a round metallic head at each end, one small, one medium. You can use the marbling tool to mix one colour into another and also to create dots of differing sizes depending on the amount of paint you use and which head.

Orange wood stick

A long stick made of orange wood, normally with tapered ends. They are ideal for picking up polish and secure items.

Glitter dust, brush and mixer

Glitter dust

Glitter dust is a dense sparkle powder used with glitter dust mixer to create fabulous designs. It is an excellent way to create extra sparkle on the nails.

Glitter dust mixer

This is used for mixing with glitter dust to create beads of product that can be applied in various designs.

Transfers

Transfers come in self-adhesive and water release formats. There are some terrific designs available which can transform nails in seconds.

Transfers

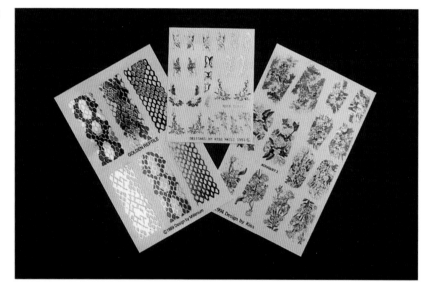

Water release transfers

Using a cotton bud dampened with water, rub the back of the transfer to release it from the backing and then slide it off with your thumb and position it on the nail.

Self-adhesive

With these transfers you simply peel off the backing sheet and attach the transfer to the nail.

Foils

Foils can give fantastic results. They have a metallic finish and come in various colours and patterns. They must be used with foil adhesive and placed with the pattern facing upwards and then rubbed onto the nail with a cotton bud.

Foil adhesive

This is an adhesive designed especially for use with foils. The adhesive goes on white and you must wait for it to become clear before applying foils. Wherever you place the adhesive is where the foil will stick.

Marbaliser kit

Every marbled design is different depending on the use of colours. A few drops of each colour are dropped into tepid water and mixed with a pin. The client's nail is then gently dragged through the water and pulled out leaving the design on the nail. The design is then top coated.

Emboss art kit

An embosser is like a syringe full of paint. It is held in the palm of the hand and the end part is pressed to allow paint to come out of the small hole in the end. This tool allows the most precise control of paint. The results are unique three-dimensional designs. Designs can be completed in three minutes and are achieved by combining three basic strokes of dots, lines and commas.

Polish secure

These could be in the form of diamonds, pearls, dazzles, flatstones, etc. and are simply pushed gently into the surface of wet polish with a damp orange stick.

Artiste's palette

This is a plastic dish where small amounts of paint can be mixed to achieve a wide variety of colours. The paint can be washed off when finished and the palette re-used.

Nail art designs

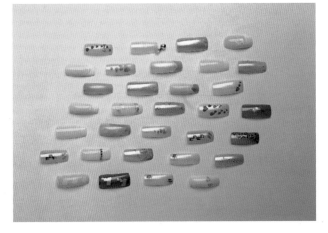

Basic nail art

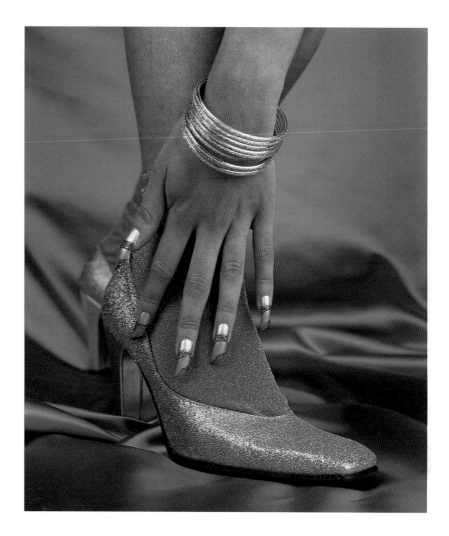

Learning objectives

In this section you will learn about:

- **freehand painting techniques**

- **how to use the most popular nail art products**

- **how to use nail decorations**

- **step-by-step way to a few popular designs**

- **how to produce a flower garden**

You are limited only by your imagination. Anyone can perform nail art, even if they feel they don't have an artistic bone in their body. It is a good idea to look around for nail art books or maybe even book onto a nail art course with a reputable company. Any help can be useful. Remember that the technicians who teach on these courses can pass on valuable tips and information from their years of experience.

In the following section we will guide you through a few very basic popular designs – out of the thousands available. Keep practising and you will soon find that your collection will build up, so that your clients have a wide choice of designs to choose from when asking for a nail art treatment.

Freehand paint techniques

Roll off

This technique can be used with any brush. Insert the brush into the paint and lower the brush onto its side. Using a rolling motion between your thumb and index finger, pull the brush out of the paint, rolling away from the paint. This will produce an even-coated brush with a sharp point. This technique is good for even lines and outlining.

Perfect circle

This technique is used to form a perfect circle. You will need a fine detail brush or medium liner. Keeping the brush straight up at all times, insert it into the paint then pull the brush up towards the ceiling. This will leave an even bead of paint on the end of the bristles. When positioning onto your work, ensure the brush still stays upright to create that perfect circle. Remember to use a light pressure for a small circle and more pressure for a bigger circle.

Mixer

This is used with a flat brush. Place one half of the brush into one colour then the other half of the brush into another colour. Keeping the brush directly upright, position it onto the nail and turn clockwise to mix the paint together – this is a good technique for creating flowers.

Swirler

Use a medium liner for this technique. Using the length of the liner, pull through one colour, turn the liner over and pull through another colour. Drawing an oval shape, twirl the brush through your fingers as you pull down the oval; this will mix the paint giving you a fabulous look for advanced flowers.

Tri-mix

Place three lines of paint in a row next to each other then, using a long liner brush, place it into the paint. Do not pull the brush through the paint, just lift it out and then place it onto your work. This creates a line of three colours which is ideal for effect work.

Flower garden

Flowers are very simple to do and look extremely effective with only a minimal amount of time and effort required to create wonderful looks. The flowers can be enhanced with diamonds or pearls placed in the centre for a more glamorous look.

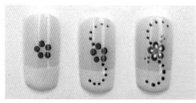

Flower design 1

Equipment needed:

- top coat
- base coat
- various colours of paint for the flowers, leaves and dots
- French manicure polish of your client's choice
- marbling tool

1   Polish all ten nails with your favourite natural French polish colours.

2   Select a darker paint colour for the base of the actual flower. Using a marbling tool, place five dots in the centre of the nail just above the white line of the French tip, using slightly more paint as these dots will form the larger petals.

3   Using a contrasting colour to that of the larger petals, take the smaller end of the marbling tool and trail dots in a five-shaped form down below the flower towards the free edge and then upwards towards the cuticle area. Remember to use only one application of paint and the dots will appear smaller as you move outwards.

4   Using a paler colour for the inner petals, use the small end of the marbling tool and place small dots towards the centre of the larger petals, leaving space for a rhinestone in the centre of the flower.

5   On just the outer edge of the petals, on either side of the flower, use the marbling tool to dot three green leaves.

6   Secure a rhinestone in the centre of the main flower with top coat. By pressing the rhinestone into a wet top coat this ensures that the rhinestone will be embedded down

Technical Tip

The amount of paint you pick up will determine the size of dot you achieve. Practise on some paper first.

into the design and remain secure without dropping out after 2–3 days. Use a wet orange stick or one tipped with blu-tac to place the rhinestone in the correct place without disturbing the top coat or design. A further top coat may be applied and allowed to dry before the client leaves.

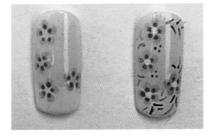

Flower design 2

Equipment needed:

- top coat
- base coat
- various colours of paint for the flowers, leaves and dots
- French manicure polish of your client's choice
- marbling tool

1 Polish all ten nails with your favourite natural French polish colours.
2 Using your marbling tool, create four flowers placed around the edge of the nail. Then, with a contrasting colour, place five larger dots around the first dots to create the petals.
3 Select a contrasting colour and using the small end of a marbling tool, add small dots to the petals near the centre and repeat on every flower.
4 Using white paint and the small end of a marbling tool, dot the centre of each flower. Alternatively you could use a flatstone or rhinestone in the centre instead of paint.
5 Using a small detail brush create V-shaped leaves and trail around each flower, following the nail shape. Add clusters of three tiny dots to define the foliage even further.
6 Apply top coat to seal the design.

Flower design 3

Equipment needed:

- top coat
- base coat
- various colours of paint for the flowers, leaves and dots
- French manicure polish of your client's choice
- marbling tool
- rhinestones

1 Polish all ten nails with your favourite natural French polish colours.

2 Select a darker paint as a base for the main flower, and using a marbling tool place five dots off-centre towards the nail fold.

3 Place three smaller dots in the opposite corner, using the smaller end of the marbling tool.

4 Trail dots from the main flower towards the free edge and also around the cuticle edge. Only use one application of paint and the dots will appear smaller as you work towards the edges of the nail.

5 Use a paler colour for the inner petals. With the smaller end of the marbling tool, place dots in the centre of the opposite corner.

6 Using a fine detail brush add V-shaped leaves around the flower. Use a pale or darker green paint.

7 Secure a rhinestone in the centre of the main flower. Pick up a rhinestone with a wet orange stick or stick tipped with blu-tac and press the rhinestone into the wet top coat.

8 Apply top coat to seal the design.

Japanese symbol

This design is so simple yet completely elegant. Practise using various colours to achieve different looks.

Equipment needed:

- top coat
- base coat
- red polish
- nail paints
- fine art or detail brush

Technical Tip

This design can look really stunning, using a combination of black, red and white. Experiment with the various combinations and also have some drawings or samples ready for your clients to choose from.

1 Apply a base coat to all ten nails.

2 Apply two coats of red polish to all ten nails, making sure there is good colour coverage.

3 Use a roll off technique with black paint and small detail brush, ensuring there is no excessive paint on the brush.

4 Use a light pressure for fine lines and heavier pressure for thicker lines. You can vary the pressure on the same stroke to create a thin then thick line, which is useful in Japanese symbols. Always remember that the area you place the brush first will have the most paint and a slightly thicker line if drawing the brush down over the nail.

5 Paint two to three lines in black paint similar to the symbol shown on the nail in the illustration. Try not to paint too many lines, keep it simple. You may want to

research some symbols with their meanings and keep a record for clients to choose from.

6 Allow the paint to dry thoroughly before applying a top coat, as most paints will look dull when dry.

7 Apply two coats of top coat for protection.

Marbling

This design is very simple to do using the marbling tool and gently swirling one colour into another. Lovely works of art can be created with this technique. Please remember not to get too carried away with your swirling because the colours will end up in one big mass – the less you swirl the better. Choose your colours carefully and do not use too many. Colours should contrast and complement one another.

Equipment needed:

- base coat
- client's colour choice of polish
- 2–3 contrasting colour paints
- marbling tool
- top coat

Technical Tip

If you find when mixing colours together that there is not enough of one colour and the others look too dominant, use your marbling tool to add some dots or larger swirls.

1 Apply base coat to all ten nails.

2 Apply two coats of polish of your client's choice, ensuring good colour coverage on all ten nails.

3 Using the large end of the marbling tool place drops of red and white nail paint onto the corner of the nail.

4 Clean marbling tool.

5 Using the large end of the marbling tool, swirl one colour of paint into the other to create a marbling effect.

6 Allow the paint to dry thoroughly. Apply two coats of top coat for protection.

Opalescent blending

Highly impressive, this technique is fabulous and looks especially good on nails with a dark background polish. These paints appear white until applied. They must be applied very thinly or you will not get the required finish. If they are applied over dark polish the effect is dazzling and strong, if applied over pale polish the effect is iridescent. This technique can create the most beautiful designs and you will need to practise with various colours to achieve different looks. Always use colours that complement one another and do not be too heavy-handed with the paint. Less paint will achieve a better iridescent look.

Equipment needed:

- top coat
- base coat
- polish of your client's choice
- opalescent nail paints
- container of water
- medium liner brush or fan brush
- palette

1   Apply base coat to all ten nails.
2   Apply two coats of polish of your client's choice, ensuring good colour coverage over all ten nails.
3   There are two methods of applying the paint before sweeping across the nail. Either apply both colours of opalescent paint in dots down either side of the nail and then use your fan brush to sweep from side to side, making sure you stop before the colours blend into one another too much. The other method is to apply a thin coat of opalescent paint onto the nail with your liner brush and sweep from side to side, working your way down the nail to the free edge. Again make sure you stop when the design looks almost like petrol and do not fall into the trap of over-blending the colours.
4   Allow the paint to dry thoroughly before applying the top coat.
5   Apply two coats of top coat for protection.

Technical Tip

You can add a second or third colour to give more depth to the design.

Striping design

Design 1
Equipment needed:

- base coat
- top coat
- client's choice of polish colours
- rhinestones
- paint colours
- striping brush or flexi-brushes
- marbling tool

1   Apply one coat of base coat to all ten nails.
2   Apply clients choice of colour polish to all ten nails.
3   Using a striping brush or flexi-brush, paint 2–4 stripes in the chosen colours, from left free edge up to right outer corner.

Technical Tip

For a good hold, make sure rhinestones are set into wet or tacky topcoat

4   Wait for paint to dry before applying top coat.

5   Apply finla top coat to each nail and place rhinestones along the stripes.

Design 2

Equipment needed:

- top coat
- base coat
- polish of your client's choice
- optional: can use black and white striping flexi-brushes
- black and white paint
- striping brush
- rhinestones
- marbling tool

1   Polish all ten nails with a bright base colour, using two coats of polish to give good coverage and colour depth.

2   Using a striping brush, place three white curved stripes from the outside edge down to the free edge. Drag the brush through the paint pot, wiping excess paint off the brush on the side of the pot. Ensure the brush is not overloaded with paint. Place the brush in the left-hand corner of each nail and lay the brush down on the nail and pull up. Do not try to use the tip of the brush to paint, as this will cause the lines to be uneven and thick.

3   Place two black stripes in between the white stripes.

4   Using the small end of a marbling tool and black polish, trail dots following the line of the stripes.

5   Secure three rhinestones at the edge and base of the stripes.

6   Apply top coat to secure the design.

Zebra print

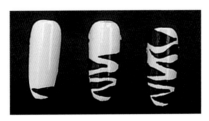

Be totally outrageous with this stunning design. Match your nails to your handbag, shoes or clothes and watch people be amazed at this designer look.

Equipment needed:

- top coat
- base coat
- white polish
- nail paints
- container of water

- liner brush
- palette

1 Apply base coat to all ten nails.

2 Apply two coats of white polish. Use a good quality polish that gives a good coverage and does not leave the nail with shadows.

3 Using a medium liner brush and black nail paint, take paint onto the brush using the roll off method and start to pull paint in lines across the nail.

4 Start by painting a short wavy line near the cuticle edge and ensure that it is filled in with no gaps, allowing the white background to be seen.

5 Paint a short wavy line from the outside edge to the middle on either side of the nail.

6 Repeat step 5 until the whole nail is completed. You can experiment with different sized lines, some going all the way across the nail and various shapes of stripe.

7 Allow the paint to dry thoroughly.

8 Apply two coats of top coat for protection.

Advanced freehand painting – Tigger

This is a superb character to paint as he just comes alive on the nail and grins back at you. You will need a medium liner brush and fine detail brush. You will be using the perfect circle technique and outlining.

Equipment needed:

- top coat
- base coat
- polish of your client's choice
- container of water
- fine detail brush
- medium liner brush
- nail art paints – yellow, orange, pink, white, darker pink for tongue and black for outline

1 Apply base coat to all ten nails.

2 Apply two coats of a colour polish of your client's choice, but remember that Tigger needs a pale background to show his features for maximum impact.

3 You will start Tigger with the eye area: draw a mis-shapen rectangle in yellow paint using a medium liner brush.

4 Draw the upper head area in orange paint, together with the ears.

5 Draw in the nose with pink paint using a medium liner brush.

6 Draw around the nose in yellow paint and create Tigger's lower face and jaw by painting two circles, one slightly larger than the other and both overlapping each other.

7 Using a deep pink paint, draw in his mouth in almost a half circle.

8 Using a black paint, draw in his stripes in the upper head area.

9 Highlight the nose with white paint and black outer highlights.

10 Using black paint and the perfect circle technique dot in Tigger's eyes and eyebrows. Using a fine detail brush, add three whiskers to each side of his face.

11 Using a fine detail brush and the roll off technique outline his face in black paint.

12 Allow the paint to dry thoroughly.

13 Apply two coats of top coat for protection.

Flat stones

Flat stones come in a variety of shapes, sizes and colours. They are polish secure items and as such adhere to wet polish. The best way to pick up flat stones is with a dampened orange wood stick; then place onto wet polish or a dot of top coat if the polish is dry.

Equipment needed:

- top coat
- base coat
- polish of your choice
- container of water
- orange stick
- flat stones

1 Apply base coat to all ten nails.

2 Apply two coats of polish of your client's choice.

3 Using an orange stick, dampen the end with water and pick up a flat stone.

4 Position onto wet polish with the flat side down. Design your own pattern.

5 Apply two coats of top coat for protection.

Rhinestones

These come in a variety of shapes, sizes and colours. They are polish secure items and as such adhere to wet polish. The best way to pick up rhinestones is with a dampened orange stick or orange stick tipped with blu-tac; then place onto wet polish or a dot of top coat if the polish is dry.

Equipment needed:

- top coat
- base coat
- polish of your choice
- container of water
- orange stick
- rhinestones

1 Apply base coat to all ten nails.
2 Apply two coats of polish of your client's choice.
3 Using an orange stick damped at the end with water or an orange stick tipped with blu-tac, pick up a rhinestone.
4 Position onto wet polish with flat side down. Design your own pattern.
5 Apply two coats of top coat for protection.

Glitter dust

This is a fine sparkly powder which looks great when applied to the nails, especially with a dark background polish. Glitter dust must be applied with a sable brush and glitter dust mixer. You must roll your brush with the mixer to pick up the glitter dust not just dip it in, as you will not be able to work with it properly.

Equipment needed:

- top coat
- base coat
- polish of your client's choice
- glitter dust
- glitter dust mixer
- sable glitter brush
- nail varnish remover

Technical Tip

Using flat stones is much cheaper than using rhinestones. Bear this in mind when doing designs on a client. If they choose rhinestones instead of flat stones warn them of the difference in price.

Rhinestones

Technical Tip

You may use rhinestones with all of your nail art techniques for dramatic effect, whether you use one or coat the whole nail with them.

1 Apply base coat to all ten nails.

2 Apply two coats of polish of your client's choice.

3 Dip brush into glitter mixer to form a ball on the end of the brush.

4 Roll the mixer on the end of the brush into the glitter to form a shiny bead of product.

5 Place the bead onto the nail and wipe the brush clean on a piece of tissue.

6 Now use the tip of the brush to position the glitter into place. Do not drag the bead over the nail as this may separate the glitter particles. Use a light circular movement first to distribute product and then press the brush to place product into shape.

7 Allow spaces of base polish to show through to create a stained glass effect.

8 When changing glitter colour make sure the brush is clean. You can clean your brush in nail varnish remover.

9 Allow nails to dry thoroughly.

10 Apply two coats of top coat for protection.

Technical Tip

You may use your flexi or striper brush with black paint to neaten the lines between the glitter. This gives a clean sharp edge. Always use paint the colour as the base colour.

Transfers

These come in self-adhesive and water release forms. Water release transfers need to be moistened on the back with a damp cotton bud until you can slide the transfer off with your thumb. Self-adhesive transfers simply peel off the backing paper and stick to the nail. Both must be covered with a top coat to seal.

Equipment needed:

- top coat
- base coat
- polish of your client's choice
- scissors
- cotton bud
- container of water

The procedure for water release transfers is as follows:

1 Apply base coat to all ten nails.

2 Apply two coats of polish of your client's choice.

3 Moisten a cotton bud with water and rub the back of the transfer. You will see the water soaking through to the transfer.

4   Slide the transfer off with the flat of your thumb.

5   Position transfer onto nail and smooth into place.

6   Apply two coats of top coat for protection.

The procedure for self-adhesive transfers is as follows:

1   Apply base coat to nails.

2   Apply two coats of polish of your client's choice.

3   Peel transfer off the backing sheet and apply to nail.

4   Apply two coats of top coat.

Foiling

Foiling is very dramatic and the effects cannot be achieved with any other medium. Foil can be bought in rolls or sheets and is supplied in the form of a metallic foil bonded onto a clear backing. The foil is released from the roll with a foil adhesive. Wherever you place the foil is where it will stick. The adhesive will be white on application and you must wait until it is clear before you place the foil onto the nail, with the pattern facing upwards. You then rub over the surface with a cotton bud to ensure adhesion of the foil to the nail; lift off the foil and you will be left with the pattern you have drawn with the adhesive.

Equipment needed:

- top coat
- base coat
- polish of your client's choice
- foils
- foil adhesive
- cotton buds
- scissors

1   Apply base coat to all ten nails.

2   Apply two coats of polish. You may leave the nail clear, but remember to use a good quality base coat as the moisture and oils from the natural nail will reduce the bonding of the foils and adhesive.

3   Once the polish is dry apply foil adhesive sparingly where you want the foil to be applied. The adhesive will be white on application.

4   Once the adhesive becomes clear apply the foil with the pattern facing upwards.

5   Rub the foil with a cotton bud to ensure adhesion to the nail.

6   Lift foil away from nail.

7   Apply two coats of top coat for protection.

Jewellery

Nail jewellery has been around for centuries and can look spectacular whether it be a simple diamond stud or a charm that is more elaborate.

There are various types of nail jewellery. Here are the main ones: press-on jewellery and post charm jewellery.

Press-on jewellery

Equipment needed:

- base coat
- polish
- top coat
- nail charm

1   Apply base coat to all ten nails.

2   Apply two coats of coloured polish to ensure good coverage on all ten nails.

3   Apply top coat and press a charm into the polish while still wet.

4   Apply a second layer of top coat after five minutes to keep the charm in place.

Post charm nail jewellery

Equipment needed:

- base coat
- polish
- top coat
- posted charm
- combi drill

1   Apply base coat to all ten nails.

2   Apply two coats of coloured polish to ensure good coverage on all ten nails.

3   Apply top coat and allow to dry thoroughly.

4   Position the drill tip 3 mm from the nail tip. Turn the drill several times to the right. When the drill touches the buffer, withdraw the drill carefully.

Safety Tip

Always make sure the natural nail is coated with an overlay before allowing your clients to wear jewellery, as the natural nails can split, get larger or – even worse – tear.

Technical Tip

You might want to advise your client to add another layer of top coat a few days later.

Drill and jewellery

5 Push charm post through the hole from the top.

6 Place the socket end of the drill into the posted charm and screw until it is in place and the charm is secure.

The art of airbrushing

Learning objectives

In this section you will learn about:

- **inspiring potential airbrush clients**
- **your charging levels**
- **airbrush equipment**
- **types of airbrush**
- **cleaning and maintenance**
- **troubleshooting**
- **types of paint, base coats and top coats**
- **step-by-step designs for a colour fade, French design, animal print and tropical design**

Christmas blue twizzle nails

The art of airbrushing

Airbrushing as a decoration for nails has become very popular over the last few years. The technique enables the technician to do designs on nails more quickly, cheaply and artistically more accurately than by hand painting, unless of course you are a true artist.

The three most popular requests for airbrushing from clients are:

- French designs
- colour fade
- animal prints

Although airbrushing can produce the most fantastic designs you will see, the initial set-up cost to introduce an airbrush system into the salon can seem quite high and it is this that puts a lot of technicians off implementing an airbrush service into the salon. However, as long as you are serious about wanting the system and you are prepared to market it, then your airbrush system can be extremely lucrative.

As well as airbrushing on nails you may use it to paint the body as well. We will touch on this briefly in the next chapter.

As with any other area of your service, you should first think about who your airbrush clients are likely to be. Just because it is classed as nail art it does not mean this is 'wacky' or way out – even your more mature clients might be encouraged to invest in a colour fade. For those clients who love the French look, you can perform beautiful designs very quickly, with the added benefit that clients do not have to wait as long for their nails to dry, as airbrushing cuts down drying time by at least half. Performing French techniques with the airbrush also means there are no lumps or bumps and every nail is the same, with neat and crisp lines.

With any new service you need to market it effectively so that you cover the cost of the equipment and training and start to earn an income. If you keep your tools and environment clean and well maintained there is no reason why they will not last for years. Most airbrush paints are very cheap and last longer than enamel. If you can convert a client to the airbrush system instead of polish, your income will grow by around 15–20 per cent per treatment.

How can you reach a new audience?

- Wear it yourself.

- Choose a client who is with a lot of people all day and do a free design (for example a hairdresser).
- Leave pictures or boards showing your designs in hairdressers, boutiques and wedding shops.
- Leave leaflets showing designs in doctor's surgeries, dentists, gyms and beauty salons.
- Have nail parties.
- Do demonstrations at women's clubs or similar where large groups gather.
- Give discounts to local hairdressers or bonuses for introducing clients.

Charges

When you paint a client's nails as part of a manicure or a new set of nails, you do not normally make a separate charge for the painting. However, if you airbrush a set of nails, this is an extra procedure and does constitute a separate charge, as it can take up to 15 minutes of treatment time. Therefore, if you can persuade a client to have a colour fade or similar finish, you can turn that 15 minutes into income-generating time and earn some extra money you would not normally take.

What you can charge for services depends to some extent on the area you work in. Obviously charges for services in cities tend to be higher than in provincial towns and villages. You need to look at other levels of charging around you to get an idea what level your charges should be. Remember this is extra income – and prices should be based on 10 fingers. Try to get some information on charges for nail treatments and other health and beauty treatments in your local area and then also from another entirely different area, and this will give you an idea of how area affects charging.

None of these designs should take more than 20 minutes from base coat to top coat. If a client wants a design that takes longer, then you need to charge by the time it is going to take you rather than a set price for the design.

It is not worth getting your airbrush set up for less than £5.00 and don't commit to one nail – the price should always be for ten even if they only want one. The minimum amount of paint you will have to put in your airbrush will do at least ten nails.

Airbrush equipment

You will need:

- a table and a good light

Airbrush equipment

Airbrushes

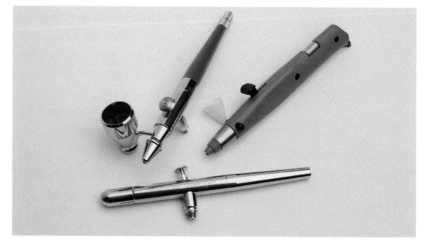

- a compressor or other appropriate air supply
- airbrush gun
- range of colours
- base coat, bond coat, top coat
- appropriate airbrush cleaner (this must be specific to the paints being used)
- cleaning station
- stencils
- masking paper or frisket
- knife and cutting board

The airbrush

Airbrushes have been around for years and were originally sold mainly through hobby shops. The range of airbrushes on the market today is quite diverse and it is easiest to purchase your airbrush from a nail art distributor, as they can advise you on equipment and offer training specific to our industry. You will need to do some careful research before committing yourself to purchasing a system. There are a number of different systems available, so make sure you choose one that can be used on nails.

You need to buy a whole system rather than just an airbrush, that is the paints, cleaner, base and top coats must all be compatible with your airbrush. It is well worth investing in a day's training with your chosen distributor or supplier to eradicate any problems you might have. Remember, education is the key to being good at what you do.

An airbrush looks like a small spray gun. They can be made from metal or resin, the latter being much lighter and easier to handle. Regardless of the material from which they are made, all airbrushes essentially work on the same principle and produce the same effect if used correctly. The system works by using compressed air to force paint out of the tip or nozzle, creating a very fine mist of paint.

Some airbrushes are easier to use than others. Ease of use is dependent on a number of factors such as:

- location of cup or paint mixer
- type of trigger action
- cleanability
- location of the air hose on the airbrush for holding comfort

Always make sure you try a few different airbrushes before taking the decision to invest your money. Every airbrush has a fluid nozzle or tip that holds a needle. When the needle is fitted into the nozzle no paint can be released but, when the trigger is pushed down and pulled back, the airbrush will start to release the paint. The further the trigger is pulled back the more paint is released.

Try to choose an airbrush with a small colour cup or reservoir. Those that have large bottles attached can be time consuming and are uneconomical for the amount of paint needed to service nails. The colour cup or reservoir can be located on the top, at the side or on the bottom of the airbrush. The paint enters the airbrush from the reservoir and is fed through to the nozzle. When using a lot of colours a smaller cup is much more convenient than having to keep cleaning a large bottle or cup between colour changes.

Make sure when purchasing your system that you can get replacement parts for your airbrush. There are two basic types of airbrush:

- single action
- double action

The single action airbrush

The single action airbrush simply releases air by depressing the trigger. This trigger has only one action and acts as the on-off switch for the air. The paint flow is controlled by a knob located somewhere on the body of the airbrush (all makes will differ slightly). When this is turned, it varies the amount of paint that will flow through when the trigger is depressed.

The double action airbrush

The double action airbrush has two functions, in that the trigger both

- releases air and
- controls the paint flow.

Most double action airbrushes release air when the trigger is pulled down and release paint when it is pulled back. The air must be released at the same time as the paint to achieve a fine mist with no spitting. Air can also be used on its own to dry a wet nail.

Cleaning and maintenance

The traditional metal airbrush has very delicate parts that need to be kept clean and lubricated for maximum effect. The newer airbrushes are a lot easier to keep clean and require little maintenance. Most of the problems nail artistes have when using an airbrush tend to be due to bad maintenance and lack of proper cleaning. Try to follow these guidelines:

- always use the recommended cleaner appropriate to the paints you use
- use an old paintbrush to clean out the colour cup
- always soak colour cups and nozzles after use
- use airbrush cleaner in a squirt bottle
- use a cleaning station to catch unwanted paint; this will reduce vapours in your breathing zone
- never place any liquid into the airbrush when the needle is not fully in position
- always clean thoroughly between each client

Troubleshooting

The table below covers a number of reasons why an airbrush may not release any paint.

No paint coming through the airbrush

Possible cause	Solution
Dried paint accumulated in nozzle	Use a toothbrush to clean or soak nozzle in cleaner
Nozzle not attached properly	Reattach nozzle
Incorrect size of nozzle for paint type	Reselect appropriate nozzle
Needle not tightened enough to allow paint through	Tighten needle
Paint particles too large	Check the paint is compatible with the system

This section also looks briefly at a number of other problems which might arise.

Bubbles in colour cup

1 nozzle has not been attached correctly
2 nozzle is damaged or cracked
3 dried paint has been left in or on the nozzle

Paint spits from cup

The air flow has been stopped before resetting nozzle.

Trigger sticks when pressed

The trigger might need lubrication.

No air flow through brush

1 remove from hose and check airflow
2 check that the moisture trap drain valve is closed
3 the air valve may be blocked or broken
4 compressor not working
5 check the fuse in the plug

Spotting of paint

1 check that air pressure is not too low
2 check the needle for damage
3 the paint may be too thick

Point to Remember

It is worth persevering with your airbrush and once you have gained confidence you will never look back. Remember airbrushing can be performed on natural nails, nail enhancements and even toes. You could even find yourself decorating your clients' mobile phones.

Compressors

All airbrushes need an air supply. You will find most suppliers of airbrush guns will offer you a range of compressors as well. You do not need a large compressor for nail designs, in fact you can use canned air, although this can be very expensive and frustrating if you are doing a lot of spraying. Although it might seem costly to invest in a good compressor at the outset, it is well worth it in the long run. If airbrushing doesn't work out for you then you can always sell your compressor on.

Compressors work on the principle that they take air from the area you are working in, compress it, then release it from the gun to push the paint out and onto the required surface. Most technicians work at between 25 pounds per square inch (psi) and 35 psi. This will vary slightly, depending on the airbrush, the paint and whether more than one airbrush is connected to the compressor. You may need to attach an air pressure regulator to the compressor to control the pressure being released into the air hose.

It is also advisable to attach a moisture trap or moisture separator to stop any moisture from spitting out from the airbrush whilst you are working. When compressed air from the compressor reaches the air hose, moisture begins to accumulate in the hose. The moisture will then form droplets that will affect the air spray from the gun if they are not collected. You can imagine how devastating it is to ruin a beautiful design by having spots splattered all over it at the last moment!

A compressor can be the most costly piece of airbrushing equipment you buy. Going to trade shows is a good way to see a number of models and try them out. Ask manufacturers for catalogues and prices before you commit yourself, and remember to look at all your options. A popular choice is a small compressor that can be easily carried around with you – particularly important if you work as a mobile technician.

Air hose

This connects your airbrush to your air supply. If you are buying a complete system these will fit automatically. If you have bought your equipment from different places you may need to purchase an adaptor, although most hoses have a $1/4$ inch thread.

Paints

These can vary greatly and it is wise to check out how easy they are to use, their prices, and the other products that go with them. Any paint can be used in any airbrush, but you need to have the appropriate cleaner for that paint. Some paints need to be diluted and you should do this before you start your treatment. Remember, time is money.

The wonderful thing about airbrush paints is that as soon as they reach the nail, they are dry (or should be!). This means you can use many colours for one design. It is worth practising on tips for a few days before you start on clients to get used to the various paints and their effects.

Paints fall into three main categories:

- opaque
- pearlised
- translucent

Opaque colours block out and give the best colour coverage. Pearlised and translucent colours are slightly see-through and will allow the colours or designs underneath to show. You need to plan your designs carefully, remembering colour and coverage.

Colours

Although you do not need to be an expert in colour theory, a basic knowledge helps when performing colour fades or more intricate designs (see the section on finishing techniques at the start of this chapter for more information).

The three primary colours are

- blue
- red
- yellow

All other colours are a mixture of these three. If you perform a colour fade with yellow and red, the overlap of colours will look orange so you will have a graduation from yellow through orange to red.

Look at the chart to see the graduation of colour. It may help to ask a client when they book an airbrushing appointment what colours or designs they would like so you can prepare beforehand.

Colour wheel

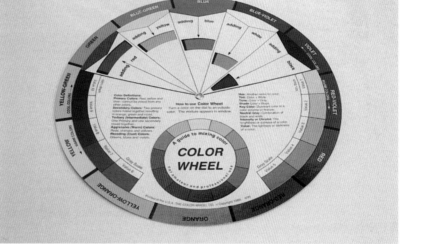

Colour pops

There are some excellent display trays on the market. Most distributors and suppliers of nail art products sell them. You could even make your own using corkboard and colour material. Use these to display your designs so that when a client enquires about airbrushing, you can show them various designs. You could just have one board with a variety of designs or different themes: various colour fades, bridal designs, Christmas designs, and so on. This is the best way to show customers your work and can be easily displayed on the salon walls, desks or at reception. You could also use colour pops, which allows you to change your display every month.

Base coat, bond coat and top coat

You will find most airbrush systems supply their own polishes to enhance the paints. It is much better to utilise those that match the paints you are using and so avoid the finished design not looking as good as it should. Your professional reputation is at stake so don't try to cut corners and save costs – buy a system, use a system as recommended by the manufacturer and it will not let you down.

- You will need to put a base on the nail to allow the paint to adhere to the nail plate. If you do not use a base coat, the paint may slide off the nail, resulting in uneven colour.
- Most paint needs a bonding agent which turns it into a polish, otherwise the design may be washed off or scratched.
- Every design should be top coated to protect it from wear and tear. It is also a good idea to retail your top coat to clients so they can add another coat a few days later. This will keep their designs looking good until they return to you.

Stencils

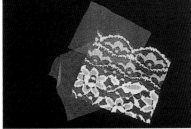

Lace

Stencils

Stencils can be made from hard or soft plastic, fabric or paper. Lace can also be used for a stunning effect. Using stencils can produce the most breathtaking designs, but you will need to perfect your spray technique before attempting to use them.

If you want to demonstrate to a client how a stencil will look before putting the design on his or her nails, spray a little paint through the stencil onto some tissue paper first. The client will then have an idea of the end result before they commit to a design. Stencils can be cleaned with acetone or polish remover and re-used.

Masking paper or frisket

This is a sticky-backed see-through plastic that allows you to make your own stencils. It is an excellent way of performing the French look on client's nails. It is very cheap to buy and easy to use. The easiest way is to take off the backing paper and lay the frisket down onto a piece of toughened glass. With a hobby knife cut out the designs you want and then pick the stencil up off the glass and lay it gently on the nail. You can cut frisket with scissors, but it can then be very fiddly trying to peel off the backing paper. Frisket is not re-useable but it is so cheap to buy that it is still very cost effective. Some companies sell pre-cut designs in frisket.

Setting up

You will need a table and a good light to work by. If using a compressor make sure you are near an electric supply and that there are no trailing leads to trip over. Plug in your compressor, attach the hose and airbrush. Make sure you have cleaner (in a squirt bottle), cleaning station, polishes and paints all to hand. Prepare a few dozen tips by base coating them and attach to a board with blu-tac or pins. These are your practice tips. You may want to set up a separate tray or trolley with all your airbrush equipment on it so it can be shared with other technicians when you are not using it. This will also prevent it cluttering up your work station. Always make sure you have plenty of tissues or terry towel around when airbrushing and that you and your client's clothes are protected by old towels or protective wear. Before you put paint into your airbrush always run a small amount of cleaner through to lubricate the pipes and tubes and to make sure the airbrush is not blocked. This will also allow the paint to move more freely. Before practising on tips or clients get used to the airbrush by practising on tissue or a white board. This will allow you to get used to the trigger, airflow and the amount of paint you need.

Here are some important points to remember:

- hold the airbrush approximately 5–8 cm from the surface to be painted
- move your whole arm and not just your wrist
- spraying near the surface will give a crisper finish
- spraying from further away will give a softer look
- press down for air
- go back to air if the paint looks wet

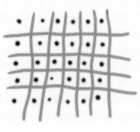

White board with dots

Use your board to practise dots and lines. This will not only help you to see where you are aiming but also to gauge how much paint is coming out. When you find that your dots are landing where you want them to, then you know your aim is right. Practise lines – this will help you to determine how much paint to use and the ratio needed of air to paint to airflow. Draw boxes and fill them in from corner to corner. If you find that the boxes look like a row of lines rather than a block of one colour this means you are too close or that there is too much paint.

Once you have perfected your technique, move on to working on your board with nail tips.

Step-by-step airbrush designs

You are limited only by your own imagination. The airbrush is the most versatile artistic tool imaginable and can produce the most incredible designs you will see. You should always practise on tips first to get the feel and touch of your airbrush. The colour range of paints is much more diverse than those you would find in a polish rack. It is even possible to mix colours to match your clients' outfits and accessories. If you are not artistic the airbrush is definitely

Airbrush designs

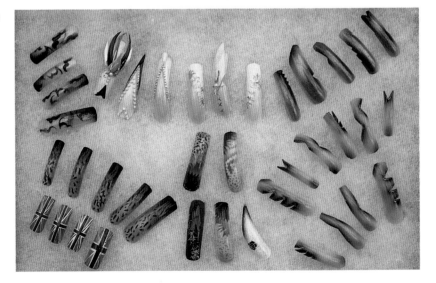

for you, as there are so many stencils and pre-cut friskets available that you do not even have to make up your own designs. Every nail artist has a day when they go blank and cannot think of what to do. A good way to avoid this is to collect pictures and colour charts from magazines and DIY stores and make up a scrapbook. This may help you to find inspiration.

Here are five step-by-step procedures for the most popular designs that are requested of nail artists.

Equipment needed for this section:

- airbrush
- compressor
- cleaner and cleaning station
- paints
- base coat, sealer and top coat
- stencils or frisket

Basic colour fade

1 Apply a base coat to clean, dry nails.
2 At this point you should have already agreed with the client which colour combination they would like. Spray the palest colour over the whole nail first and make sure the colour depth on all ten nails is the same.

Colour fade

Technical Tip

- A good colour fade is one where you cannot distinguish where one colour ends and the next colour begins.
- Always choose colours that will complement one another.

3 Take the second colour, which should be darker than the first, and spray across the nail diagonally starting at the free edge and working towards the middle. Work the colour back down towards the free edge and take the colour back up again, but this time only half the previous surface should be covered. Finally spray into the tip in the corner to get good colour depth.

4   If desired, take a third colour and repeat step 3 but only work in the bottom quarter of the nail at the free edge. Do not forget to come back down on the free edge to increase colour depth.

5   Very carefully apply bonder or sealant if the paints require it. This will turn most paints into what we would consider a polish. The application of sealers and bonders can enhance or ruin a beautiful design. You need to apply the bonder liberally and not allow the bristles of the brush to scratch the surface, as this could drag the paint down the nail.

6   Apply a good quality top coat that will keep your client's design looking good for weeks.

7   Once your client has had time for their nails to dry it is time to clean off any paint oversprayed on their skin. You can use a cotton tip with a small amount of polish remover, remembering to oil the skin afterwards to counteract any drying. Alternatively, most paints should come off if your clients wash their hands. There is obviously a risk doing this that the nails are not dry, so check them first.

Chevron French with stripe

1   Apply a base coat to clean, dry nails.

2   Spray chosen French colour all over the entire nail.

3   Having already prepared your frisket in a V-shape, place it on the nail, covering the top two thirds of the nail and leaving the free edge exposed.

4   Spray the exposed nail with chosen colour, making sure you have good coverage along the edge of the frisket.

5   Peel off frisket very carefully and re-attach further down the nail, still leaving a gap to spray on the white. The further down you move the frisket the bigger the stripe

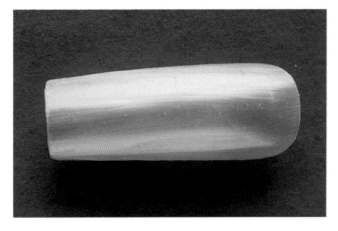

Base coat application for French

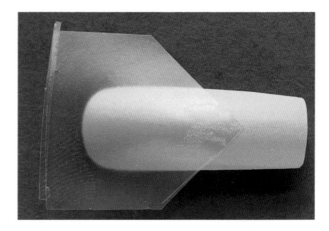

Frisket on French nail

will be. Spray white onto the remaining exposed free edge, making sure you get good coverage and that no other colour can be seen through. Remove the frisket gently to expose the finished nail.

Colour sprayed on free edge

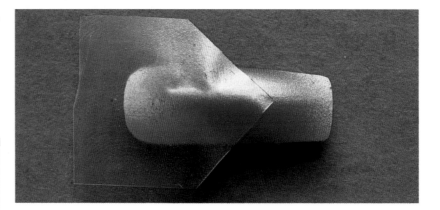

Technical Tip

- If the paint is applied too thick or too wet it will come away when the frisket is peeled off. If this happens then alter your technique.

- Be consistent when placing the frisket as this will ensure that all of your stripes are the same width.

- Be sure to line up the point of the V at the same place on each nail so the chevron is not distorted.

6 Very carefully apply bonder or sealant if the paints require it. This will turn most paints into what we would consider a polish. The application of sealers and bonders can enhance or ruin a beautiful design. You need to apply the bonder liberally and not allow the bristles of the brush to scratch the surface, as this could drag the paint down the nail.

7 Apply a good quality top coat that will keep your client's design looking good for weeks.

8 Once your client has had time for their nails to dry it is time to clean off any paint oversprayed on their skin. You can use a cotton tip with a small amount of polish remover, remembering to oil the skin afterwards to counteract any drying. Alternatively, most paints should come off if your clients wash their hands. There is obviously a risk doing this that the nails might not be dry, so check them first.

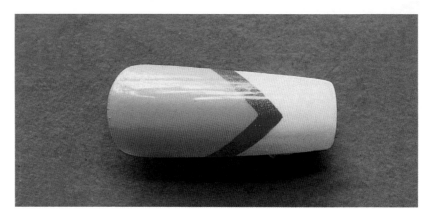

Finished French nail

Step-by-step animal print

Animal print

1   Apply a base coat to clean, dry nails.

2   Spray with the chosen base colour over the entire nail, making sure you have the same coverage on all ten nails. When choosing colours for your animal print it is a good idea to use a paler colour as the base and to pick other colours that will complement one another.

3   Spray a second, slightly darker colour on each end of the nail, the cuticle and the free edge.

4   Spray with a deeper colour down the side of the nail making sure you cannot determine where each colour starts and finishes. Build up the colour on the edge to give an illusion of depth.

5   Make sure the surface of the nails dry and lay an animal stencil lightly over the nail holding down either side of client's nail with your two fingers. The nearer the stencil is to the surface of the nail the crisper the resulting design. Spray with your darkest colour, usually black, up and down in a vertical line ensuring a good coverage. Gently take the stencil away and go on to the next nail.

6   Finish with steps 7 and 8 given for the chevron French design above for sealant, top coat and cleaning the skin.

Fancy French

1   Apply base coat to clean, dry nails.

2   Spray the selected base colour over the entire nail and repeat on all 10 nails.

3   Cover the top two-thirds with a pre-cut piece of frisket that has a curve. This will create your smile line. Spray white paint over the free edge.

4   Remove frisket carefully, then use a small abstract stencil to create a random pattern with two selected colours.

Step 2 – spray nails pink

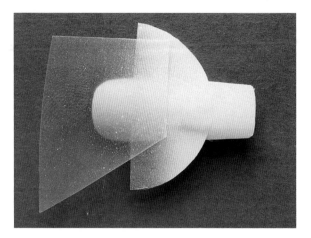

Step 3 – frisket on pink nail

Step 4 – stencil

Step 5 – seal the design

Step 6 – clean the skin

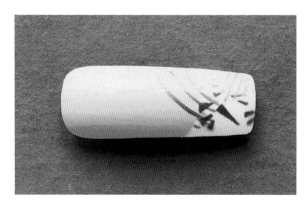

Finished nail

Technical Tip

Use different shapes such as curved lines, triangles or wisps.

5 Repeat the steps given for sealant as above.

6 Repeat the steps given for top coat and cleaning the skin as above.

Tropical paradise

1 Apply a base coat to clean, dry nails.

2 Cover the bottom half of all ten nails with frisket and spray the top portion of the nails with a two-colour fade. This will represent a sunset, so choose colours that will complement this.

3 Using a stencil with a small hole, hold the stencil just above the frisket and spray a yellow sun.

Step by step tropical design

4 Remove the frisket, turn through 180°, replace the frisket and spray a two-colour fade on the bottom portion. By turning the frisket you are protecting the top portion.

5 Remove the frisket, apply a stencil with a palm tree and spray in an appropriate colour.

6 Repeat the steps given for sealant, top coat and cleaning the skin as above.

Selection of airbrush designs

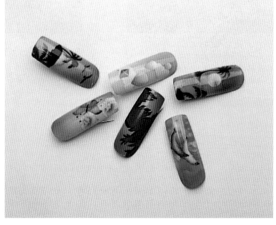

Technical Tip

Try changing the colour to create a night scene. You could also hand paint white waves or birds for more detail.

Taking nail art to the next dimension

Learning objectives

In this section you will learn about:

- **advanced nail art techniques**

- **when 3D nails can be incorporated into salon treatments**

- **a step-by-step zebra print design**

- **setting nail bindis into acrylic nails**

- **cut outs and acrylic 3D nails**

No longer do nail technicians have to restrict themselves to performing nail enhancements on their clients. The nail industry is becoming a very exciting place to work. Customers in general have become more adventurous and wearing nail art is now considered quite normal and no longer as unnecessarily ostentatious. You will always find that your clients fall into two categories: the conservative and the adventurous. It will be the latter group who are willing to let you experiment on their nails and who will love the looks you can create with 3D nail art. We have already looked at the basics of nail art and airbrushing. These are both skilful techniques that need to be learnt and practised, but now we are going to examine a relatively new area of work – creating artistic designs with more than just your nail products.

It's a great idea to practise new designs on tips before trying to recreate them on clients. The Nail Trainer is an excellent tool to use for this practice, as it acts like a real hand and, while it allows you freedom of movement, it also gives you an idea of the restrictions working on a real hand will bring. You can also save your designs to show your clients, allowing them to choose the ones they like the best.

If you decide to introduce 3D nails into your salon make sure you include this service on your price list and set your prices to take into account the extra artwork you will be performing. You will find that doing any intricate work will take much longer and your time is what the clients are paying for. You might also need to add in the cost of any extra jewels or products that you use. However, be sure to warn your clients of the extra cost.

Clients are continually demanding more and more from us and we need to keep up to date with fashions, trends, colours and styles. No longer do they just want a polish, but they are looking for nails that will match their outfits, hair, jewellery, shoes and much, much more. Look around you to see what can be incorporated into your nail art kit – items such as sandwich bag ties, feathers, bindis, chains and a lot more. Never say no and always strive for new ideas. Look through magazines, hair and make-up books, nail style books for anything and everything that will give you inspiration.

If you look at nail technicians who have dared to be different, you will see how successful they are – not only with their salon clients but they are frequently sought after by photographers, designers, models and pop stars for their innovative designs with nails.

Salon nails

When you look at trade magazines and nail style books you will see the most outrageous designs on nails and wonder how they are done. These are obviously unwearable and are usually for photographic or catwalk use. In fact that is why 'The Untouchables' Nail Art Team called themselves by that name, purely because the nails that they create cannot be worn in normal daily living – they are untouchable and unwearable. However, these nail styles – just like catwalk clothes – can be scaled down for our clients to wear in their everyday lives. It is possible to create a 3D look that is wearable and stunning without too much time and expense and which can be rebalanced quite easily.

For example, rhinestones are easy to set into UV gel or acrylic before it is cured and so will last a lot longer than normal. You can create beautiful designs with coloured acrylics set onto a clear tip or sculpting form that will grow out with the natural nail. Even fibreglass can be used to create beautiful 3D designs. Practise as much as possible and if you develop a design you like, wear it on one finger and see what reaction you get from clients. We find that anything a technician wears, their clients will want too – what better way to sell your skills than by wearing them.

Step-by-step zebra print

You will need:

- files and buffers
- manicure tools
- cuticle cream or oil
- clear tips or sculpting forms
- white acrylic powder
- black acrylic powder
- monomer
- clear, pink and natural acrylic powder

1 Perform a mini manicure on the cuticles using cuticle cream or oil, making sure all excessive non-living tissue is removed.

2 Gently buff the surface shine from the natural nail surface to remove any oil and bacteria.

3 Dehydrate and cleanse the nail with an appropriate product.

4 Apply clear or normal tips depending on the design you want to achieve. Make sure the contact area is cut out as small as is practical and *do not blend* into the natural nail.

5 Cleanse the nail again with a dehydrator, making sure you do not touch the tip as this will cloud the area.

6 With the white powder, build acrylic into small sections up the nail. You can take the design over the entire nail or just up to the flesh line, it really depends which look you want. You may find using a smaller brush than normal will help you achieve finer lines.

7 Fill in the gaps with black powder, trying not to overlap too much. If you do, do not worry as the nail can be buffed to take the shadow away.

8 Buff gently to take down any height in the product and wipe with cleanser to remove dust particles.

9 Apply either clear, natural or pink powder to the rest of the nail. Remember, clear will look best as it will show the design off well, but if your client has any damage or marks on his or her natural nail you might want to camouflage these with natural or pink powders.

10 Buff nails to a high shine and oil.

Step-by-step embedding bindis

You will need:

- files and buffers

- manicure tools
- cuticle creams and oils
- clear tips or sculpting forms
- UV gel or clear acrylic powder
- 10 bindis of the same design

You may use bindis or rhinestones, jewellery, even tiny dried flowers, shells – the list goes on.

1 Perform a mini manicure to make sure all excessive non-living tissue is removed.

2 Remove the shine from the natural nail plate.

3 Cleanse and dehydrate the natural nail plate with an appropriate cleanser.

4 Apply clear tip in the same way as described above or fit the sculpting forms.

5 Cleanse the nail to remove all dust.

6 Apply a small bead of acrylic or gel in the area where the bindi is to be placed and set the jewel into it. Press gently until the bindi is in correct place and then apply product over the rest of the nail.

7 Buff to a high gloss finish and apply oil.

Technical Tip

Try not to set the bindi too near the cuticle as this will make the nail very bulky and proud and difficult to buff down. The easiest and better looking position is right on the stress line.

Technical Tip

You could use white paint in a henna design over free edge to add to artwork, after nails have been buffed and shined.

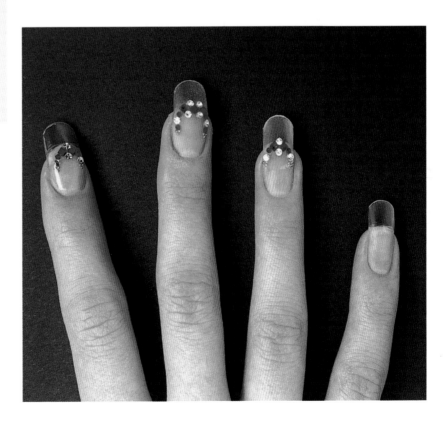

Step-by-step cut outs

You will need:

- scissors
- files and buffers
- sculpting brush
- liquid and powder
- drill
- airbrush equipment
- airbrush colours
- selection of rhinestones
- top coat

1   Take an extra long, curved tip and cut either side of the free edge to form a point.

2   Take a drill and make two or three holes in the tip.

3   Take beads of liquid and powder and place onto nail tip in various shapes. Work acrylic with the tip of a brush,

remembering the time constraints this product works to.
Try to work from the cuticle end of the tip to get a
teardrop effect coming down the nail.

4   Once the product is dry, spray nail tips with airbrush
colours. Fade colour in and out of the beads of product to
give shadows and highlights.

5   Seal the design with airbrush sealant or an appropriate
top coat.

6   Apply a final top coat and embed three of four
rhinestones across the design to complement the colour
and give added texture.

7   Once dry, nails can be attached to models' nails for a
photoshoot or catwalk show.

These nail designs are obviously intended for photographic
purposes and should not be worn in normal circumstances.

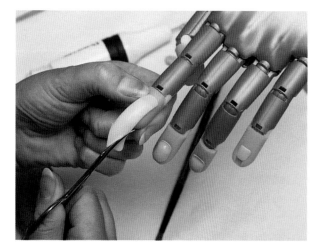

Step 1 – cut outs

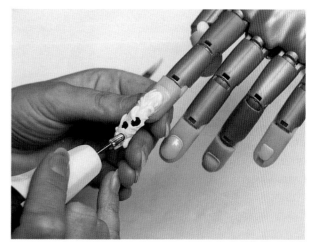

Step 2 – drill

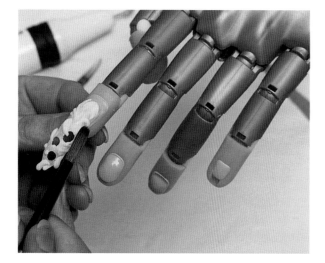

Step 3 – adding liquid and powder

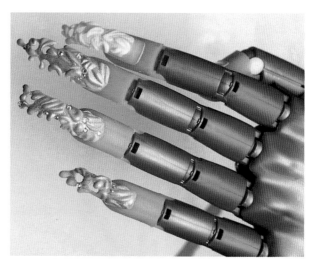

Step 4 – sculpting

You can tone down your more inventive designs for your salon clients.

Remember that you are limited only by your imagination. If you have any spare time just sit with your nail kit, your Hand Trainer and design yourself some incredible nails. Enjoy being *creative*.

Technical Tip

Use your hand trainer to work on this type of nail as it will give you a good idea of what position the designs will take when applied to a real hand.

Chapter summary

There are many companies that offer nail art courses, some basic and others more advanced. After reading this chapter and following the basic step-by-step guides you could incorporate simple designs onto your clients' nails without having to attend a course. This chapter will also help those who are not particularly artistic and feel they need some inspiration to get started. You can refer to this chapter throughout your training and career to help with colour, finishing techniques, simple nail art designs and – for those who are more adventurous – the airbrushing and 3D work.

Photographic and competition nails

This chapter is one of the most exciting as it covers competition, photographic and catwalk nails. All of these areas of work are relatively new to the industry and all three will be better suited to those technicians with some experience than to those who have just completed their basic training. Competition nails are becoming increasingly popular and the competition circuit is getting harder, with new talent entering each year. This chapter will take you through the rules and regulations involved in entering a competition, choosing the right model, what the judges will be looking for and the rewards not just of winning but also of enhancing your skills for your clients.

This chapter looks at the key differences between catwalk nails and photographic nails and the benefits of getting involved in this side of the industry. Also discussed is the equipment you will need to have, the key people involved in this type of work and what type of experience you will need to have to be able to get work in the first place.

Whether you are an experienced technician or just starting out, this chapter will make interesting reading and hopefully inspire you to stretch your capabilities and enter a new field of work.

In this chapter we will consider the following aspects:

- **winning nails**
- **photographing nails**
- **catwalk nails**

Winning nails

Learning objectives

In this section you will learn about:

- **how to recognise the perfect model**
- **applying thin, beautiful nail enhancements**
- **setting up a nail station for maximum points**
- **what the judges are looking for**
- **types of competition**
- **the rewards of entering competitions**

Competition work is nerve-racking, but extremely rewarding. The key is to enter to compete against yourself, as you should always be trying to stretch your capabilities to the limit. Any technician who can do a beautiful set of competition nails will also be able to do the best photographic nails. You will see, when you enter the nail industry, that the same technicians enter competitions time and time again. There are very few people who win straight-away. You will need determination and skill to be able to succeed.

Competition winner accepting trophy

Types of competition

Entering competitions can greatly improve your skill in the salon. The detail that you will have to work to in a competition will make you look critically at the work you are doing within the salon and adapt your techniques to enhance your clients' nails. It is impossible to perform competition nails on your clients as they are not hard-wearing and would break soon after they left the salon, but you can certainly use your skills to perfect the overall look. A set of competition nails will take you $2^1/_2$ hours to complete; salon nails average about $1^1/_2$ hours.

If you are not sure whether you should enter competitions then listen to friends and colleagues. If they are constantly telling you how wonderful your skills are at the desk, then maybe it is something you should consider. It is relatively inexpensive to enter and competitions are usually held at Nail and Beauty Shows throughout the year, so you will have plenty of opportunities to attend and enter a number of times in a short period of time.

There are various categories that you can enter at competitions. The one that we will concentrate on in this section is Nail Enhancements.

Here are the categories that currently run at most shows:

- manicure – with written test
- nail art – not 3D, just flat nail art such as painting
- fibreglass
- gel
- liquid and powder
- sculpting – using any system
- virgin or rookie – for technicians who have never entered before
- winner of winners – for technicians that have won previously

In this section we will discuss how to prepare nails for the three nail systems, what the judges are looking for and finishing techniques. Whilst it is very flattering that people around you encourage you to enter competitions, you will have a better chance of winning if you are absolutely sure what the criteria for winning nails are and what the judges want to see. You need to know how to achieve this and achieve it consistently, not just occasionally.

There are five main areas to look at before attempting a competition entry and you will need to achieve them all before you are likely to win.

Practice

It is virtually impossible for any technician, no matter how wonderful their skills, to win a competition without practising. Do not leave this to the week before the competition. Practise all the time in your work on clients, they will be really pleased with that little bit of extra attention to detail. You will need months of practice and critical appraisal of your work before you will feel ready to enter.

Consistency

You will need to be consistent in every area of your work. You cannot leave any area to chance, you need to be confident that on the day you are capable of creating beautiful nails every time you do a new set. It relieves the pressure slightly to know that you are as good as everyone else but just need to perform better than anyone else on the day. Consistency is the key word. Every nail should look the same, have the same length, the same 'C' curve and profile.

Brush technique

Looking at the way you apply product will save you valuable time that you need for finishing off. Whether it is liquid and powder, gel or fibreglass the way you apply your product will affect not only the look of the nails but also the confidence you have to finish off in the allotted time. Stress can be disastrous when you are under pressure at the end of your $2^{1}/_{2}$ hours. Make sure that you practise your product placement until it becomes second nature.

Finishing and filing techniques

Every nail should look exactly the same all the time. If your product has been applied perfectly then there should be less filing to do. You will need extra files at a competition than when you are working in the salon. For instance, when buffing to a shine it is a good idea to take a new file for each nail. You should be able to see a mirror image of yourself when looking into the nails at the end – there should be no scratches, no cut cuticles, all the arches in the right places and beautiful 'C' curves, not flat nails.

It would be highly beneficial to book a one-on-one session with a competition winner, as they can pass on their speed and finishing techniques and give you great tips for winning.

Courtesy of Katherine Rae

Your competition set-up

So what do you need on the day? Try to gather together all
tools, products and equipment at least a week before – there
has been many a technician seen rushing around just before
the competition starts, trying to buy products from stands
that have not yet opened. Be organised, it is less stressful.
The following is a basic checklist for those essential items
you will need on the day:

- towels and tissue or couch roll
- uniform
- table lamp
- extension lead for lamp

- small table decoration – maybe a flower arrangement
- small jar for sterilising solution
- appropriate solution to sterilise and disinfect tools
- nail products in clean containers
- new files and buffers – plenty of them
- manicure tools
- cuticle oil and creams – check if these are allowed
- red polish

The following points will help your performance to go smoothly:

- Choose a good quality polish with good colour coverage.
- Have at least one finishing buffer for each finger on the unfinished hand.
- Use a tip box with few rather than many tips in it.
- Make sure you have prepared your model's cuticles the day before.
- Size tips on your model the day before to save time.

Desk set-up

Have all your equipment prepared the week before and check it again the day before. There will be floor judges looking at the way you have set out your nail station and whether you are working safely and using all the proper procedures. They will also want to see that your working area looks clean, neat and attractive. Make sure you take into account all of these points as the marks you might lose could make all the difference between first and second place.

Appearance

Dress as you should do in the salon: white jacket or top, just a wedding band, small watch, stud earrings and long hair tied away from the face. You could also lose valuable points by ignoring the industry dress code and attending a competition dressed inappropriately. As the industry is moving towards a more professional stance, the judges will be looking for all those entering to be setting the standards – as indeed they should.

Your model

The model you choose to work on can make a huge difference to the end result. It is not just their nails that should be taken into account but their personality as well. Choose someone that you feel comfortable with, someone who will help *you* to relax and critique the nails during the competition. It is amazing how much support your model can give you and if you can find one who is also a nail technician this will be an added bonus. When searching for a model you will need to take the following points into account:

- your model should be a helpful partner during the competition
- the model's hands should be neither too large nor too small
- the model's skin should be smooth, with an even skin tone and no imperfections
- the model's nail beds should be long and slim, with a very small free edge
- the nail beds should be pink and healthy, with no damage
- the model should have a calm personality and be able to advise you throughout of how much time you have left
- choose a model you can practice on a month before and whom you can meet a few days before to prepare her cuticles and natural nails

Try to practise as much as possible on anyone who will allow you to and each time you work concentrate on perfecting a different area. If you think that your ego will be shattered by losing then do not enter competitions. Be a good sport, whether you win or lose. Be supportive of the other nail technicians sitting around you and they will help you too.

Even if you do not win, you will have learnt something that you can take back to the salon and your clients. The skills you have practised and used will dramatically enhance your work. Your clients will respect you for trying and hopefully it will motivate you to enter further competitions.

So what are the judges looking for?

You will have only $2^1/_2$ hours to produce a set of perfect, thin, sleek and polished natural-looking nails. The shape and design is up to the competitor, but it is easier to judge the 'C' curve and lower arch on a square or square rounded nail.

Here are some of the points the judges will be looking for in a perfect competition nail.

1 *Consistency* of the upper and lower arch. This can be

Technical Tip

- Do not try anything new on competition day. This could be costly in time or points.
- Use the Nail Trainer to practise your skills; this practice hand is invaluable for working on your skills at any time of the day or night.

achieved by perfect product placement at the stress area, as this will parallel the lower arch line of the sidewalls.

2   The *stress point* should be consistent across all ten nails. Make sure the stress area bead never covers more than one half of the visible nail plate and that it is applied in exactly the same spot on every nail to achieve consistency.

3   The *cuticle area* should be clean, neat and with no signs of abrasion. The judge will feel each nail to see if there is a ridge between the product and the natural nail. Leave a tiny free margin so that the product can be buffed into the natural nail.

4   The *free edge* should be consistent in shape and smoothness. Measure each one with an orange stick to check length.

5   The *'C' curve* should be crescent-shaped and neither too flat nor too curved. A crescent shape is what the judges will be looking for when they look down the 'barrel' of the nails. This is easier to achieve by keeping the flat side of your brush always facing the curve of the nail – rotate your brush as you work.

6   The *sidewalls* should fit perfectly into the grooves with no 'glitches'. The judges will be looking for a perfect tip fit and no matter which system you are using a badly fitted tip will show through. Watch your tip sizing and make sure it is exact from sidewall to sidewall and sitting straight on the hand you are working on.

7   The *underside* of a tip or sculpted nail should be free from dust and excess product or adhesive. The judges will be looking to see if there is an excess of adhesive or seepage of too much product. Have some orange sticks tipped with cotton wool prepared to dip into remover and clean up immediately if this happens. You can also use these later to clean off any excess dust.

8   *Product application* should be crystal clear with no bubbles or white spots. The judges will look to see if there are any ghost shadows from the tip application or shadows in your white powder application and also that your smile line is smiling and looks like a knife edge. To achieve a perfect crisp smile you may need to backbrush – although this should never be done in the salon many technicians use it in their competition work. To eliminate any possibility of bubbles in your product application leave the bead on the nail for a few seconds before you start to press. This will allow the chemical reaction to get going before you start to press into place.

9 *Surface smoothness* is very important on both hands but you will need to pay more attention to the hand that will not have polish. If you finish buffing the polished hand and apply polish it means you have time to concentrate on achieving the highest gloss shine on the other hand. The judges will be looking to see that you have no scratch marks showing at all. Use only the finest abrasives to finish the nails, the harsher the abrasive, the deeper the grooves you will put into the nail surface. This will mean extra buffing and you will not have time. Keep to a strict method of buffing each nail so they all look consistent.

10 Your *polish application* needs to be perfect. You will not be using a base coat or top coat so it will be difficult to disguise bad application. The judges will want to see an even, consistent application, no seepage and good coverage on all five nails. You must make sure you know which hand it is you need to paint, there have been many technicians who have lost marks by polishing the wrong hand. Look at the free edge and make sure the polish is buffered to cover the white. Use a small art brush with a nail dehydrator to clean up any seepage or small glitches around the sidewalls, cuticle or free edge.

If this has not put you off, then get practising and find out when and where the next competition will be held. When you register, make sure that you have received the rules and regulations and read them carefully to make sure you are not disappointed in any way. Ask colleagues who have already been on the competition circuit for tips, book in for some training with a competition winner, but at the end of the day it is up to you to *practise, practise, practise.*

The judges will use a judging sheet to mark your nails and at the end of the competition this will be given to you to keep. If you are unhappy about your marks, the judges will allow you time to go over why they have marked your nails in that way. Judges are usually very experienced nail technicians themselves so it is worth listening to their constructive criticism and learning from it. Judging is a very difficult job which has to be done in a very short space of time. They will not know whose nails they are judging so it is impossible for them to be biased in any way.

Some people are naturally competitive and thrive on competitions, others have to be coaxed into it, but competitions are a good way of developing your skills. You are really only competing against yourself to achieve the ultimate set of nails. *Good luck.*

TIP & OVERLAY

CONTESTANT# _____

JUDGE _____

TOTAL SCORE _____

PLACEMENT _____

	PINKY	RING	MIDDLE	INDEX	THUMB	PINKY	RING	MIDDLE	INDEX	THUMB	TOTAL POINTS
All 10 Nails #1 CONCAVE & CONVEX Consistency of degree & convex/concave shape											
#2 STRESS POINT Location & consistency of arch											
#3 GROOVE WALLS Quality of edge from nail grove											
#4 FREE EDGE Smoothness & consistent shape											
#5 CUTICLE Smoothness & skin											
#6 UNDERSIDE Cleanliness & tip fit											
#7 LENGTH CONSISTENCY											
Unpolished Nails #8 SURFACE SMOOTHNESS Buffing & smoothness											
#9 PRODUCT CONTROL Air bubbles, product application, clarity, smile line & tip application & blending											
Polished Nails #10 SURFACE FINISH Smoothness and consistency of polish											
#11 CUTICLE Neatness & finished quality											
#12 OVERALL COVERAGE Coverage on all edges											
#13 OVERALL WORKMANSHIP Overall appearance & presentation consistency											

JUDGE'S COMMENTS: _____

_____

_____

TOTAL SCORE
POINT SYSTEM
2 points = perfect
1 point = average
0 points = below average

Judging sheet

Lights, camera, action

Learning objectives

In this section you will learn about:

- **planning commercial and trade photographic nail shots**

- **photographing your own designs**

- **making use of additional materials such as hair, make-up and airbrush body art**

- **presenting a final image**

- **creating a portfolio of work**

How to create a great photograph

Design your nails and then create the rest of the picture. Remember that the nails are the focal point of the photograph and don't lose them in the overall picture.

Your design should be natural, creative and inspiring to your audience. Study other great nail shots and make a list of the points you see. Be creative and don't put up boundaries for yourself, anything is possible. This section will guide you through the areas you will need to know about before embarking on a career in photographic nails, whether this is taking your own work shots or working for a photographer.

Planning your photographic work

Organising a photographic shot takes a lot of planning before the event otherwise a number of things can go wrong. This may be extremely expensive and it can be very upsetting if your pictures do not turn out the way you had hoped. You need to decide first whether or not you will be using a professional photographer or doing the photography yourself. Carry out some research first to get ideas on looks and themes. Use trade magazines, consumer magazines, films and television. The Internet has a number of different sites where you can find inspiration. If you already have an idea, share it with friends and benefit from their valuable input.

The initial plan

- research ideas
- decide on a theme
- design your nails
- budget for a photographer, developing costs, a model and props
- budget for a professional hairdresser and make-up artist
- put the plan in writing and include letters to key people
- set a date, let the key people know the schedule and times, and collect your props

The blueprint

You will need to design a blueprint for your picture. To keep the costs down and to avoid wasting time, organise yourself and look at the following points:

- What are you trying to get?
- How will you make the nails the main focus?

- Which position of the hands will most complement the nails?
- Should you include props or not? Will they complement the nails?
- What colour scheme will you use?

It is quite a recent development that the consumer press, photographers and other professionals have begun to recognise nail technicians as stand-alone artists. In the past, at most photo shoots and catwalk shows, it was the make-up artist who painted or decorated the models' nails. That has now changed and nail technicians can choose to make photographic work a full-time career.

Being creative is a very big part of being a nail technician and without this creativity new techniques and images would never come into being. Every technician loves to see work that stretches the imagination of clients and professionals alike. In this section we hope to take you on an exciting journey through the steps required to plan your work and create a beautiful portfolio to present to potential agencies or clients.

Most images – whether it be hair, make-up or nails – fall into three main categories:

- natural or commercial
- fashion or avant-garde
- fantasy

All technicians can create their own opportunities by entering competitions, staging fashion shows and getting involved in photographic shoots.

The detailed plan

You will need to consider the picture as a whole, but still keep the focus on the nails. Depending on the look you want to achieve you might need to look at the following:

- background colour
- clothing, accessories and jewellery
- nail art, body art – tattoos, body paint, henna

A checklist such as the one below will help you to plan for the day and so save time and possibly expensive mistakes.

- Sketch the idea and make notes – this will give you a design plan to work to.
- Decide on the model (use the model checklist) and give them a time to arrive. Allow for hair and make-up if it is being used.

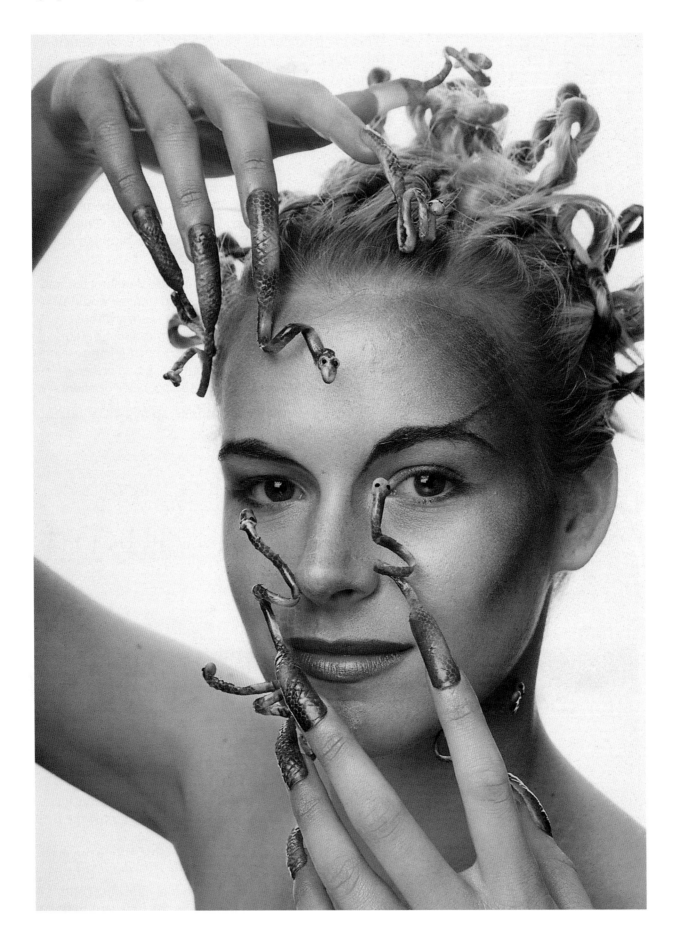

- Meet with the photographer beforehand so he or she knows what equipment to bring and what look you want to achieve. Show them some pictures to give an idea of what you want.

- Make a list of who is responsible for what and give it to each person with a briefing to ensure that everyone understands what is required of them.

- Make sure all the props are ready the day before the shoot.

- Work out the schedule for the day. A photographer's time is very expensive you don't want the photographer sitting around idle whilst hair and make-up is being done.

- Make sure you have adequate lighting, if not arrange for extra lighting.

- Make sure you have a lot of film so different angles and looks can be taken. You will find that once the shots have been developed some will be unsuitable for various reasons.

The model

The model is probably the most important person in the whole process. Choose the wrong model and you could lose the look of the whole picture. It goes without saying that a hand model needs gorgeous hands but if you are using the body, hair or face you need to check these too. Do not assume that because someone is a model that every part of his or her body is perfect. Here are two checklists for you.

Choose a model with beautiful hands and skin:

- long, slender fingers (watch for crooked fingers or large knuckles)
- wrinkle-free skin
- light to no body hair on hands or arms
- even skin tone
- no scars or abrasions
- small bones
- young hands shoot best

Choose a model with beautiful natural nails:

- long, slender nail beds
- medium 'C' curves (if these are too deep they can make enhancements look thick)
- medium-sized nail plates (neither too small nor too large)

- deep, dramatic smile lines
- flat to slightly arched upper arches (too much natural curve makes nails look thick)
- straight sidewalls
- even pink colour
- no abrasions or damage in nail beds
- thin, neat cuticles

Natural nails

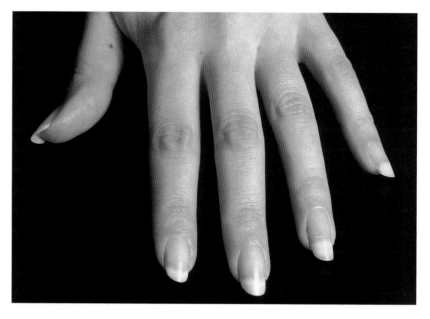

Photographing your designs

Once you have designed your nails, found a good model and decided on a location, you need to design your picture. Don't choose a model who has wonderful hands if she does not have the type of face or hair you want when these are to be included in the picture. You need to look at the props you might need in relation to the end look that you want. In this section we will take you through the steps to setting up a mini studio and doing a shoot of a front cover.

The studio will need the following equipment:

- table or equivalent prop
- 35mm camera
- professional or portrait film
- tripod to hold the camera steady
- at least two 30cm silver reflector flood lamps
- two 250-watt blue photo flood bulbs
- close-up lens if you require intricate work
- appropriate props, such as background materials, paper, etc.

Position the table in the centre of the room and make sure it is stable. Cover with material appropriate for the shot being taken. The two floor-length reflector lamps with 250-watt flood bulbs should be placed either side of the table and the tripod with the camera close up to the desk. The lamp bulbs are specially designed to cast a bright light that will not distort the true colours of your picture; you will not need extra flashes.

Make sure the shutter speed is set at 125th of a second and that the F stop is at F8 or higher.

When you have set up all the equipment properly put your model in place and arrange your props around them. Make sure you stress to your model how important it is not to move after you have positioned his or her hands.

Studio set-up

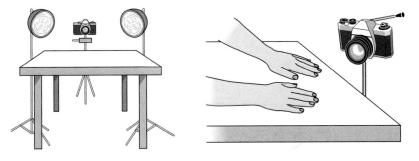

The look you are trying to achieve will determine how near you position the camera to the nails.

Remember to position the hands for the maximum impact. If you can see the underneath of the nail, make sure that it is tidy. If photographing from the side, make sure the sidewalls are neat. Look at the nails from every angle through the camera to find the look you want before using up expensive film.

Before you finish try taking a few shots from a different angle – sometimes the camera does not complement what you want to achieve.

It is a really good idea to link in with a local photographer to get hints and tips or find a good book so that you can develop a better understanding of what is going on.

You are limited only by your own imagination and you should never assume something is impossible. The following photo checklist will help you to prepare for the shoot:

- Always look through the lens once the shoot is in position to check it is the picture that you want. Move the fingers, hands or props as necessary to get the right look.
- Make sure the model's hands look natural and relaxed.

- Watch for movement; the model should be aware that any slight movement can spoil the picture.
- The nail design should stand out as the main focus and not blend into the background.
- It is a good idea to take a polaroid before using the film to give you an idea of what the picture will look like.
- Remember the camera adds weight and picks up any inconsistencies – make sure the nails are perfect.

To produce nails as shown in the photo the nails are first prepared using white and black acrylic. The extensions are sculptured onto the natural nails using a zebra design. The model, wearing a silver bikini, places her hand over her chest and, with the airbrush, white paint is sprayed over her chest, arm, hand and fingers. Using black paint, a zebra stripe is sprayed through a large stencil. A final spray of gold gives the whole look a softer shimmer. The model must keep her hand in position while the photographer takes the picture.

Additional materials

Make sure when designing your picture that your props do not overshadow the nails. The model's hair should match the look you are trying to achieve. Look at the fashion of the moment, including colours. There are a number of hair products on the market, such as washout coloured mousses or clip-in hairpieces. You can use twigs, ribbons and a wide range of hair accessories in your model's hair. If hair is going to be a big part of the picture make sure you choose a model with good hair. The make-up on the market today also incorporates every colour you could possibly think of. You can use false lashes, bindis, and body jewellery. If you want to use diamantes use an eyelash adhesive and not a nail adhesive to attach them to the skin.

If using material in the background consider its texture and colour and make sure it will not overshadow the nail design.

Airbrushing is probably the most versatile decorating tool you can use for nails and body art. It is worthwhile thinking about attending a course and investing in equipment if you want to embark on a photographic career. Airbrushing is covered in Chapter 7.

Wedding nails

Creating a portfolio

If you decide that you wish to become a full-time photographic nail technician, you will need to have a professional portfolio. Most agencies or photographers will want to see some of your work before they decide whether to use your skills.

You will need a good, if possible leather-bound, book with plastic inserts. If you cannot find leather then use a book with a hard plastic cover – but remember that first impressions count. If your portfolio is being sent by courier or post it will need to stand up to some rough treatment. Make sure it has no more than twenty pages. You must make sure that you have a duplicate of everything in the portfolio just in case it goes astray.

Select a range of work to put in your portfolio, such as:

Christmas nails

- a natural nail shot
- a hand and foot shot
- a polished nail picture
- a hand only shot
- a head and hand shot
- a nail art shot
- if possible, a fantasy shot
- any professional shots you already have, such as a front cover or campaign shot

The more exciting and diverse you make the images in your portfolio, the more likely interested potential clients will be to book you for their photographic shoots.

Working within the media industry can be very exciting and rewarding. However, be prepared to work for a while for very little return as you will need to prove your worth with photographers, agencies and editors. It is a good idea to get yourself signed up with an agency as they will find work for you and do all the administration and booking of jobs. Make sure they know your availability and also what work you are capable of; if nail art is not your forte then do not attempt it, just stick to what you know. You will find that working on a photo shoot can mean a lot of sitting around doing nothing or alternatively rushing around trying to manicure ten models in one hour. Do not have too many expectations as you may be disappointed. Just enjoy your work and learn from each experience.

Technical Tip

Remember that the camera shows every little mistake so you must work to the finest detail. It is not worth cutting corners as this will give you a bad reputation and your career could be seriously affected.

Grim reaper

Grim reaper

Catwalk nails

Catwalk nails

Learning objectives

In this section you will learn about:

- **what type of work you need to cover**

- **the communication skills needed backstage with key people**

- **what to wear**

- **the type of kit you will need for every eventuality**

- **fashion trends**

Working backstage at Fashion Shows, especially for big events such as London Fashion Week can be a very challenging and exciting experience. It is very unlikely that you will ever work alone in an environment such as this, so learning to be part of a team is vitally important. There is always a team leader in charge of hair and make-up who designs the total look to complement the designers' clothes and accessories. The team leader is responsible for deciding who does what, when and to which model.

This type of work is mainly available through an agency. You may be lucky enough to have a contact with knowledge of your skills who can get you work. If you have built a healthy reputation for professionalism and artistic work you will definitely get this type of work and be given repeat work by

Nail team

people you have worked with before. Fashion work is well-known for being poorly paid but the raised profile you will get from this type of work more than compensates. A good reputation is built on:

● good timekeeping
● being versatile and able to cover a range of treatments
● the ability to work safely and quickly
● working well under pressure
● being able to work as part of a team
● not being a sensitive little soul – there are some very fraught stylists around

The kinds of work you will be asked to perform backstage include:

● manicures and pedicures
● nail repairs on fingers and toes
● polishing
● hand painting
● airbrushing
● texturing using materials
● 3D work
● extending artwork from nails onto hands and feet

Working environment

There may be, if you are lucky, a meeting a few days before a show with stylists, hairdressers and make-up artists. Very rarely would you meet the designers themselves until the day of the fashion show. It is usually the designer's stylist who liaises with all the other professionals and coordinates every aspect of the show.

Working environment

In many cases, it is the make-up artist and the look he or she creates that determines the nail style for the day. You will need to check the following details before the show if you are to have any input into the nail style for each look:

- the overall theme of the show
- clothes, colours and textures
- make-up – colours and style
- hair – simple, avant-garde or fantasy
- how many models there are and who will be wearing what

You will need to ask the make-up artist for a list of all the models coming on the day so that as you complete each model's nails you can tick them off your list. This list is invaluable for three main reasons:

- You will know how many models you have to do on the day.
- You will know the colour scheme and clothes for each model.
- You can mark off the models you have finished. This will allow you to leave time for the models who will arrive at the last minute. The more important the model, the later he or she will arrive – this is because they are in demand and may have more than one show in a day.

You will need to wear old clothes as some of the work could involve crawling around a very dusty, dirty old warehouse floor to paint models' nails. You may have to work around hair and make-up stylists, which could involve sitting on a cold floor in cramped conditions, being trodden on by

Models backstage

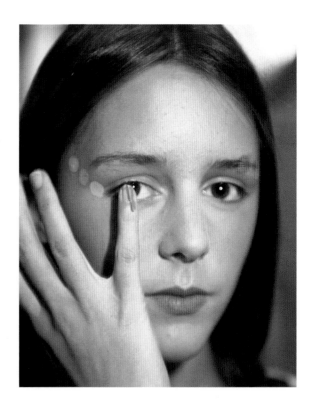

stressed hair and make-up artists. You may also have to work in very poorly lit conditions.

If none of the above has put you off, here is a list of the kit we suggest you will need. Remember this will depend on what is required on the day. Even if you have been told that only natural nails are required, take some polishes with you just in case. Designers have been known to change their minds ten minutes before a show, so always have a full kit ready.

- base coat, top coat and quick dry
- range of colour polishes and enamels
- massage and hand lotion
- cotton wool, cotton buds and tissues
- polish remover
- towels
- cuticle creams or oils
- files and buffers
- range of coloured paints
- range of coloured glitters
- selection of nail art brushes
- nail tips and adhesives
- nail art decorations, such as rhinestones and flat stones
- extras.

Catwalk show

Catwalk show London Fashion Week

Airbrush kit

It is probably not worth dragging a compressor and airbrush kit along with you if you really do not need it. Check with the make-up artist that they will not need you to do any spraying onto fingers and toes.

Final helpful tips

- Make sure you have arranged and received your pass in advance of the show.
- Try to get a list of the models as soon as possible and make sure you have it with you.
- Check in with the make-up artist or team leader on arrival.
- Wear old clothes.
- Take a full kit to meet the notified needs of the show – and a bit more to allow for a change of plan.
- Work as quickly as possible, but do not forget your own reputation with regards to the quality of your work.

Technical Tip

It is very important to make sure you have secure and hard-wearing cases to carry your kit in. Remember you will be travelling around quite a lot, although most of the work will probably be in London. However, the easiest way to travel is probably the train or tube so your cases will take a lot of battering. Think carefully when investing in cases to ensure that they last a long time.

Catwalk show

Chapter summary

The three areas of work that this chapter discusses are all very exciting ones to be involved in, but are all very different and specialised. The information contained within this chapter, is as comprehensive as we can make it at the time of writing, as these are skill areas which are still being developed. Ideally, we would recommend you find an experienced technician who has already worked in these fields and pick his or her brains for ideas, tips and information or their apprentice for six months. Always be prepared to stretch yourself and your abilities to the next level.

The next step

The 'next step' means exactly that. It is for the more experienced technician wishing to go into more advanced areas of work and will require a few years' experience. This chapter deals with the skills required to manage other people. There are a many management courses available at colleges and private training centres. You may not have the opportunity to attend a formal course but you may progress through the ranks of a salon naturally. This chapter will help you identify the key areas to managing people effectively. It also covers the skills needed to become a trainer or teacher and gives information on how to become an NVQ (National Vocational Qualification) Assessor. If you are considering teaching at a further education college, you will find that most will require this qualification.

As your career progresses you may find yourself being asked to give presentations or to demonstrate your skills in front of an audience. This area of work requires special skills and experience and these are identified and explained in full in the following sections.

In this chapter we will consider the following aspects:

- **managing people**
- **becoming a trainer**
- **presentation skills**
- **demonstration skills**

Managing people

When starting out on any new career path you should set yourself short- and long-term goals. If you know where you want to take your career, setting goals will allow you to identify the skills or qualifications you will have to acquire to achieve your ultimate target. The nail industry demands a variety of technical skills, good people skills and a high standard of professionalism – standards which are rising as the industry branches into new areas and new opportunities. For instance, as recently as the mid-1990s nail extensions were usually taught in further education colleges by beauty therapy teachers. Colleges are now looking for teachers with expert knowledge of nail treatments and the skills to back this up.

Knowing your strengths and weaknesses will help you choose the correct path for you and plan your future within the nail industry. Always remember to build on your strengths, but do not ignore the weaker areas as these can always be improved upon.

How to develop personal management skills

If you are going to be a successful manager you will need to manage yourself effectively first. How can you do this? First look at your aims, whether you are capable of achieving them, and whether you can manage your time effectively.

Efficient use of time implies less stress, better results, good organisation and a happy team. Try the following self-assessment exercise to identify if you have the criteria needed of an effective time manager.

1 Am I a perfectionist?
2 Do I manage my time at all?
3 Do I put off doing things?
4 Do I plan my tasks for each day?
5 Do I control my time or does my time control me?
6 Do I meet deadlines?

7 Do I delegate?

8 Do I prioritise?

9 Do I constantly achieve my daily targets?

10 Do I waste time?

To be able to manage yourself and your time you will need to set yourself daily goals *and achieve them*. Use a planner to do this and look at the tasks that are the most important. There will be jobs that must be done daily, some weekly and others less often. Do not leave the most important jobs to mount up because they then become problems.

Setting yourself goals can avoid problems arising but always make sure your approach is flexible enough to allow for other priorities that may arise unpredictably.

A good manager will create a working environment with:

- trust between co-workers
- enthusiasm from all members of staff
- a good working environment for all staff
- a happy and relaxed atmosphere for clients

To establish this kind of working environment a manager will need to consider:

- the aims and objectives of the salon
- how these aims can be achieved
- a clear staff structure

Members of staff need to know that they can trust their manager to be able to deal with all sorts of problems, whether they arise internally or concern an unhappy client. To be able to do this the manager must have the right type of character. There are three main character types:

- aggressive
- passive
- assertive

A person who is too aggressive will only cause problems and staff will usually feel this person is unapproachable. Someone who is passive will be indecisive and unable to motivate staff. An assertive manager, however, will be able to:

- control any situation that arises
- support other members of staff
- demonstrate self-motivation

- gain respect from others
- be confident
- be honest
- be efficient
- encourage teamwork
- delegate and negotiate

To be an effective manager you will need to anticipate problems before they arise, always be in control, set high standards for yourself and your staff and always be forward-looking. The manager's role can sometimes be a lonely one, especially if you are a manager of someone else's salon. In that role the manager has to represent both the staff and the owner. You will obviously need to have a good working relationship with the proprietor and be able to report honestly what is going on within the salon. You will also need to consider the staff working under you and be able to represent their needs to your bosses. In effect, you must gain the trust of both the staff and the owner to be able to do your job effectively.

Creating a good working environment

A good salon manager has ways to keep staff motivation and morale high. It is very easy, especially if you are a working manager, to let the daily routine of a salon carry on to an established pattern, without monitoring whether it is working to its maximum potential. Staff need to know that you are interested in their welfare if they are to remain loyal and work hard. There are ways to achieve this in addition to the obvious factors such as a pleasant working environment, good pay and perks. Morale and loyalty in particular can be improved by implementing programmes for:

- staff meetings
- staff training
- staff appraisals

By holding regular staff meetings and offering training you will encourage your staff to do their jobs confidently and competently.

Staff meetings

Regular staff meetings can perform a number of functions:

- staff concerns can be identified and addressed
- staff can be informed of any new products or equipment
- staff are made to feel they are part of a team

- staff structure and reporting line can be clarified
- the concerns of management can be expressed
- any forthcoming changes in staff structure or the working of the salon can be explained

Staff training

If you establish a good programme of staff training it will have the following benefits for your business:

- staff will be kept up-to-date on new products
- staff will constantly be developing new skills
- staff will be motivated to sell retail products
- existing skills can be refreshed and updated
- creation of job satisfaction
- evaluation of existing skills and setting of targets
- allows everyone to keep up-to-date with new Health and Safety issues
- it can expand skills to include additional skills, for example in fire evacuation or First Aid

Any technician who does not actively seek further training each year will miss out on new products and techniques in what is a fast-moving industry. Staff meetings will identify how members of staff would like to develop and a manager should keep abreast of these ideas and maybe attend workshops with their staff. If the manager no longer performs nail treatments on a regular basis, this will enable him or her to keep up-to-date with the staff or at least understand and be aware of what they are doing.

Staff appraisals

Staff appraisals will not only improve staff relations but can also identify an individual's needs, strengths and weaknesses. It is an employer's responsibility to give each individual employee a Job Appraisal Review (JAR) at least once a year. Appraisals should normally be conducted by an employee's direct line manager, who is assumed to have a stronger relationship with the employee and to be in a better position to interview them. The purpose of an appraisal is to assess an employee's performance in the following areas:

- strengths and weaknesses
- areas where improvement might be made
- technical skills
- future potential
- personal aims for the future
- promotion prospects

- job satisfaction
- self-assessment by employee

This process should allow the manager to:

- improve communication
- show an interest in the employee's career
- identify any training needs
- identify any individual needs
- target any future goals
- give constructive advice
- identify any areas of work that need attention
- maintain a good working environment
- deliver staff satisfaction and make employees realise they are important

If you are carrying out a staff appraisal you will need to be an excellent communicator. You must let the employee know that you value the time spent looking at their working relationships and the work they carry out. This will give them the confidence to discuss such issues as their aims, any problems or grievances, and where they see their future within the salon. The interview should be conducted in a quiet room or, if this is not possible, after work when everyone else has gone. The details of the interview should be recorded and both parties should sign this record to agree what has been discussed. Appraisal records must be kept in a locked filing cabinet, as they are confidential documents for management's eyes only.

There are many other areas to consider when thinking of taking a management position and you will need to consider all of these. There are far too many for us to write about in this book and we suggest that you consult one of the many excellent books available. There is a bibliography at the end of the book.

Becoming a trainer

Learning objectives

In this section you will learn about:

- **the sort of experience needed to become a trainer**
- **types of training establishments**
- **the NVQ framework**
- **the skills required of an assessor**

There are many different ways of teaching nail skills and we will endeavour to cover the main ones in this section.

It is important to remember that nothing can take the place of experience, so we would recommend that a minimum of three years experience in the field should be the basic requirement before anyone embarks on a teaching career. This is not only for your students' sake but also for your protection. You will need a good sound knowledge of the whole industry before you can realistically stand in front of a class of beginners or technicians who are looking to advance their skills further.

When you apply to a training centre they will want to know what qualifications and experience you have. Having excellent nail skills will not necessarily make you a good trainer. Training and teaching need special skills and some of these cannot be taught, they are part of our character. One of the main traits of a good teacher is patience. Remember back to your own schooldays and the subjects you were best at – they were usually the lessons where the teacher got along with you and your classmates.

Think about the nail training courses you have attended and learn from them: What were their good points? What did you not like about them? Which ones did you learn from and were they any where you came away feeling you had learnt very little?

Teaching requires a smooth, polished performance – done well this looks easy and should come automatically to an experienced trainer. For those just starting out it can only be achieved through careful planning of each training session.

Training establishments

If you decide that this is the career route you would like to follow there are two main areas to consider:

1 further education colleges
2 private training schools

Colleges of further education

Colleges of further or adult education will normally ask for at least 3 years experience and some formal teaching qualification, for example the Further Adult Education Teaching Certificate. They will usually invite you to a formal interview and may ask you to give a small presentation on your subject. If they offer an NVQ (National Vocational Qualification) they might also ask you for a Vocational Assessors Award (D32/D33).

Note: as of 2002 the Vocational Assessors Award will be replaced by a new Unit L28 of the Training Development Standards. Those already holding a D32/D33 will not have to undertake the new award as the D32/D33 qualifications will still be valid.

Private centres

Private schools or training centres are usually financed by product manufacturers and may have different guidelines for their in-house trainers. They may ask for the evidence of experience or nationally recognised qualifications, or they may not, but what they will be looking for in their trainers is an in-depth knowledge of their products, systems and procedures.

Most good product companies will provide you with training on all the features and benefits of their products and systems. They might also want to train you in their way of delivering information to potential students. You might find that they will allow you to train from your own premises under their umbrella, or that they want you to travel to their own location. They may even want you to go out on the road as trainers within local hair and beauty suppliers.

Before committing yourself to a private training school or product supplier make sure you have a written contract with them. This should state:

- how much they are going to pay per hour, per day or per student
- whether they will provide your demonstration and training kit
- how many hours per day, week or month they want you to work
- whether they want you to be exclusive to them
- whether they want you to work at trade shows, and if so how many per year
- what expenses, if any, you will be entitled to (e.g. travel, overnight, etc.)
- whether you will get a discount on their products
- what training they will provide for you

Be sure to negotiate a new contract every year that benefits you and your training establishment. Help them to develop their training by making sure you encourage feedback from your students on both the training and the products. Make sure that the company or centre offers good back-up in the form of training materials such as training notes and handouts. This could be very expensive if you are expected to provide them yourself.

If you are considering entering the world of training then try to find a colleague who is already training and who will allow you to shadow them for a few weeks. This experience could be invaluable and may actually help you decide whether or not teaching is for you!

The NVQ framework

The government proposed a review of all qualifications in 1985 which led to the establishment of the *National Council for Vocational Qualifications* which is now known as the *Qualifications Curriculum Authority*. From this 1985 review came a new set of qualifications called **National Vocational Qualifications (NVQs)** in England and Wales and Scottish National Vocational Qualifications (SNVQs) in Scotland. These qualifications are based not just on academic ability but also on a person's skills. The standards for each qualification are set by a National Training Organisation or NTO. The NTO for the Hair and Beauty Industry is called **HABIA**, the Hair and Beauty Industry Authority.

The NVQ framework is based on five levels of attainment which provide students and employers with a clear indication of the achievement level of students who have completed an award.

Level 1

This is the lowest level and is for those persons who carry out tasks which assist others in a higher position or which require supervision.

Level 2

This is the level concerned with the knowledge of how to carry out basic treatments without supervision, for example a manicure or pedicure.

Level 3

This level begins to look at the managerial role and more advanced treatments, in the hair and beauty field this includes treatments such as reflexology, aromatherapy and nail extensions.

Level 4

This level is more relevant to a manager or salon owner and will require extra skills such as responsibility for others and the allocation of resources.

Level 5

This is the highest NVQ standard attainable and is equivalent to the standard of academic postgraduate studies.

The NVQ system allows students to learn their skills in a variety of establishments, even in their own workplace, and over a period of time that suits their level of skill and commitment to training. It is the student who decides when they are ready for assessment and these assessments can be carried out by trained assessors in the workplace or at a training centre.

The structure of the NVQ

Every NVQ has a title and is then divided into *units*. These *units of accreditation* are mini qualifications in their own right and it is possible for a student to build up units over a period of time to gain a full NVQ Award. The unit structure of NVQs also allows individuals to choose which units suit their particular needs. Even if students do not complete a whole NVQ, they will still receive a certificate for each successful unit completed, which will constitute evidence of their level of attainment.

A unit comprises three areas:

1   performance criteria

2   range statements

3   underpinning knowledge requirements

Performance criteria

Performance criteria or PCs describe the physical activity required for each part of a treatment and all PCs have to be met in order to claim competence. All PCs within every element have to be completed to pass each unit and students are graded as either *competent* or *not yet competent*.

Range statements

Range statements describe the activities, tools, equipment and treatments that need to be covered in each element. There are strict guidelines for the assessor on those aspects that *they have to see being performed* and those where evidence from other sources can be used.

Underpinning knowledge requirements

Underpinning knowledge requirements defines areas where the student has to prove that not only do they know how to perform treatments but that they have the background knowledge necessary to perform their job safely and effectively. Assessment of the requirements can include assignments and projects given to them by their assessor and could also be in the form of written and oral questions.

Within each unit there are four elements that have to be covered to prove competence. These four elements in health and beauty, for example, include the preparation of the work area and the client, safe working practices, working over a range of conditions and treatments, and maintenance and aftercare. Anyone undertaking a unit of an NVQ has to demonstrate competence in all four elements before being accredited with that unit.

The idea of NVQs is that they should:

- be without fixed periods of study – students will work at their own pace
- be open to all
- assess candidates when they feel ready
- be based on what the student can do regardless of when and how it was learnt
- allow students to build units at their own pace
- award units on evidence that is sufficient, valid, authentic and reliable or current

The skills required of an assessor

To be able to assess properly you should have a good sound knowledge not only of the NVQ system, but also of the qualification you are assessing. A good way to ensure this – if you have not already been through the NVQ system – is to take the award you are assessing yourself. At least you will then understand what you are expecting to see your students do themselves.

You will also need to understand the types of evidence that a student can collect towards his or her award:

1 Primary evidence is *by* the student.
2 Secondary evidence is *about* the student.

An example of primary evidence is natural performance in the workplace, written and oral questions, videos and simulation. Secondary evidence includes certificates, trophies, peer reports, products and witness testimonies.

An assessor cannot teach whilst assessing or assess whilst teaching. A clear understanding must be given to each student that they are being assessed, by what criteria, when it will take place and who their assessor will be. They should always be given guidance and the relevant documentation to help them understand how the assessment process works.

It is essential for an assessor to remain as unobtrusive as possible when performing an assessment and this will ensure that the treatment is conducted in a professional manner with no interruptions which might put off a nervous student. It can be nerve-racking, even for an experienced technician, to be watched.

Lastly it is imperative that the student is given *feedback* immediately at the end of the assessment session and that the assessor's decisions are recorded on the relevant paperwork. Feedback should be a two-way process and the student should also be allowed to question any assessment decisions. As long as an assessor has used the performance criteria within the national standards and not their own set of standards, there should be no problems with a student being found non-competent. You can explain that they have been assessed against the national standards and point out where they have fallen short. Always give praise where it is due and constructive feedback where skills need to be improved.

A good assessor is firm but fair. He or she needs to make sure that the national standards are adhered to when assessing but at the same time be supportive and approachable for their students.

If you are looking to train as an NVQ Assessor make sure that you choose a college or private training company that will give you all the information you need and take you through the physical assessing skills as well. Try to find a colleague who will recommend a company they have used which offers good support. Try to spend some time with an experienced assessor before going it alone, as the paperwork can be confusing at first. As with any new skill, it takes time to become proficient and assessing is no different; make sure you have a support structure in place.

Technical Tip

It is easy when assessing to fall into the trap of imposing your own standards on the students, especially if you have not taught them and find the standard of work not quite as high as your own. As an Assessor it is your job to assess only against the national standards and you must be clear about what they are. If you have any problems of interpretation contact HABIA or the Awarding Body you are working with.

Presentation skills

Learning objectives

In this section you will learn about:

- **preparing for your audience**
- **developing and preparing visual aids**
- **preparing and structuring material**
- **various types of equipment**
- **delivering the presentation**
- **questioning techniques**
- **the qualities needed in a presenter**

The idea of giving a presentation fills many people with apprehension, and brings to mind addressing large groups of people using all the latest high-tech equipment. In fact, most nail presentations are given to quite small groups and in recent times the term presentation has been specifically applied to a semi-formal or formal talk to one person (e.g. a sales representative or a customer) or to a small group (of up to ten people), which will inform and/or motivate the audience to take some kind of action. That desired action could be, for example, a change of attitude towards new equipment or systems, the purchase of a product or service or how to improve technical skills.

Putting across information and thereby instigating a desired action is the most important objective of a presentation. Business presentations are more likely to be persuasive than purely informative; a training presentation on a newly purchased computer system will be more informative than persuasive. You cannot proceed to give a presentation until you have clarified your objectives.

As in all aspects of communications, the first stage in giving a presentation is to prepare. The work involved can be set out under the following headings:

- preparing for your audience
- gathering data and information
- developing and preparing visual or audio-visual aids

We will consider each stage in turn.

Preparing for your audience

You will naturally want to think about your audience. They could be, for example, other colleagues, your superiors, customers, people from other organisations, trainees, or members of the public. In each case, you will have to prepare a slightly different method of delivery.

With your colleagues, you will need to be technically competent; with superiors well prepared and positive; with customers and outsiders friendly and courteous (acting as an ambassador for the company you represent); and with trainees careful not to overload them with new ideas and materials.

You will also have to give some additional thought to the make up of your audience, as it may contain people from different backgrounds, with widely differing levels of knowledge and experience. It is best to pitch your approach to those with the least knowledge, although towards the end of the presentation you can dwell briefly on more advanced or detailed points.

By inviting questions or comments at the end, you can cater for the better informed, and make them feel they have achieved something by attending the presentation.

The only way that you can prepare for this aspect is to find out who is likely to be in the audience. The more you can find out about them, the better able you will be to direct your material appropriately.

Gathering data and information

The first step is to gather material for the main body of the presentation. You can then put together the introduction and the conclusion. As the presenter, you must spend plenty of time obtaining as much information on your chosen topic as possible. It doesn't matter if you have too much – it is easier to discard the surplus than to find out too late that you are short on material.

You are going to make a presentation because you are in some way qualified to do so, usually because of a combination of knowledge and experience. However, you may need to add to your store of knowledge, perhaps to fit what you want to say into a broader context. Therefore, you may need to do some research by asking others or looking up things in magazines, books or on the Internet.

Preparing and structuring the material

Having gathered the required material, you need to plan the length of your presentation. Once you have determined its length, you will have to add in natural breaks for the audience and – as a guide – listeners' attention will start to waver after about 35–40 minutes maximum, at which stage you will need to take a break or risk losing them.

- It is a good idea to find a way to ensure that everything you want to say will be covered in the time you have allocated. A general rule of thumb is that you may overrun by 10 per cent of the time allocated, but whenever possible this must be avoided.

- Do not try to cover more than is physically possible. Within a 30–40 minute presentation you should try to cover no more than three or five main themes or points. These main headings may have sub-headings, but never try to include more than four or five main themes within this timescale.

- Selecting the main points must be done carefully, so that you can stress all the important aspects of your chosen topic.

- Once you have prepared the main topics, you can consider the introduction, in which you will state the main theme or purpose of the presentation, and outline the areas and topics you propose to cover.

- Finally, the conclusion (finish) will summarise the main points.

- Any aid that you can use as a presenter is a bonus – whether they be memory joggers or lesson plans. They can be of such invaluable help that we will consider them in detail.

Developing and preparing visual or audio-visual aids

When using the term 'visual aids' people often tend to think of slides, overhead transparencies, or something to write on such as black- or whiteboards, flip charts, etc. In fact, people can be visual aids, as can pieces of equipment or even ordinary things like documents and forms.

This concept can be expanded further to include all the senses and, as such, anything can be used to demonstrate a point. As a presenter, you must try to enliven your presentation without letting the aids take over your presentation. Therefore, imagination and ingenuity are important tools and will be based on your experience and confidence.

Try placing yourself in the audience, looking at your presentation, and ask yourself whether the presentation will be:

- theoretical, abstract or academic?
- complex or difficult to understand?
- on a new or unusual topic to them?
- difficult to put across verbally without illustrations?
- of vital importance to the audience?
- full of detailed information?

If the answer to any of these questions is yes, then visual aids of some kind are essential. In any event, the use of these aids will help you to keep your audience's attention, to emphasise and underline your message, and to ensure that your audience remember it.

However, do not forget that visual aids *supplement* the spoken word, not *substitute* it.

We will now consider some of the traditional visual aids.

Overhead projectors

Rules of use:

- transparencies should be on clear, acetate sheets and should be well prepared beforehand
- keep the message short and simple and avoid overloading transparencies with data or information
- each acetate sheet should be carefully numbered in sequence – everybody drops the pile at least once in their career!

Care must be taken when enlivening a transparency not to get carried away:

- keep the message short and simple
- use diagrams, graphs, etc.
- use colour where you can
- use material which can be clearly seen by those furthest away from you

There are a few important points to remember when using an overhead projector:

- never use a projector without trying it out first
- make sure you can switch it on and off easily, and know how to adjust the focus.
- always have a spare bulb handy
- make sure the lens and surface are clean and free from dust.
- photocopied extracts are not recommended, the print will normally be too small
- the siting of the projector is very important: everybody must be able to see the screen, which is sometimes just the wall
- you must also remember that, for best results, the screen should be tilted away at the top

Other major faults you must plan to avoid are:

- leaving the OHP on for long periods during explanations, as the fan can be quite noisy and distract the group
- having the room too bright, or casting a shadow on the screen
- exposing all the points on a sheet at once as this can distract attention from the points that you are making – blank off the points that you do not want them to see with a piece of paper
- pointing to the image on the screen: you should use a pointer or pen on the acetate itself, remembering not to leave it there when you have finished

Black- and whiteboards

It is very rare these days to find blackboards anywhere other than in schools. They are likely to have been replaced by whiteboards, which are more user-friendly. Whichever you use there are problems, so be prepared and bear in mind the following tips:

- The board must perfectly clean at the start and you must write in large letters.
- Bright sunlight shining on the board can make it difficult for everyone to see, so ensure that it is sited effectively by checking that everyone can clearly read it.
- Plenty of chalk or spare pens must be available in case you run out.
- Care must be taken to ensure that difficult words are not misspelled, as this will detract from the point of using the aid.
- Writing whilst you are talking is a difficult task that

requires practice – do not assume that this will come to you overnight.

Flipcharts

Flipcharts are now very common and are often used in other work situations, such as brainstorming. The virtues of this medium are:

Technical Tip

If you want to make notes to jog your memory you can write them on the flipchart with a soft pencil – the audience will not be able to see the writing but you can.

- you can carefully prepare what you want to write before the event
- when you have finished with a set of ideas, all you need to do is flip over and the next set is there
- you can always recap by turning back
- you can move the flipchart to the best place for all people to see it
- you can use different coloured pens to stress particular main points

Videotapes

There are many suitable types of videotape on the market, which you can use to enhance your presentation. However, take care that they do not take over from the lesson. Their use must be carefully planned and rehearsed in relation to the points that you are making. The following tips should be applied:

- The time you have and the length of the film should be taken into account.
- You will need to have everything set up prior to the presentation, so that all you have to do is switch it on after you have given the introduction.
- You should explain to the group the major points so they know what to look for – this will encourage their attention.
- Using the pause button and freezing the tape for a short while, can be useful to make a point, but do not overdo it.

Handouts

Handouts have the advantage that they summarise what you have to say and, for those people who don't take notes, your handouts are their only record of the event.

To prepare effective handouts, try to avoid the following points:

- using poorly typed or badly prepared notes

- spelling mistakes
- giving them out before the start, people will start to read them and lose interest in what you have to say

Be careful to determine which aids would be best suited to your presentation. Look at the advantages and disadvantages of each format, taking into account the opportunity at the venue to position screens, etc. where everyone can see them, the expense and reliability of the equipment, and any difficulties in transporting it. Check to make sure that vital services and back-up are available, for example power points, extension leads, spare bulbs, flipchart packs, marker pens, chalk, dusters, etc.

Recheck your own plan to ensure that you know exactly when in the presentation each aid will be used, but most importantly work out how to put the visual message over in a clear, lively, short and professional manner.

Delivering the presentation

A successful presentation depends upon you concentrating hard on the four Ps: preparing, practising, polishing and persuading.

Having prepared, you should be clear in your mind what you propose to put over to your audience, what visual and other aids you will be using and you should have checked that all of your aids work and that back-up and spares are in place. You must now look at the presentation environment. Leave nothing to chance: ensure that the following points are dealt with, preferably well in advance.

- Electrical power points and leads, overhead and wall lighting all work. Can you dim the lights from a dimmer switch close to you or do you need someone to operate the lights?
- If you have problems projecting your voice then consideration should be given to using a microphone. Before you use it live, however, try out the volume and clarity with someone sitting far away from you. Never use a hand-held microphone, as your hands may be required for other tasks or the microphone will become a distraction for you. Make sure the acoustics at the venue will allow you to be heard everywhere in the room if there is no microphone system.
- Can you adjust the presenter's table or lectern where your notes are to be put? Is there sufficient room for you to put out your papers, transparencies, handouts, etc?

- Look at the seating arrangements and try to ensure that you are going to be well away from an entrance or exit so that people entering late will not upset you. Setting out the seating in a horseshoe shape is better than straight rows – more people can see you clearly.
- Temperature and ventilation must also be considered. If the room is cold people will want to get away as quickly as possible; if it is hot or stuffy the audience will be only half awake. Even opening a window slightly can solve this problem.

Rehearsing the presentation

Practice makes perfect, at least that's the theory, so effective rehearsal can begin at home or anywhere convenient. To begin, start by practising in front of a mirror where not only will you be a distraction to no one but yourself, but you will see yourself in the way your audience will.

Some other suggestions for presenting are:

- rehearse standing up
- imagine the audience is sitting in front of you, and speak as loudly as you would on the day
- initially concentrate on the verbal presentation, trying out the visual aids comes once you have mastered the verbal sequence
- ask someone else to check a final rehearsal
- a dress rehearsal in the actual room is a bonus, if it can be arranged
- four or five rehearsals at least are recommended for those who are new to presentations
- work at your 'opening' and try linking it to something topical to gain the audience's attention immediately
- polish your conclusion
- summarise clearly and if your presentation aims to encourage your audience to a particular action, make that clear at this point, but do not unnecessarily prolong this part of your presentation

Questioning techniques

Questioning has a very important role within the presenter's armoury and a number of purposes within instruction:

- to test by checking learners' knowledge

- to teach by making learners reason out answers for themselves
- to create activity and keep learners mentally alert

In all cases, the wording must be clear, unambiguous and discourage questioning of the presenter.

When asking questions of learners follow this procedure:

- *pose* the question
- *pause*
- *pounce* (select a learner)

By using this technique, you give everyone a chance to think about the question that you are asking, and by not nominating someone to answer, at this stage, everyone has to be prepared to reply if selected. The pause is obviously there for everyone to have an opportunity to think about the question. Lastly nominate the learner that you wish to answer the question, but be prepared to ask someone else should you not get the response that you are seeking or you could ask another person to confirm whether the first answer is right or not.

The following points should be avoided when asking questions of learners, whether they are written or oral questions:

- *Ambiguity*. There should be no doubt about what is being asked and the response that is sought.
- *True/false*. Such questions encourage guesswork and should be avoided.
- *Yes/no*. If asked, the answer given must be justified.
- *Oral test of skills*. The only effective test of a skill is a practical performance test. Skills should *not* be described orally.
- *Tests of expression*. Where powers of expression are *not* required to be tested, questions which demand such powers for an adequate answer should not be asked.

When learners ask questions the following points should be applied:

- *Relevance*. If the question concerns a point already taught, it should be referred back to the learners to check whether or not it is generally misunderstood. If the question reveals an omission in the instruction, the instructor should rectify it immediately. If the point is yet to be taught, the learner should be told that it will be covered at a later stage. Do not disturb the logical progression of the lesson to deal with it out of sequence.

- *Irrelevance.* If the question is genuine, it should be dismissed quickly but constructively without discouraging the learner. If it is a deliberate 'red herring', it should be dismissed immediately.

- *The unknown answer.* If the answer to a relevant question is *not* known, the *only* recourse is to admit as much and accept the loss of face entailed. On no account pass the question back to the class in the hope that a bright learner might know. The correct answer must be discovered as soon as possible and the learners informed. If you promise to find out an answer and give it to the learners later, failure to do this will result in a continued loss of face for you as an instructor.

The qualities needed in a presenter

As a presenter your own personality will always be one of the factors that students will home in on, and as such you must be aware of it. Bearing this in mind, all presenters should strive to develop the following personal characteristics as a step towards improving performance.

When you are starting out, remember that just because you have presented one lecture it does not mean that you can rest on your laurels.

Confidence

You can only become confident in your ability to lecture if you know your subject matter. As a presenter, this must be the first priority – you must acquire a complete knowledge of the subject, and present with instinct, be fully audible, and vary the rhythm, speed, volume and pitch of your voice to avoid monotony.

Movement

Remember that continually moving whilst speaking distracts attention from what is being said, as do nervous mannerisms, repetitive use of phrases such as a-ha, okay, alright, etc. Always plant your feet and do not move around when speaking, unless to make a point. Arm movements should be kept to a minimum and not waved around all over the place.

Personal appearance

What the audience first sees will make an impression on them even before you speak. By paying attention to your personal appearance, you are taking the first steps towards a professional approach, which in turn will instil confidence in your learners.

Attitude

As a presenter, you should always try to be:

- *Fair* – no favouritism or discrimination should be shown to any of the learners that you are responsible for.
- *Firm* – maintain a tight control over your learners and do not allow them to usurp authority.
- *Friendly* – be approachable and try to establish a 'rapport' with your learners.

Diligence

If you are going to get the best from your learners then the first step is ensuring that you prepare yourself. This will require painstaking and persistent attention to detail.

Enthusiasm

The more enthusiastic you are about what you are doing, the more enthusiastic your learners will be to learn. You should never undermine your own enthusiasm for a subject that you are responsible for delivering as this is a valuable quality to have as a presenter.

You may find, however, that not all the subjects you have to present will arouse your enthusiasm. But you will see from all the facts discussed so far that if you make the effort then your learners will gain from it.

The skills of a demonstrator

Learning objectives

In this section you will learn about:

- **the types of work and environments available for demonstrators**
- **the skills required**
- **how to organise a demonstration**

The work of a demonstrator

You will need good technical, practical and oral skills if you want to do demonstration work. You will also need to be confident and able to talk to one or maybe hundreds of people whilst working. Most big companies taking stands at trade shows will want experienced technicians to demonstrate their products and they will also need a good sales technique.

Your audience could be:

- a class of students
- other professionals at trade shows
- other technicians in salons
- the other side of a camera for filmed shows or lectures

You will need to prepare yourself for each demonstration and make sure it is targeted appropriately for your audience. Every audience will want something different and you need to be clear about the level to which you are demonstrating.

For a demonstration to any audience you will need to look at three main areas:

- preparation
- delivery
- evaluation

Preparation

Whatever the size of your audience, you will need to prepare your demonstration thoroughly so that you do not look unprofessional. Decide what your objectives are and what you want the outcome to be. Whether you are showing students how to apply a tip for the first time or demonstrating the most advanced airbrush techniques under camera, you still need to be properly prepared. The following points should be taken into account when planning your demonstration:

- plan the most effective time for the demonstration
- consider the room or hall and decide if it provides the right surroundings for you
- familiarise yourself with the equipment and make sure it is in good working order
- make sure you have any additional materials you need such as posters, videos, examples, handouts, etc.

- estimate the time needed for the demonstration
- plan the content of the demonstration and give yourself time guides so that time does not run away with you
- have completed examples or pictures of any work ready to hand out
- make sure all products and tools are in good working order and up to date

Delivery

You will need to adjust the level of the demonstration to meet the needs of your audience. Always remember to consider those technicians in the audience who have the least experience. It is important to take all students through the skill they are learning step by step, covering every point. For instance, there is no point in demonstrating a specialist manicure if your listeners do not know how to perform a basic manicure. You will need to be clear and precise, stress any key points and include essential extra information such as Health and Safety issues throughout the whole demonstration. Always encourage questions, but make sure this will not put you off your flow.

Consider the following points when delivering your demonstration:

- use your own experience to explain what you are doing
- summarise all the key points towards the end
- ensure that your audience can see what you are doing
- ensure that they can hear you clearly
- make sure you talk to the audience and not to the hands you are working on
- explain any technical terms that may be new to your audience
- make sure that you move at the correct pace so they can see what you are doing
- ask questions and relate what you are demonstrating to the audience's experience

Evaluation

The only way to constantly improve the way you work is to evaluate your own skills and performance. It is a good idea when performing on stage to ask a colleague to video your demonstration from beginning to end. There will be no better critic of your work than yourself.

You will also need feedback from your audience, however; if they have found your performance lacking in any way you need to know this so you can improve the next one. We teach because we want to pass information on to help others learn and we cannot be classed as good teachers if our audience has not absorbed the knowledge we went there to pass on. At the end of any demonstration, even if it is on a nail stand at a trade show, remember to:

● ask questions
● test the audience's knowledge
● encourage individuals to practise the skills they have just seen you use

Demonstrating for a product company

If you want to get work as a demonstrator for a product company you will have to make sure that you:

● know all the features and benefits of their products
● have excellent technical ability in their use
● are approachable and friendly
● have a good sales technique
● are well groomed at all times
● wear nails which reflect those you are demonstrating

Most product companies will ask their top trainers to work on stands at trade shows because they know and trust their work. This does not mean to say you cannot get work as a demonstrator, but you will need to make yourself known to your supplier and build a good relationship with them, maybe even starting off as part of the sales team. It can be very rewarding to meet the same technicians year after year on stands at trade shows and it is certainly good for business. Companies will appreciate your loyalty.

Chapter summary

After reading this chapter you may find that the areas of work mentioned are just not for you. They all require confidence, experience and a thorough knowledge of products and the industry as a whole. This type of work is very rewarding and satisfying and many technicians feel, after a few years behind a nail station, that they want a change. Even if these areas do not appeal to you at the moment, we hope they made interesting reading and have given you a broader knowledge of the nail industry and the range of work open to nail technicians.

Knowledge reviews

Chapter 1

1 What are the different career routes you can take?

2 Name some advantages of working in a 'nails only' salon.

3 What safety factors should you consider when working as a mobile technician?

4 List the equipment you would need for a salon.

5 What security precautions could you take within the salon to ensure a safe working environment?

6 What skills would you look for in a good receptionist?

7 What information should be available on your price list?

8 How could you effectively control your stock?

9 What is stock rotation and what does it mean to a nail salon?

10 What do features and benefits mean to you?

11 Explain how you can sell whilst working.

12 Give three different ways of taking payments.

13 How would you deal with complaints?

14 What characteristics would you look for when interviewing a potential employee?

15 Why is it so important to have a written contract with employees?

16 What are the advantages and disadvantages of being self-employed?

Chapter 2

1 What does the Health and Safety at Work Act mean to you as a nail technician?

2 What other pieces of legislation do you need to be aware of?

3 Where should your First Aid box be kept and what should it contain?

4 Why should every salon have an accident book?

5 How often should electrical equipment be checked by a qualified electrician?

6 Why is good ventilation so important for places where nail treatments are performed?

7 Give three reasons how dust and vapours could potentially do harm if not controlled properly.

8 What fire evacuation procedure would you take in the event of a drill?

9 Which types of fire extinguisher would be suitable for a nail salon?

10 What would you do if any nail product splashed into the eyes?

11 Describe how you would deal with a product spillage.

12 Why should a nail technician not wear contact lenses?

13 What is the correct procedure for disposing of salon waste?

14 How can you avoid cross infection from tools and products?

15 Name three ways in which metal tools can be sterilised or disinfected.

16 Give ten ways of protecting you and your clients when working in the salon environment.

Chapter 3

1 Define professional ethics and what this means to a nail technician.

2 Give four examples of professional ethics towards colleagues.

3 Explain ways of ensuring good personal hygiene.

4 Why is it so important to have an industry dress code?

5 How could a salon lose clients through unprofessional conduct of its staff?

6 How can body language affect relationships with clients and colleagues?

7 Why is it so important to build good relationships with colleagues?

8 What are the goals of a client consultation?

9 What are the possible implications of not carrying out a client consultation?

10 What could result from not keeping client records up to date?

11 How could a client's lifestyle affect the treatment you are performing?

12 Why is it so important to ensure that your client has signed their treatment plan and record card?

13 What can happen if you do not choose the best treatment for your client?

14 What are the consequences if clients are not given specific aftercare for the treatment they have received?

15 Why is it so important that you and your client are seated correctly throughout the treatment?

16 Think about four ways you could develop yourself within the salon environment.

Chapter 4

1 Why is it important to recognise contra indications when performing nail extension treatments?

2 Name five common nail disorders where you could still work on a client by adapting the treatment.

3 List four nail disorders that cannot be serviced by a nail technician.

4 List four common skin disorders encountered by nail technicians.

5 Name four disorders that can occur on the feet.

6 What are the characteristics of a healthy nail?

7 What are the major parts of the natural nail?

8 List four factors that can influence natural nail growth.

9 How many layers are there in the epidermis?

10 What structures does the dermis contain?

11 What are the main functions of the skin?

12 What is the relationship between blood and lymph?

13 Name four different massage movements?

14 What are the effects of massage?

15 What specific aftercare advice would you give a client having a pedicure treatment?

Chapter 5

1 List five ways of ensuring safe working practice with chemicals.

2 What does COSHH stand for?

3 Name three ways in which chemicals can enter the body.

4 Why is it necessary to dehydrate the nail before commencing treatment?

5 What is an oligomer?

6 What three pieces of PPE can be used when performing nail treatments?

7 What is odour and is it safe?

8 Explain what 'breathing zone' means to you.

9 What is a catalyst?

10 What is MMA?

11 What is the process of polymerisation?

12 What generally causes the product to separate from the nail plate?

13 Explain the safe methods of using solvents.

14 What are the effects of formaldehyde?

15 Name three reasons yellowing of a product can occur.

16 Why should you never mix components from different manufacturer's systems?

Chapter 6

1 Give three different types of fabric that can be used in a wrap system.

2 Name three advantages of using a wrap system.

3 Describe how you would remove a wrap system.

4 When would you use tips as opposed to free-form sculpting?

5 Why is it so important to educate clients about the treatment and systems you are performing?

5 Describe how you would apply a primer.

6 What are the important factors when fitting a sculpting form onto a client's natural nail?

7 What could happen if your acrylic product is too wet?

8 Why is it so important to follow manufacturer's recommendations for times of curing gels under a UV lamp?

9 What two different types of plastic are tips made from?

10 Describe how you would tailor a tip to fit your client's nails and the key areas where you would ensure complete contact.

11 What products would you need for a manicure treatment?

12 What types of specialist manicures can be offered in salons?

13 List the steps involved in preparing a client for a pedicure treatment.

14 What is the key difference between a manicure and pedicure treatment?

15 How often should a client return for further treatments in:

- manicures?
- pedicures?
- nail extensions?

Chapter 7

1 Which tools would you need in your kit to carry out nail art designs?

2 List the main products required in a nail art kit.

3 What are the three primary colours?

4 Why is a good knowledge of colour important to a nail artist?

5 Why is it important to consult with your client on colour and design?

6 What are the properties of a good base coat?

7 How do polishers differ in colour and consistency?

8 What are the steps in a pearl polish application?

9 What are the different ways of polishing a french manicure?

10 What factors would you take into account when advising your client on a nail art design?

11 How would you apply rhinestones without destroying the shine?

12 What advice would you give a client to help them keep their design as long as possible?

13 List all of the equipment needed for an airbrush treatment.

14 Describe the different parts of an airbrush and how they work.

15 What are the benefits of airbrushing in comparison to other art techniques?

16 How can you advertise and market airbrushing and nail art treatments?

Chapter 8

1 Describe how to set up a studio.

2 What are the best ways to position your model's hands for the camera?

3 What props could you use when taking a photograph of the hands?

4 List the key factors you need to take into account when planning a photo shoot.

5 What characteristics should a perfect model for photographic or competition work have?

6 How and when would you prepare your model for competition day?

7 What personal characteristics should you have to enter the competition circuit?

8 What are the judges looking for in a set of winning nails?

9 What competition categories are there?

10 Why is current fashion so important when designing nails for catwalk shows?

11 Who are the key people you need to link with backstage at a fashion show or photographic shoot?

12 List the equipment you would need to take to a fashion show.

13 How can you find work within the fashion industry?

14 What range of pictures should you have in your portfolio?

15 What are the benefits of entering competitions, fashion and photographic work?

Chapter 9

1 Which characteristics would you need to become a teacher/trainer?

2 What qualifications would a school or college be looking for when recruiting a teacher/trainer?

3 What experience would you need before embarking on a teaching career?

4 Which types of training establishments could you teach in?

5 What is the difference between a teacher and an NVQ Assessor?

6 What qualities and skills should an NVQ Assessor have?

7 What does NVQ stand for?

8 How many different levels are there within the NVQ system?

9 What is the structure of any NVQ?

10 Who are HABIA and what is their role?

11 How would you plan for a demonstration at a trade show?

12 Explain the various methods of evaluating performance in the classroom or as a demonstrator.

13 Why is it important to evaluate your performance at regular intervals?

14 As a trainer, how could you keep updated on what is happening within the industry?

Bibliography

Almond, E. (1992/2000) *Manicure, Pedicure and Advanced Nail Techniques*. Thomson Learning, London.

Baran, R. and Dawber, R.P.R. (1994) *Diseases of the Nails and Their Management*, 2nd ed. Blackwell Scientific, Oxford.

Green, M. (2001) *Salon Management*. Thomson Learning, London.

K-Sa-Ra (1999) *All You Need to Know About Nail Art*. Oceana Books, London.

Milady's Art & Science of Nail Technology (1997) Milady Publishing, New York.

Rigazzi-Tarling, I. and Franklin, F. (2000) *Creating an Excellent Salon*. Hodder and Stoughton, London.

Schoon, D.D. (1996) *Milday's Nail Structure & Product Chemistry*. Milady Publishing, New York.

Glossary of terms

Abrasive Material used to shape and redefine nails

ABS Acrylonitrile-butadine-styrene; the polymer, or resin, from which most tips are made

Absorption One of the routes of entry into the body, of liquids through the skin

Acetone A solvent that efficiently removes nail extensions

Acrylates Family of monomers used in light curing gel products

Activator Speeds up a reaction in the fibreglass system

Adhesion When molecules on one surface are attracted to molecules on another

Adhesive A chemical that causes two surfaces to stick or bond

Aftercare advice Information given to clients to help them maximise their investment on treatment through home use of products and correct care procedures

AHA Alpha hydroxy acid

Allergic reaction Adverse response by the human body caused by contact with a substance to which that body is sensitive

Apex The high point which is just above the stress area

Arteries Vessels in the body that carry oxygenated blood from the heart around the body

Bacteria A single-cell organism capable of causing disease

Bacterial spore A dormant state of some bacteria, spores can become active under certain conditions

Blood A nutritive liquid circulating through the blood vessels

Body language Non-verbal communication which includes body positions and movements, facial expressions, etc.

Breathing zone 1m. sphere extending around your head and mouth from which you draw all the air you breathe

Capillaries Tiny, thin-walled blood vessels

Carpal tunnel A small passage in the wrist which houses a nerve that runs from the fingers into the arm

Catalyst Substance that activates or controls a chemical reaction

Cell The smallest and simplest unit capable of life

Chemical Everything that you can see and touch except light, sound and electricity. One of the building blocks of all matter

Chemical reaction What happens when two or more chemicals come together, usually resulting in a new substance or substances being formed

Consultation The process of gaining information on a client's needs and requirements

Contact area The well area of the tip just above the stop point

Contact dermatitis Inflammation of the skin caused by touching certain substances

Contamination To make impure, infect or corrupt a substance

Contra action A possible adverse reaction caused by a treatment

Contra indications A reason why a treatment should not be carried out

Corrosive Substance that can cause visible and sometimes permanent damage to skin

COSHH Control of Substances Hazardous to Health

Cure The process of turning a liquid into a solid

Cuticle The seal at the base of the nail plate

Cyanoacrylates Family of monomers that can be used with low light gels and instant adhesives

Dehydrate To remove water or dry out

Dermatitis Inflammation of the skin

Dermis The deep layer of skin under the epidermis

Disinfectant A substance capable of removing or reducing disease-causing organisms

Disinfection The process of removing or reducing disease-causing organisms using a disinfectant

Distal The farthest attached end

Effleurage A stroking movement during massage

Epidermis The top layer of skin

Eponychium The seal of colourless skin on the underside of the cuticle attached to the nail plate and cuticle

Ethyl methacrylate (EMA) A monomer most commonly used in acrylic nail systems; causes far fewer allergic reactions than MMA

Exhaust A ventilation system that removes vapours and dust to the outside of the workplace

Extension Artificial addition enhancing the length of a natural nail

Fibreglass The weave or material within the wrap system

Formaldehyde A substance that causes the nail plate to stiffen

Free edge The portion of the nail that extends beyond the nail plate

Free radical A excited molecule responsible for many chemical reactions

Fumes Tiny solid particles suspended in smoke

Furrows Ridges, horizontal or vertical

Gels Thickened liquids (oligomers)

Glue Adhesive made from proteins (normally animal)

HABIA Hair and Beauty Industry Authority, National Training Organisation which oversees qualification standards covering nail technicians

Habit tic Nervous disorder; picking at nail plate

Hang nail Small tear or split in the cuticle

Hapalonychia Soft nails

HASAW Act Health and Safety at Work Act

Histamine Chemical released by the body to protect against harm from an unwanted substance or irritation

Home care advice Recommendations given to clients to ensure they continue to benefit from the treatment once they are at home

Hygiene Standard of cleanliness aimed at preventing cross infection and secondary infection

Hyponychium The protective seal at the distal end of the nail unit

Ingestion One of the routes of entry into the body, by eating or drinking

Inhalation One of the routes of entry into the body, by breathing

Initiator A molecule that starts a reaction

Irritant A substance capable of causing inflammation of the skin, lungs, eyes, throat and nose

Keratin A group of fibrous proteins found in the skin, hair and nails

Koilonychia Spoon-shaped nails

Lamellar distrophy Flaking and peeling of the nail plate layer

Lateral To the side

Leukonychia White spots on nails

Lifting Separation of product from the natural nail bed

Liquid When talking about nails this term normally refers to monomer

Lower arch The curve of the extension from the sidewall to the edge of the tip

Lunula (half moon) Proximal end of nail plate, a white area formed by immature keratin cells

Lymph A clear straw-coloured liquid circulating in the lymph vessels and lymphatic system of the body

Mantle An area of skin that covers the matrix, the proximal nail fold

Matrix The area below the proximal nail fold where keratinisation takes place

Methacrylates A family of monomer used in several types of nail system

Methacrylic acid A commonly used acid found in primer

Methyl methacrylate (MMA) A monomer no longer used by manufacturers due to severe allergic reactions

Micro-organisms Term used for microscopic living creatures

Mix ratio The mix of powder and liquid used to create nail extensions

Molecule Basic chemical building block

Mono Meaning one

Monomer Single molecule chain, in the nail industry usually used for the liquid in liquid and powder systems

MSDS Material Safety Data Sheets, providing information on safety in the USA

Muscle Contractile tissue responsible for the movement of body parts

Nail bed Area under the nail plate

Nail plate The hard layers of keratinised skin at the tips of fingers and toes

Nail tips A plastic tip used to extend the length of the natural nail

NVQ National Vocational Qualification

Odour Caused by vapours in the air

Oligomers A single chain that is several thousand monomers long, but not long enough to become a polymer

Onychia Infection in or on the nail plate

Onychoclasis Broken nail, normally at the free edge

Onychocryptosis Ingrown nail

Onychogryphosis Claw nail

Onycholysis Separation of the nail from the nail bed

Onychomadesis Loss of nail plate at proximal nail fold

Onychomycosis A fungal infection normally present under the free edge of the nail

Onychophagy Nail biting

Onychorrhexis Split or brittle nails

Overlay A thin coating applied to the natural nail or applied over natural nail and tip

Paronychia Bacterial infection in the side of the cuticle or nail wall

Pathogens Disease-causing micro-organisms

Perionychium Lateral nail fold which creates a seal at the sidewall

Petrissage A compression movement during massage

Poly Meaning many

Polymerisation A chemical reaction that converts monomers to polymers

Polymers Many units of molecules, or monomers, joined together to make a polymer chain

Powder In the nail industry, a finely ground polymer powder

Preparation To prepare the natural nail for a nail treatment

Pre-tailor Adjustment of tip before fitting

Primer Substance that makes the nail plate more compatible with certain overlays

Proximal The nearest attached end

Psoriasis A skin or nail disorder

Pterygium Excessive forward growth of the cuticle

Resin A cyanoacrylate adhesive used in the fibreglass system

Risk assessment The procedure of ascertaining and controlling any potential hazards

Routes of entry Passageways by which chemicals can enter the body

Sanitation To reduce pathogens from a surface, e.g. hair, skin, nails

Sculpting form Paper or metal aids placed at the end of the free edge to lengthen nails without the use of a tip and then removed once application has taken place

Sculptured nail Nail extension extended beyond the free edge without the use of a tip

Ski jump A nail plate that curves upwards as it leaves the free edge

Smile line The natural nail area where nail leaves the nail plate; free edge; when referring to the extension this is the clean white line in zone one

Solute A substance that has been dissolved in a solvent

Solvent Substance capable of dissolving another substance

Splinter haemorrhage Tiny longitudinal streak of blood under nail plate

Sterilisation Total destruction of all micro-organisms

Stop point The thicker part of the tip under the stress area where the free edge will fit

Stratum corneum Surface layer of skin within the epidermis

Stratum germinativum Where cell division takes place within the epidermis

Stratum granulosum Outermost living layer within the epidermis

Stratum lucidum Clear layer of skin found in the second layer of the dermis

Stratum spinosum Where the keratin is made, also within the epidermis

Stress area Zone two, the area which has to withstand the wear and tear of everyday life; this should be the thickest part of the nail

System In this context 'system' refers to the three media: fibreglass, UV gel, liquid and powder

Tapotement A percussive movement during massage

Toluene A substance used to dissolve ingredients into nail enamels

Trachyonychia Extreme roughness of the nail surface

Upper arch The curve of the nail from the cuticle to free edge

UV (ultra violet) Invisible light above violet in the spectrum

Vaporisation The process by which a liquid is converted into a gaseous state

Vapour A gas. This would be a liquid at room temperature

Veins Vessels which collect blood from capillaries and return it to the heart

Ventilation Replacing stale air with fresh air

Volatile A liquid that evaporates rapidly

Wrap The term used in the fibreglass system for the material used to overlay natural nails

Zone one The area that extends from the nail plate

Zone three The thin area around the cuticle

Zone two The stress area

Index